Rust for C++ Developers

Leverage your C++ expertise to write safer and faster systems code in Rust

Dan Olson

<packt>

Rust for C++ Developers

Portfolio Director: Kunal Choudhary
Relationship Lead: Srishti Seth
Project Manager: K. Loganathan
Content Engineer: Sujata Tripathi
Technical Editor: Riya Agarwal
Copy Editor: Safis Editing
Indexer: Pratik Shirodkar
Proofreader: Sujata Tripathi
Production Designer: Salma Patel
Growth Lead: Vinishka Kalra

First published: March 2026

Production reference: 1240326

Published by Packt Publishing Ltd.
Grosvenor House
11 St Paul's Square
Birmingham
B3 1RB, UK.

ISBN 978-1-83620-651-4
`www.packtpub.com`

With thanks to my family for their grace, patience, and faith as we walk this road together.

– Dan Olson

Contributors

About the author

Dan Olson is a seasoned C++ developer with over 20 years of experience in the video game industry. A dedicated programming language enthusiast, he began transitioning projects from C, Python, and C# to Rust after its 1.0 release, impressed by its safety and performance. Dan now helps developers explore Rust's potential to elevate software quality and maintainability.

About the reviewer

Nejc Galof is an expert software developer from Slovenia with around 10 years of experience in software engineering, specializing in computer vision and signal processing. He works at SICK, developing high-performance software solutions for industrial and enterprise applications. While he has a strong background in C++, he now primarily develops in Rust, leveraging it to build safer, faster, and more maintainable software. Nejc enjoys exploring cutting-edge programming languages, tools, and technologies to deliver practical and innovative solutions to complex technical challenges.

About the reviewer

[illegible]

Table of Contents

Chapter 7: Understanding Iterators 121

Chapter 8: Object-Oriented Programming 139

Preface

It's hard to avoid Rust if you spend much time reading about programming on social media. While it has been in stable release since 2015, among the myriad programming languages, it still feels young and perhaps unfamiliar to many. Yet companies such as Google and Microsoft have been vocal about embracing this language and its unique security and safety advantages.

Rust excels in many of the same areas as C++. Especially for low-overhead, high-performance programming, very few other languages compete with C and C++ as well as Rust. This alone makes learning it worthwhile for any C++ programmer looking to expand their technical toolbox.

This book is about Rust, but it's written specifically for C++ programmers. Throughout the book, we'll look at Rust through the lens of C++. We'll highlight the similarities and differences between the two languages, with an understanding that we can lean on our existing mastery of C++ to quickly understand the concepts Rust introduces.

The path we'll follow mirrors my own journey learning Rust. As a C++ professional for over two decades, I feel that my time with Rust has benefited me in several ways, including how I think about writing C++ code. I hope you'll come away from this book with a similar feeling.

Who this book is for

This book is for C++ programmers who wish to learn about Rust: what it is, what it endeavors to solve, and why we'd want to use it in the first place. Every chapter is written specifically for C++ programmers, and thus, an intermediate to advanced knowledge of C++ will be helpful for our discussions comparing the two languages.

What this book covers

Chapter 1, Why Choose Rust?, gives us a brief introduction to the history of Rust and the technical trade-offs that have so many people excited about the language.

Chapter 2, Working with Rust Syntax, walks through the syntax of Rust, with each example compared directly to C++ where possible.

Chapter 3, The Rust Safety Model, shows exactly how Rust achieves its safety and security guarantees, which is fundamental for understanding how to use the language in practice.

Chapter 4, Managing Rust Projects with Cargo, explores Rust's excellent build, project setup, and dependency management tooling.

Chapter 5, Data Structures, explains how the Rust standard library represents common containers such as vectors, sets, and maps.

Chapter 6, Reading and Writing Files, reveals how Rust manages I/O operations and error handling when dealing with files and other kinds of I/O streams.

Chapter 7, Understanding Iterators, demystifies Rust's functional-style iterators and how they end up generating efficient code.

Chapter 8, Object Oriented Programming, shows Rust's unique take on object-oriented programming and explores how we can use Rust's functional and object-oriented features together in the same program.

Chapter 9, Working with C++ in Rust, explores interoperability between C++ and Rust, showing how the two languages can work together through Rust's foreign function interface.

Chapter 10, Optimization in Rust, details how we can find bottlenecks and measure improvement in Rust programs and explains how our intuitions about performance from C++ can be adapted to Rust.

Chapter 11, Multithreading in Rust, shows how Rust's safety guarantees extend to multithreaded programs and gives us several techniques for working with threads in Rust.

Chapter 12, Metaprogramming with Macros, discusses Rust's powerful macro system and works through examples of each of the many types of Rust macros.

Chapter 13, Continuing with Rust, provides information and suggestions about how to continue with Rust as a hobbyist, as a professional, and as a member of the community.

Appendix, Setting up a Development Environment, contains a step-by-step guide to setting up Visual Studio Code and a Rust development environment.

To get the most out of this book

The version of Rust used in this book is 1.82.0. Code examples will work on Linux, macOS, or Windows. They can also be explored in the Rust Playground found at . Help installing Rust and a compatible text editor can be found in the *Appendix*.

Download the example code files

The code bundle for the book is hosted on GitHub at `https://github.com/PacktPublishing/Rust-for-CPP-Developers`. We also have other code bundles from our rich catalog of books and videos available at `https://github.com/PacktPublishing`. Check them out!

Download the color images

We also provide a PDF file that has color images of the screenshots/diagrams used in this book. You can download it here: `https://packt.link/gbp/9781836206514`.

Conventions used

There are a number of text conventions used throughout this book.

`CodeInText`: Indicates code words in text, database table names, folder names, filenames, file extensions, pathnames, dummy URLs, user input, and Twitter handles. For example: "In recent standards, those languages have introduced the `stdint.h` and `cstdint` headers, providing fixed-width types such as `int32_t` or `uint64_t`."

A block of code is set as follows:

```
struct Vector3 {
    x: f32,
    y: f32,
    z: f32,
}
```

Any command-line input or output is written as follows:

```
checkpoint 1
checkpoint 2
checkpoint 3
drop
checkpoint 4
```

Bold: Indicates a new term, an important word, or words that you see on the screen. For instance, words in menus or dialog boxes appear in the text like this. For example: "To avoid this, it's best to use `Copy` for structures that are conceptually **"plain old data,"** or **POD**. "

> **Note**
>
> Warnings or important notes appear like this.

> **Tip**
>
> Tips and tricks appear like this.

Get in touch

Feedback from our readers is always welcome.

General feedback: If you have questions about any aspect of this book or have any general feedback, please email us at `customercare@packt.com` and mention the book's title in the subject of your message.

Errata: Although we have taken every care to ensure the accuracy of our content, mistakes do happen. If you have found a mistake in this book, we would be grateful if you reported this to us. Please visit `http://www.packt.com/submit-errata`, click **Submit Errata**, and fill in the form.

Piracy: If you come across any illegal copies of our works in any form on the internet, we would be grateful if you would provide us with the location address or website name. Please contact us at `copyright@packt.com` with a link to the material.

If you are interested in becoming an author: If there is a topic that you have expertise in and you are interested in either writing or contributing to a book, please visit .

Share your thoughts

Once you've read *Rust for C++ Developers,* we'd love to hear your thoughts! Scan the QR code below to go straight to the Amazon review page for this book and share your feedback.

`https://packt.link/r/1836206518`

Your review is important to us and the tech community and will help us make sure we're delivering excellent quality content.

Free benefits with your book

This book comes with free benefits to support your learning. Activate them now for instant access (see the "*How to Unlock*" section for instructions).

Here's a quick overview of what you can instantly unlock with your purchase:

DRM-Free PDF Version

Download DRM-free PDF and ePub copies of this book.

7-Day Packt Library Access

Get 7-day unlimited access to 8,000+ books and videos. No credit card required.

Available for first-time Packt+ trial users only.

Next-Gen Reader Access

Read this book on Packt Reader with progress sync, dark mode and note-taking.

How to Unlock

Scan the QR code (or go to `packtpub.com/unlock`). Search for this book by name, confirm the edition, and then follow the steps on the page.

UNLOCK NOW

Note: Keep your invoice handy. Purchases made directly from Packt don't require one

Part 1

Understanding Rust Basics

In this first part of the book, we'll explore the basics of Rust, including the technical benefits of the language and its tooling. You'll see Rust syntax in the context of equivalent code in C++, when possible. By the end of this part, you'll be able to read most Rust code and understand where and why Rust chooses different trade-offs from C++. You'll be able to create a basic project in Rust, and you'll have a good understanding of the tooling that supports the Rust ecosystem.

This part of the book includes the following chapters:

1

Why Choose Rust?

If you've decided to read this book, you may already have some idea of how Rust can be useful to you in your career or personal projects. Maybe you've used some software written in Rust and want to delve a little deeper into the language. Or perhaps you're interested in learning a new programming language just to challenge yourself. It could even be the case that a well-meaning coworker or friend told you that Rust is a "C++ killer" or that learning it will help you write better C++.

Whatever the reason, let's take some time at the outset to address the question of why programmers should be interested in Rust in the first place. We'll examine where Rust came from, see some examples of software using it, learn where it stands in the ever-expanding field of programming languages, and discover how we can use the Rust language, tooling, and community to help us create excellent software.

In this chapter, we're going to cover the following main topics:

- A brief history of Rust
- How Rust can improve software
- Crates and the Rust ecosystem

Note

Your purchase includes a free PDF copy + exclusive extras

Your purchase includes a DRM-free PDF copy of this book, 7-day trial to the Packt+ library (no credit card required), and additional exclusive extras. See the *Free benefits with your book* section in the *Preface* to unlock them instantly and maximize your learning.

A brief history of Rust

When examining a programming language, it can be helpful to understand the historical context in which it was created. What are the problems it was created to solve? What about the trade-offs it chooses? What group of people does it appeal to most? To answer those questions, we'll follow Rust through its journey from one man's personal project to a language that's powering both web browsers and operating systems on millions of devices today.

Early beginnings at Mozilla

Rust was started in 2006 as a personal project by Graydon Hoare, an engineer working for Mozilla Research. His new language was designed to be practical from the start rather than just a research project that would forever be obscure. In fact, he was specifically targeting "frustrated C++ developers" by aiming at the space in the programming language landscape traditionally occupied by C and C++.

C and C++ are distinguished from other programming languages in two primary areas: the level of control they give developers over memory and their minimization of language-imposed runtime overhead. Many languages make compromises in at least one of these areas. While it doesn't necessarily make them bad languages, it does make them useful for different things. The trade-offs chosen by languages such as C and C++ still make sense for many software projects, especially those that cannot tolerate any performance or memory overhead.

As we would expect from any language aimed at frustrated C++ developers, Rust was designed to make similar trade-offs as C and C++: minimizing runtime overhead while maximizing control. Minimizing runtime overhead is an easy choice, but there are some tricky parts about maximizing control over memory that Rust's design needed to revisit. Even the best programmers make mistakes. And when programmers make mistakes with memory, the consequences can range all the way from strange behavior that comes and goes randomly to exploitable security holes that enrich hackers at the expense of our users.

Now we can begin to imagine why Graydon Hoare and the C++ programmers around him were frustrated. They wanted to make fewer mistakes, but the tools they had available weren't really giving them the help they needed. Rust is their gift to us, the C++ programmers who keep making these same mistakes and need a little help. And Rust's idea is to give that help to us by making us divide our code into "safe" and "unsafe" sections. Most of our Rust code will be "safe," operating under a set of compile-time restrictions that work together to free us from the burden of many specific memory-handling bugs.

For the small amount of our code that needs extra control, we can use "unsafe" Rust code and rely on tests and other verification methods to prove that it works correctly. If we make our choices well, this significantly reduces the surface area of the code we must painstakingly validate. What was a daunting task for large software projects suddenly turns into an achievable one.

When Mozilla saw a prototype of Rust that Hoare had been working on, they quickly recognized the problems it addressed and decided to put the new language to work on the software they knew best: web browsers. Mozilla started a project called **Servo**, which had the primary purpose of creating a new, safe, and secure browser engine from the ground up in Rust. The Servo project funded much of Rust's early development and catapulted it from one man's personal project into a formidable competitor in the crowded programming language scene. But most tech companies weren't ready to start moving their software projects to Rust just yet.

Stabilizing the language

Code written early in the language's development can look unrecognizable to Rust programmers today. Parts of the language were changing rapidly as the developers sorted out the syntax and standard library they wanted to create. The pace of change was necessary for the language to evolve into what we know today, but it meant that anyone interested in using Rust at the time had to update or even rewrite their code with every new release. This wasn't a situation that invited serious long-term interest in the language from the wider software industry.

In May 2015, this situation was resolved, as Rust reached its stable 1.0 release. After so much churn, the developers finally felt confident that the feature set of the language would no longer need to change significantly from release to release. Being "stable" didn't imply that the language was anywhere close to finished, but the 1.0 release came with a stability guarantee. The developers promised that any Rust program written from then on would still work without modification when using any future release of the language. But won't a language with a stability guarantee like this just continue to grow indefinitely? Especially in languages that have been around for a long time, the inability to deprecate features is a thorn in the side of both users and language designers. C++ has dealt with this by choosing strategic ways to break compatibility in places that are deemed low impact, but still, the evolution of the language is hampered by its requirement to support several decades worth of legacy code.

Seeing the problems C++ and other long-lived languages had encountered, the designers of Rust knew to plan for this situation from the start. They devised a concept called **editions** for making changes to the language. A new edition is allowed to make significant changes to the language, including adding new reserved keywords, deprecating and removing features, and changing language semantics. New editions of Rust are released at roughly three-year intervals. The 2018 and 2021 editions each brought a host of interesting additions to and removals from the language. While most Rust programmers choose to migrate their code to the newest edition to get the benefit of the new features, older editions are indefinitely supported by the compiler, providing compatibility guarantees for anyone who judges it to be too risky or time-consuming to move their project forward to the new edition.

With the stable 1.0 release behind and a solid plan in place for evolving the language going forward, Rust was finally positioned for companies beyond Mozilla to start experimenting with the language in their own projects. And sure enough, in the years after stabilization, the language began a slow and steady growth in popularity across the wider tech industry.

Expanding into new territory

One of the first major victories for Rust came out of the Servo project at Mozilla. After several years of development on the new browser project, Mozilla decided to begin replacing parts of the C++ code in its Firefox browser with Rust components that had been developed for Servo. Starting in late 2017, Firefox began to ship to end users with Rust code enabled. Although safety was one of the main focuses of the Servo project, runtime speed improvements came along for the ride. This release of Firefox, dubbed "Quantum," boasted a significant speedup in rendering thanks to CPU parallelization improvements made in Servo using Rust.

As early as 2018, Amazon began using Rust to improve its AWS cloud services. Their public support of Rust started with the announcement of Amazon's Firecracker VM, which powers some of AWS's serverless offerings. In a 2020 blog post, Amazon praised Rust for its focus on performance and reliability, while revealing that several additional AWS services, including their cloud storage and compute offerings, were now using Rust in some form as well. This dependence on Rust led Amazon to hire several key Rust contributors to ensure that the language can continue to meet their needs as well as the needs of the wider community.

Similarly, Rust caught Microsoft's eye as early as 2019. The Microsoft Security Response Center, which manages handling of security issues in Microsoft products, stated that 70% of the most severe security issues they handle are caused by memory safety issues... the exact thing Rust aims to prevent. Microsoft released some helpful open source Rust code for working with Windows APIs, but it wasn't clear how exactly they were planning to use Rust in their products at this point.

In the meantime, Google was quietly embracing Rust for its Android operating system and Chromium browser. Google's investment was surprisingly large; in the year 2022 alone, they measured over 1,000 individual internal contributors to their Rust projects. Google also applied its internal analysis processes to its Rust programmers, finding that two-thirds of them felt confident contributing to a Rust code base in two months or less. Most material for Rust beginners emphasizes that it is a language with a steep learning curve, but Google's experiences suggest it might not be a very large hurdle after all for experienced engineers.

One of the most surprising adopters of Rust ended up being the Linux operating system, which is historically written in C and assembly. Chief maintainer Linus Torvald's abrasive rant against C++ became famous when contributors suggested allowing it into the kernel in 2007. Thus, it came as a shock to many when he appeared to be cautiously supportive of efforts to add Rust as a kernel development language. After several months of careful work by a small group of maintainers, Rust accomplished what C++ could not when it was merged into the kernel in late 2022.

In March 2023, another surprise came out of Microsoft that finally shed some light on how they had been using Rust behind the scenes. Microsoft had been experimenting since 2020 with rewriting parts of the Windows operating system in Rust and was now ready to start shipping it to end users. The first insider builds of Windows 11 shipped Rust code to users in May 2023, making Windows the third major operating system after Android and Linux to ship with kernel code written in Rust. As with Linux, the amount of Rust code in the Windows kernel remains small, but Microsoft engineers have stated that they intend to expand the usage further beyond their initial trials.

Today, Rust is known to be a part of three of the top five operating systems by user count, two of the three largest web browser backends, and several offerings from cloud providers. Rust has appealed to frustrated developers in these areas and more, many of which have traditionally been dominated by languages such as C and C++. While most system-level code is still written in C or C++, Rust has a clear and rapidly growing foothold in the tech industry that will keep it relevant for many years to come.

How Rust can improve software

For us to choose Rust, it must present a compelling set of features that create a meaningful improvement over the status quo. In this section, we'll examine a few aspects and features of Rust that make it a great choice for reliable and high-performance software.

High level, low level

I'd like to start by sharing one of my favorite examples for Rust beginners: reading a file and producing a hash. Solving this problem in C++ probably begins with an extensive search for an appropriately licensed library that both implements the needed algorithm and happens to be compatible with whatever build system we're using. There are several tools to help with this problem in C++, but none of them are installed by default with every C++ toolset.

I like to use this problem just to show that Rust is easy to use out of the box. Grabbing dependencies is trivial, and a simple program in Rust actually looks simple. Try not to be overwhelmed by the unfamiliar syntax or specifics of the program. We'll learn all of that as we go through the book. Instead, I'd like you to focus on the brevity and simplicity of the process.

To create a new Rust project, I can create a skeleton project in my terminal or shell application and add an appropriate library to do the hashing for me in a few seconds of typing. In this example, we're using Rust 1.82.0, but any future version of Rust will work identically:

```
$ cargo init hash
$ cd hash
$ cargo add sha256
```

The program itself is only a handful of lines in the `src/main.rs` file created by Cargo:

```
use sha256::digest;
fn main() -> Result<(), std::io::Error>   {
    for argument in std::env::args().skip(1) {
        let file = std::fs::read(&argument)?;
        let hash = digest(file);
        println!("{}: {}", argument, hash);
    }
    Ok(())
}
```

Compiling and running the program can then be handled in one step:

```
$ cargo run -- src/main.rs
```

This passes the `src/main.rs` file containing our code as an argument to our program, which, in turn, will print out the hash of the file:

```
src/main.rs: 327268ae21b5c28adea2e290af7f35bca3baa1089fa7bd4a22193743196f7eb8
```

When examining a program like this, I like to reference Alan Perlis's idea about high- and low-level programming languages from his timeless *Epigrams on Programming*:

"*A programming language is low level when its programs require attention to the irrelevant.*"

While the preceding Rust program might not be perfect, it's clearly not low-level by Perlis's standards simply because of how much the programmer is able to happily and safely ignore. Memory allocation and error handling are hidden behind straightforward abstractions, and even the types of variables are elided. I'm also guaranteed that the program won't crash or invoke any unexpected behavior since I have written it entirely in safe Rust.

The tooling was trivial to interface with as well. I didn't have to think much at all about creating a new project or adding a dependency. I did have to look up the name and documentation of the dependency I needed to add, but as we'll see next, this is often painless as well. A programmer with Rust in their toolbox can rapidly put together solid, well-performing programs due to the high-level nature of the language and its static safety guarantees.

And yet, Rust also allows us to dip as far into low-level programming as we need to solve our problem. If a safe abstraction for memory or file I/O is not giving us enough control, we can create our own memory allocation or read buffering strategy. If Rust's safety checks are preventing us from making an optimization, we can disable them as long as we're comfortable with the risks.

But by default, Rust often exposes simple APIs for simple tasks. In fact, one of Rust's strengths in general is making great choices by default.

Safety by default

Microsoft, Google, Mozilla, and many others are investing in Rust because they have all noticed the same problem in their software products. Different groups from within these companies have looked at the statistics and found that around 70% of the most severe bugs and vulnerabilities in their products are the result of memory safety issues, such as buffer overruns or use memory after it has been freed.

Rust's default "safe" configuration is protected from the most common bugs stemming from memory misuse. While there are several memory-safe languages out there, many compromise by adding runtime overhead in the form of a garbage collector. Rust's method, as we'll see in *Chapter 3*, works without significant runtime overhead by statically tracking the ownership and lifetime of memory as it flows throughout the program.

Rust also helps us write robust multithreaded code. The Rust designers recognized that the same compile-time rules that protect programmers from memory bugs can also be extended to protect users from a common multithreading problem called **data races**. As the Servo team at Mozilla found out, this can unlock significant speed improvements by creating opportunities for parallelism in code where it was thought to be too difficult or tricky to get right in other languages. In the end, Rust's default safe configuration protects programmers and users from many costly errors that C++ developers are exposed to directly. Certainly, the C++ community has made huge efforts around standardization and tooling to squash these bugs, but the process of catching them is still onerous and costly.

To achieve Rust's guarantees on a C++ project, a team must use a specific subset of language features, a specific style guide, static checkers to make sure everything is compliant, and special runtime configurations such as LLVM's undefined behavior sanitizer, address sanitizer, or thread sanitizer. In Rust, all that's needed is to compile and run the program.

Performance and memory

The ability to write programs with minimal overhead is something that C++ got right, and no language lacking that ability could ever be a serious competitor to C++. Happily, Rust exposes a similar feature set to C++ when it comes to performance and memory usage, meaning that it's decent at both out of the box.

Like the Clang compiler for C++, Rust is built on top of the LLVM Project's compiler architecture. This gives Rust a world-class optimizing compiler backend with support for several different CPU architectures right out of the box. Several other language-level optimizations familiar to many C++ programmers, such as move semantics and **Single Instruction, Multiple Data (SIMD)** intrinsics, are also featured in Rust, as we'll see in later chapters.

Rust is generally very memory-efficient as well. Rust has no garbage collection overhead by default, instead using scope to manage allocation and deallocation. Rust can be quite flexible with memory allocation strategies, though. The default allocator can be globally swapped out if a different allocator provides better performance for the use case. Also, embedded Rust programs targeted to microcontrollers often run in a mode that removes heap allocations from the language. These can then be replaced with fixed-size versions of the same types of containers that don't use the heap, or whatever else fits the needs of the program. Many different allocation methods are represented in the collection of open source libraries created by the community.

Modern language and tooling

We already saw how easy it can be to use Rust's tooling to create projects and add dependencies. This is just one of the many things Rust gets right just by virtue of being newer. This pattern has been seen repeatedly in the software world. A new project can often move faster than its competitors because it's able to learn from the mistakes and challenges the older project ran into and can design from the ground up to avoid them.

Rust has had the opportunity to learn from languages outside of the structural and object-oriented styles embraced by C++. There's a small but identifiable functional programming lineage in the language design. The original Rust compiler was first written in a lovely functional language called **OCaml**, so this influence shouldn't come as much of a surprise to us. The most obvious feature coming from functional programming in Rust is known as **sum types** or *algebraic data types* in some circles, but for most C++ programmers, it's probably best to think of it as *tagged unions*. As we'll see in *Chapter 2*, tagged unions enable convenient and powerful abstractions and are the core of Rust's error-handling mechanism.

Rust has other interesting types built directly into the language as well. **Ranges** represent a series of consecutive integers and can either be finite or infinite. **Slices** represent a reference to a series of contiguous values and are stored together as a pointer and a count, such as C++20's `std::span`. This makes trimming or resizing operations using slices `O(1)` cost. Iterators are also in Rust, although they don't have much to do with C++'s iterators. Rather, they expose a functional interface for operating efficiently on lists of objects that can be a powerful way to express many looping constructs.

In the years since C++ was initially designed, software testing has grown in importance significantly. Rust's designers recognized this and added a test runner to the language and build tooling. Similarly, code-formatting and documentation generation functionality come by default with any new installation of Rust. These features are almost a default expectation from any serious new programming language, but sadly, not available by default with much of the most popular C++ tooling.

We already briefly saw Cargo, Rust's build and package management solution. Next, we'll explore how this tool and the wider Rust ecosystem can give our programs a significant boost.

Crates and the Rust ecosystem

Typically, newer languages live or die not only on the strength of their language design but on the strength of the libraries provided through both their standard and their community. The most interesting language design in the world will still fail to gain any traction if every programmer who picks it up finds that they need to implement their own JSON parser or socket library. Due to general excitement around Rust and its initial development requirement of creating the Servo browser, Rust has very good library coverage of the most common libraries and techniques. For most of us, this means we can spend less time looking around for suitable dependencies and more time writing our program.

The anatomy of a crate

Rust calls both programs and library dependencies **crates**. There doesn't appear to be any solid technical reason for this terminology, but perhaps it makes sense to think of these as crates of code. After all, in Rust, a crate defines the unit of compilation. C++ defines each `.cpp` source file as the unit of compilation (often called the **translation unit**), but in Rust, the compilation unit encompasses one or more source files making up a single crate.

Crates can be either libraries or individual programs, called **binary crates**. The root of each crate contains a `Cargo.toml` file listing the dependencies on which it relies. A library crate will start with `src/lib.rs` as its top-level file, while a binary crate will use `src/main.rs`. Library crates might also ship one or more binaries alongside them. These can be placed as individual files in the `src/bin/` folder underneath the crate, with the name of each binary being the name of the source files. Each additional source underneath the crate's `src/` folder represents a

module that can be imported by other source files in the crate. Functions and data types can either be local to an individual module or exposed to the rest of the crate.

These files and paths represent Rust's idea of "convention over configuration" when it comes to source code layout. Because the unit of compilation is a crate and because the source files within the crate are very rigidly laid out, any crate can be compiled using a simple set of rules. There are several build systems for C++, but each needs to handle the complexity of preprocessor headers and macro definitions while also dealing with libraries that have no consistent conventions around source layout or inclusion. Nearly every C++ project needs to be handled in a different way. Rust's persistence in avoiding these problems is one of the main reasons that Cargo, its build and dependency management tool, is so highly regarded.

Adding dependencies on community crates

Both library and binary crates can be uploaded to the main repository for Rust community code at `https://crates.io/`. This site provides a searchable list of all community crates that can be easily imported into a Rust program. As we saw with the hashing example earlier, adding a dependency can be as simple as using the `cargo add` command in your crate's root folder. On a build, Cargo will check its local cache against the requested versions of the crates required and download the source code for each crate it needs to compile.

> Note
>
> **About code licensing**
>
> It's always important to check the software license of the code you're importing into your project to ensure that it's compatible with your software project. Much of the Rust community chooses to dual-license their code under the Apache and MIT licenses, which allows them to be used in closed-source projects. But this is not the case across the board. There are several good tools for checking the licenses of your program's dependencies at `https://crates.io`.

This may be a level of convenience that C++ programmers are unfamiliar with or skeptical about. Why would we want to download code at build time? Doesn't this tie us to external infrastructure that could go down at any time, leaving us unable to build our project? In short, yes, this is a risk. But a common one outside of the C++ ecosystem, where languages such as JavaScript and Python have similar package repositories. If this is a concern for your organization or just a risk you're not willing to take as a programmer, Rust has ways around this, which we'll explore in *Chapter 4*.

Summary

We've learned how Rust was developed initially to appeal to frustrated C++ programmers and noted how the teams behind several important pieces of software are gradually moving their work to use Rust. We explored some of the language's safety guarantees and language features, as well as its excellent tooling and strong library of open source code created by its community.

Taken together, these make a compelling set of reasons to choose Rust, but by far the best reason to jump into the language is that it's a joy to use. Because of its strong safety guarantees, there's no need to worry about many of the things we must normally worry about when coding in other languages. There's a curious freedom in writing or reviewing Rust code. One can focus only on the actual logic of the program itself instead of using constant vigilance to avoid serious missteps such as crashes and memory safety problems.

In *Chapter 2*, we'll take a deeper look at Rust's syntax and learn how to use its major language features more effectively.

Get this book's PDF version and more

Scan the QR code (or go to `packtpub.com/unlock`). Search for this book by name, confirm the edition, and then follow the steps on the page.

UNLOCK NOW

Note: Keep your invoice handy. Purchases made directly from Packt don't require an invoice.

2

Working with Rust Syntax

Now that we have an idea of the benefits Rust can give us, it's time to start examining the syntax. In this chapter, we'll illustrate Rust's basic syntactical concepts in the context of the corresponding C++ code. In the following code examples, we'll first see the Rust syntax for each concept and, whenever possible, follow it with the closest equivalent we can create in C++. By seeing the two languages together, we'll have a much easier time understanding the similarities and differences between them.

We will tackle the topics roughly in order of similarity to C++, from most to least similar.

In this chapter, we're going to cover the following main topics:

- Declaring variables and structures
- Using functions and methods
- Moving around the program
- Understanding generic programming
- Learning pattern matching

Technical requirements

The examples in this chapter use Rust 1.82.0, but they will also work with any newer version. If you need help installing Rust, please refer to the *Appendix*.

Rust code can also be entered into the Rust Playground, which is available online at `https://play.rust-lang.org/`. The Rust Playground is highly recommended for exploring the syntax examples in this chapter.

Declaring variables and structures

While programmers might associate our work with writing code, much of the behavior of our programs revolves around declaring data instead. Thus, we'll look at declaring and using variables and structures first. The concepts should all feel very familiar to C++ programmers, but we'll learn about the basic syntactical and behavioral quirks that separate Rust from C++.

Using simple variables

Declaring a simple variable is straightforward in both languages. Let us first look at how this is done in Rust:

simple_variable.rs

```
let some_int : i32 = 0;
```

And next in C++:

simple_variable.cpp

```
const int some_int = 0;
```

Even with this simple example, we can immediately observe several interesting things about Rust. The `let` keyword introduces a name that we can use to reference a piece of data. In C++, we might call this a variable declaration, but in Rust, it's often referred to as a *let binding*. This keyword and terminology are a small part of Rust's functional programming lineage.

We can also note that, unlike C++, the type is placed after the name, separated by a colon. Many languages created in recent years prefer to place the type in this position because it simplifies the language's grammar. It is also important because Rust is a type-inferred language, meaning that in many cases the type is optional information and may be omitted entirely.

We should also notice that common integer types in Rust are *fixed-width*, meaning that they encode the number of bits they contain. For some programmers, this is a welcome change from C and C++, where an `int` or `long` can represent different numbers of bits based on the platform and architecture in use. In recent standards, those languages have introduced the `stdint.h` and `cstdint` headers, providing fixed-width types such as `int32_t` or `uint64_t`. While this is an excellent improvement, it requires coding standards, code review, and perhaps static checking to ensure its use. Meanwhile, most of Rust's integer types have predictable sizes encoded into the name.

This is a pattern we'll see repeatedly. Rust has learned a great deal from the languages that preceded it and strives to make the best choice the default choice in many situations. Even from this simplest of code comparisons, we can observe another case of improved default behavior in that Rust treats variables as immutable by default. Not only do we encounter mutability less frequently in most real code, but it also has several additional implications for Rust's safety-checking strategies. Therefore, in Rust, mutability must be explicitly specified.

mutable_variable.rs

```
let mut some_int : i32 = 0;
```

In comparison, mutability is the default in C++:

mutable_variable.cpp

```
int some_int = 0;
```

Having used the `mut` keyword as part of our `let` binding, the compiler will now allow us to alter the contents of `some_int` in later code. We're giving the variable an initial value in these code examples, but Rust does not require variable initialization even for immutable variables. Unlike C++, though, it will error at compile time if a variable is read before being initialized. It's most common in Rust to initialize all variables.

It should be mentioned that `let` bindings like the ones we have been examining are only used for function-local variables. Global variables in Rust must use either the `const` or `static` keyword in place of `let`, cannot infer or omit their type, and must be initialized.

Learning array syntax

Next, we'll examine the syntax used by Rust to represent arrays:

simple_array.rs

```
let some_array = [0i32, 1, 2, 3, 4, 5];
```

And in C++:

simple_array.cpp

```
const int some_array[6] = {0, 1, 2, 3, 4, 5};
```

First, we notice that declaring an array also begins with the `let` keyword in Rust, and that our array is again immutable by default. This code also uses a syntax we haven't seen yet. We have attached the `i32` type directly to a literal integer. Rust uses this syntax to give programmers a way to explicitly choose a specific type among the various types available when using an integer literal. Most often, this is done when the type is not explicitly specified as part of the declaration. We could use this syntax on every element in the array, but it would be needlessly verbose.

Rust also supports a terse syntax for initializing an entire array to a single value:

```
let some_array = [0i32; 6];
```

The number before the semicolon is the value used to initialize each element, and the following number is the size of the array. There is no direct C++ equivalent for this syntax, although it can be approximated if the array is to be initialized to zeroes:

```
int array[6] = {};
```

In our Rust examples, the type of this array is `[i32; 6]`. Like C++, the length of the array is part of the type. Unlike C++, the array has no concept of decay to a pointer type in Rust. Rust instead has the concept of a *slice*, which is a pointer-size pair much like `std::span` in C++. We will examine slices in depth in later chapters.

Working with structures

Rust has no `class` keyword. Instead, it groups pieces of data together using structures that look much like C++ at first glance. We'll imagine a structure representing a three-dimensional vector as our example:

simple_structure.rs

```
struct Vector3 {
    x: f32,
    y: f32,
    z: f32,
}
```

simple_structure.cpp

```
struct Vector3 {
    float x;
    float y;
    float z;
};
```

The differences between the two languages here are somewhat small. Rust still chooses to put the type after the name of the member. Here, we use the `f32` type to specify a single-precision, 32-bit floating point number, matching C++'s `float` on most architectures. Also, we notice that Rust does not use a trailing semicolon when defining structures.

When we declare an instance of the structure, the differences between the two languages begin to emerge:

structure_declaration.rs

```
let some_vector = Vector3 {
    x: 0.0,
    y: 0.0,
    z: 0.0,
};
```

structure_declaration.cpp

```
const Vector3 some_vector = { 0.0, 0.0, 0.0 };
```

Here, we see an interesting exception to the rules we've encountered in Rust syntax so far. Previously, a colon always meant that a type would follow, but this isn't the case here. When declaring a structure, the colon is used to separate the name of the member from its value. Just in case you're wondering, Rust does indeed require us to specify a value for every member in the structure by name.

Perhaps recognizing that this can be cumbersome, the Rust developers provided two variations on the structure declaration syntax to improve the clarity of the code and reduce some of the typing required. First, if a variable with the same name as the structure member exists in scope, we can omit the value portion. This makes the following two declarations identical:

```
let x = 0.0;
let y = 0.0;
let z = 0.0;
let vector1 = Vector3 { x: x, y: y, z: z };
let vector2 = Vector3 { x, y, z };
```

Second, if an existing structure of the same type is in scope, we can initialize a new structure using its values. Continuing from the previous example, we can write some code that takes advantage of this:

```
let vector3 = Vector3 { x: 1.0, ..vector1 };
```

This syntax means that we wish to initialize the x member only and to copy the remaining values from `vector1`.

While these syntactical tricks help in some cases, large structures can still be cumbersome to declare. In typical Rust code, we find that this syntax for declaring structures isn't used very much. Instead, the community has settled on a series of conventions that make structures much easier to use. But to understand those conventions, we'll have to learn about Rust's syntax for declaring and calling functions.

Using functions and methods

As important as data is, C++ and Rust programs both need functions to accomplish anything useful. We'll now look at how Rust approaches the syntax for functions and methods. Conceptually, the two languages have very similar behaviors, but Rust's functional roots lead to an interesting twist in how functions are often implemented that we'll now explore.

Functions and block expressions

Using our `Vector3` structure from the previous section, let's write a function to add two vectors in both Rust and C++:

add_vectors.rs

```
fn add_vectors(left: Vector3, right: Vector3) -> Vector3 {
    Vector3 {
        x: left.x + right.x,
        y: left.y + right.y,
        z: left.z + right.z,
    }
}
```

add_vectors.cpp

```
Vector3 add_vectors(Vector3 left, Vector3 right) {
    return {
        left.x + right.x,
```

```
        left.y + right.y,
        left.z + right.z
    };
}
```

From this example, we see that Rust functions start with the `fn` keyword and that their return type follows the `->` operator on the right side of the function header. Some light linear algebra notwithstanding, the body of the function should already be understandable to us because it simply uses the Rust structure declaration syntax to declare a new `Vector3`. But there's something missing in the Rust version that may be confusing. Where is the `return` keyword?

What we're seeing in action here is another Rust concept with its roots in functional programming. In Rust, as in C++, a *block* is enclosed by braces and contains one or more *statements*, each followed by a semicolon. However, each block in Rust may also end with an optional *expression* that does not end with a semicolon. When this expression is present, the type and value of the block itself are treated as the type and value of the final expression. If a block has no final expression, it has the type `()`, which is similar to the `void` type in C++.

This means that the value of a block can be assigned to variables or, as we see here, represent the return value of a function. The term for a block used this way in Rust is a *block expression*. Block expressions are an important and frequently used concept in Rust code. There is no direct equivalent, but there are two somewhat similar concepts in C++: the so-called *Immediately Invoked Function Expression* (which is beyond the scope of this book) and the C++ conditional operator, sometimes called the ternary operator:

ternary_operator.rs

```
fn absolute_value(x: i32) -> i32 {
    if x < 0 { -x } else { x }
}
```

ternary_operator.cpp

```
int absolute_value(int x) {
    return (x < 0) ? -x : x;
}
```

While we haven't looked at control flow yet, the Rust version of the `if` expression should be familiar enough to be understandable in this case. This function makes use of block expressions twice. First, the value of the `if` expression is the value of the last expression in the branch that is taken. Then, because the `if` expression is the last expression in the function, the entire function takes on the value of that expression. The `return` keyword exists in Rust and could be used in this function, but it's more common for Rust code to omit it for brevity.

Using methods to add behavior to structures

Like many other languages, Rust distinguishes between *methods* and other types of functions. A method is a function that operates on an instance or *object* of a specific type.

The `add_vectors` function we created above took two `Vector3` structures and returned a new `Vector3` containing their sum. However, a function like this could also work quite nicely as a method. As a method, we would want it to use the current object as one of the two arguments while passing the other. Let's examine a few different ways to accomplish this in both Rust and C++:

vector_method.rs

```
impl Vector3 {
    fn add(&self, other: Vector3) -> Vector3 {
        Vector3 {
            x: self.x + other.x,
            y: self.y + other.y,
            z: self.z + other.z,
        }
    }
}
```

vector_method.cpp

```
Vector3 Vector3::add(Vector3 other) const {
    return {
        this->x + other.x,
        this->y + other.y,
        this->z + other.z,
    };
}
```

The first thing we note about this example is that Rust strictly separates the code that defines the data contained in the structure from the code that defines functions implemented for that structure. All methods in Rust must be inside an `impl` block. This likely seems unusual to C++ programmers, but it keeps both the structure and implementation clean and, as we will see later, feeds into Rust's strategy for generic programming.

The second new piece of syntax we see is the `&self` argument. Much like the `this` pointer in C++, the `self` keyword represents the object on which this method is being called. Also, like C++, the & operator turns the type into a reference, although it is used as a prefix for the type in Rust rather than a suffix as in C++. As we might expect by now, in Rust, references are immutable unless specifically declared otherwise.

As an example of using a mutable `self` reference, we can change this method to perform vector addition and assignment in a single step, much like the += operator in both Rust and C++:

mutable_self_method.rs

```
impl Vector3 {
    fn add_assign(&mut self, other: Vector3) {
        self.x += other.x;
        self.y += other.y;
        self.z += other.z;
    }
}
```

After calling this function, the contents of the structure will be updated to contain the sum of the data in the object and the `other` vector. Since the function requires `self` to be mutable, attempting to call this on an object that was not declared mutable will fail.

Rust calls all functions associated with a structure *associated functions,* but only refers to an associated function that has the `self` argument as a method. By omitting the `self` argument, we create an associated function that's similar in behavior to what C++ refers to as a static member function.

There's a special convention around this used by many Rust programs that was alluded to earlier. Many structures in Rust code provide a `new` function with no `self` argument as a convenient means of initializing the structure. This function is like a constructor in C++, but in Rust, the `new` function has no special behavior. Providing such a function is done entirely by convention.

Let's look at an example of our `Vector3` structure:

```
impl Vector3 {
    fn new() -> Vector3 {
        Vector3 {
            x: 0.0,
            y: 0.0,
            z: 0.0,
```

```
        }
    }
}
```

The designers of Rust chose to implement neither the default argument nor the function overloading features of C++, so multiple constructor-like functions may need to be provided for each struct. The conventions around `new` and other constructor-like functions followed by the standard library and most of the Rust community are outlined by the Rust API guidelines, located at `https://rust-lang.github.io/api-guidelines/`.

Calling functions and methods

The last aspect of functions we need to examine is how to call them. Continuing to use our `Vector3` structure, we find that there are many syntactical similarities between Rust and C++ code when it comes to calling functions and methods:

function_call.rs

```
let left = Vector3::new();
let right = Vector3::new();
let sum = add_vectors(left, right);
```

function_call.cpp

```
const Vector3 left = { 0.0, 0.0, 0.0 };
const Vector3 right = { 0.0, 0.0, 0.0 };
const Vector3 sum = add_vectors(left, right);
```

Calling a function in Rust has a nearly identical syntax to that of C++. Here, we also see a call to the `new` function for the first time. Calling an associated function in Rust uses the `::` operator to join the function's name to the name of the structure.

Next, we'll examine calls to the immutable and mutable method versions of the vector add function we made. We'll likely find no syntactical surprises here either. First, we'll see the immutable calls:

method_call.rs

```
let left = Vector3::new();
let right = Vector3::new();
let sum = left.add(right);
```

method_call.cpp

```
const Vector3 left = { 0.0, 0.0, 0.0 };
const Vector3 right = { 0.0, 0.0, 0.0 };
const Vector3 sum = left.add(right);
```

Now, with mutability:

mutable_method_call.rs

```
let mut left = Vector3::new();
let right = Vector3::new();
left.add_assign(right);
```

mutable_method_call.cpp

```
Vector3 left = { 0.0, 0.0, 0.0 };
const Vector3 right = { 0.0, 0.0, 0.0 };
left.add_assign(right);
```

As we see, the syntax for calling a function is very similar between the two languages. However, when talking about method calls, we should note that Rust always uses the `.` operator to access members. Unlike C++, there is no `->` operator.

With the ability to define and call functions added to our Rust toolbox, we're now ready to learn about Rust's control flow constructs.

Moving around the program

In our programs, we often want to take different paths through the code based on the state of the program. Conditional execution and looping are collectively called *control flow* and are essential to understanding all but the simplest of programs.

Using conditionals

The most straightforward form of control flow is the simple `if` statement, and we'll find that, in Rust, it shares many similarities with C++. Let's imagine that we are computing an average and want to guard against a divide-by-zero operation:

simple_if_statement.rs

```
let mut avg = 0;
if count != 0 {
```

```
    avg = sum / count;
}
```

simple_if_statement.cpp

```
int avg = 0;
if (count != 0) {
    avg = sum / count;
}
```

In Rust, we see that parentheses are not syntactically required for an `if` statement, and we'll find that this is true for all other control flow statements as well. This saves a little typing, but it also, thankfully, preempts a lot of arguing about how exactly whitespace and parentheses should be combined for each type of statement. Parentheses are still used for grouping expressions and enforcing precedence in Rust, just as in C++.

In Rust, though, it's not very common to see a mutable initialization like this one. We'd more likely see the preceding code written using an immutable variable initialized with a block expression:

```
let avg = if count == 0 { 0 } else { sum / count };
```

What about `else if`? Again, it's nearly the same as C++, but we should also note that braces are required in Rust even for single-line `if` and `else if` blocks:

else_if_chain.rs

```
if i % 3 == 0 && i % 5 == 0 {
    println!("fizzbuzz");
} else if i % 3 == 0 {
    println!("fizz");
} else if i % 5 == 0 {
    println!("buzz");
}
```

else_if_chain.cpp

```
if (i % 3 == 0 && i % 5 == 0)
    std::cout << "fizzbuzz" << std::endl;
else if (i % 3 == 0)
    std::cout << "fizz" << std::endl;
```

```
else if (i % 5 == 0)
    std::cout << "buzz" << std::endl;
```

A final thing to point out here is that simple and compound conditionals in Rust are often identical to those in C++, using &&, ||, !=, and == operators exactly as C++ does.

Using loops and breaks

The simplest way to loop in Rust is to use the `loop` keyword to create a loop that never ends:

infinite_loop.rs

```
loop {
    println!("waiting...");
}
```

infinite_loop.cpp

```
while (true) {
    std::cout << "waiting" << std::endl;
}
```

A loop that never ends is of questionable utility on its own. Typically, we exit the loop using the `break` keyword when some condition is met in both languages.

Another way to write a loop that exits after a condition is met is to use the `while` keyword.

while_loop.rs

```
let mut i = 0;
while i < 10 {
    i += 1;
}
```

while_loop.cpp

```
int i = 0;
while (i < 10) {
    i += 1;
}
```

As we've seen with other keywords, the only difference between the two languages here is that Rust does not use parentheses as part of the loop syntax.

In the previous example, we were just looping through a specific number of integers, which is a great thing to do using a `for` loop. Here, we finally begin to see some meaningful differences between the two languages:

for_loop.rs

```
for i in 0..10 {
    println!("{}", i);
}
```

for_loop.cpp

```
for (int i = 0; i < 10; i++) {
    std::cout << i << std::endl;
}
```

Rust always pairs the `for` keyword with a corresponding `in` keyword, making it much closer to C++'s *range-based for loop* than a traditional C-style `for` loop. In Rust, the loop will iterate over the elements of whatever follows the `in` keyword. This could be an array, a container, or, as in this case, a *range* of integers.

Ranges in Rust have a first-class syntax, either `start..end` to define an *exclusive range* that does not include the final number or `start..=end` to define an *inclusive range* that does include it.

The last looping topic we'll examine is nested loops. Occasionally, when nesting loops, we want to use `continue` or `break` to affect the outer loop rather than the inner one, which is their default behavior in both Rust and C++. In C++, our options are usually to use `goto`, which Rust lacks, or to restructure the code to add additional checks. Rust's solution is to allow the `continue` and `break` keywords to take an optional *label* that will specify which loop to affect.

break_to_outer_loop.rs

```
'outer: for y in 0..200 {
    for x in 0..320 {
        if finished() {
            break 'outer;
        }
    }
}
```

break_to_outer_loop.cpp

```
outer:
for (int y = 0; y < 200; y++) {
    for (int x = 0; x < 320; x++) {
        if (finished()) {
            goto outer;
        }
    }
}
```

Rust is somewhat strict in how these labels are used. First, the label name must start with a single quote character. They can also only be used to refer to enclosing loops, and they can only be used by the `break` and `continue` keywords. This feature is not a replacement for the goto keyword, but it does implement one of its most common usages in C and C++.

Understanding generic programming

Generic programming is the practice of writing a single function or structure that can work with more than one set of types. C++ implements generic behavior with *templates* and the **Standard Template Library** or **STL**. Despite some syntactical similarities, Rust's approach to generic programming is quite different than C++. This can make it challenging to provide equivalent C++ code examples, but we'll still use them to illustrate concepts whenever it's practical.

Using generic structures

The easiest place to start with generics is a structure. Let's extend the `Vector3` type we've been working with to allow for the use of a different base type.

generic_vector3.rs

```
struct GenericVector3<T> {
    x: T,
    y: T,
    z: T,
}
```

generic_vector3.cpp

```
template <typename T>
struct GenericVector3 {
```

```
    T x;
    T y;
    T z;
};
```

The Rust syntax is a little more compact, but not much of a departure from C++'s syntax.

If we want to specify a method on a generic Rust structure, we must use a generic `impl` block:

```
impl<T> GenericVector3<T> {
    fn new() -> GenericVector3<T> {
        todo!()
    }
}
```

You might have noticed that the generic parameter `T` is listed twice. This is a confusing quirk of Rust for many beginners. The generic parameter placed directly after the `impl` keyword makes that generic type available for the entire rest of the `impl` block. The generic parameters are then used immediately after the structure name as well because the structure that we are implementing is generic.

We also used the standard `todo!()` macro here to indicate that the code will be filled in later. If the code is executed, the code will cause the program to exit with an error message indicating that the function is not yet implemented. We're still missing one small piece required to be able to provide a meaningful implementation for this function, so we'll just make a note of the syntax for now.

In addition to types, Rust also provides a feature called *const generics* that allows us to use integer types as generic parameters. These are much like *non-type template parameters* in C++. An example usage might be to create a vector type that can support any size.

const_generic.rs

```
struct ArbitrarySizeVector<const N: usize> {
    values: [f32; N]
}
```

const_generic.cpp

```
template <size_t N>
struct ArbitrarySizeVector {
```

```
    float values[N];
};
```

We haven't seen `usize` yet, but it is one of the few integer types in Rust that has an architecture-dependent size. In this case, it's the size required to address any location in memory: 4 bytes on 32-bit architectures and 8 bytes on 64-bit ones.

To declare a new object with a specified size, you must use the operator with both the most unfortunate syntax and the most unfortunate name in all of Rust: the *turbofish* operator, `::< >`.

```
let vec = ArbitrarySizeVector::<3>::new();
```

This operator must be used in any situation where the compiler does not have enough information to determine the generic type or value we require.

Specifying generic behavior with traits

Generic data structures are a great tool, but to write generic code, we need to understand what Rust calls *traits*. A trait might be called an interface in some other languages. A trait definition specifies a set of functions that must be implemented for any structure implementing that trait. Let's look at a simplified version of Rust's standard `Add` trait:

```
trait Add {
    fn add(self, rhs: Self) -> Self;
}
```

In this code, `Self` is a special keyword that represents the type of the `self` parameter, which wouldn't otherwise be known because the trait could be implemented for several different structures. Armed with this trait definition, we can provide an implementation for our custom `Vector3` type:

```
impl Add for Vector3 {
    fn add(self, rhs: Self) -> Self {
        Vector3 {
            x: self.x + rhs.x,
            y: self.y + rhs.y,
            z: self.z + rhs.z,
        }
    }
}
```

Notice that we're using the same `impl` keyword that we saw before when implementing associated functions, but this time we're implementing a trait, or interface, specifically for our structure. With this trait imported into our code, we'll be able to use the `add` function exactly as if it were a regular method with the `x.add(y)` syntax.

You may be wondering what advantages implementing behavior as a trait provides. After all, we could have just used the `add` function we implemented earlier as part of the structure rather than the generic trait. It turns out that traits are the missing piece we are looking for when it comes to implementing generic functions.

If you're familiar with C++ template resolution, you may know that templates can only be type-checked after they are expanded or *instantiated*. This design choice can at times lead to confusing error messages from the compiler. Rust makes the opposite choice and instead requires the programmer to provide enough information to allow the Rust compiler to type-check all generic code before expansion or *specialization*.

The way that Rust does this is by requiring the programmer to specify *trait bounds* whenever a generic type is used. Using the preceding simplified `Add` trait, we can implement a free `add` function that accepts any structure that implements our trait:

```
fn add<T>(left: T, right: T) -> T
where
    T: Add,
{
    left.add(right)
}
```

This code uses a `where` clause to specify the trait bounds for this function. This *bounds* the possible set of structures that can be passed to this function to only those implementing the `Add` trait. Because the compiler knows that every structure passed to the function will implement the `Add` trait, it knows that it is valid to call the `add` member function on any value of type `T` in this function. By requiring trait bounds, the compiler can fully type-check the function before knowing the specific types that will be used with it.

Returning to `GenericVector3<T>`, we can now understand that we need to use a trait bound to do anything meaningful with our generic function:

```
impl<T: Default> GenericVector3<T> {
    fn new() -> GenericVector3<T> {
        GenericVector3 {
            x: T::default(),
```

```
            y: T::default(),
            z: T::default(),
        }
    }
}
```

Here, we specify the standard library's `Default` trait bound, which provides the `default()` function for us to use inside our generic function. This time, the trait bound is not specified in a `where` clause. I did this on purpose because Rust syntax often allows either a `where` clause or the `T: Default` syntax used here. Either syntax may be seen in Rust code bases when reading code.

This is only a small overview of traits and trait bounds. We'll encounter them and see many more examples of their usage as we go through the book. Some of the concepts transfer from C++, but don't worry if traits don't make sense quite yet. For now, we are most interested in familiarizing ourselves with the syntax conventions Rust uses for traits and generic programming.

Learning pattern matching

Pattern matching is where the functional programming roots of Rust shine through the most and is also one of the aspects of the language that allows us to craft APIs that are a joy to use. Pattern matching is used in almost every non-trivial Rust program, and understanding it is essential to be able to read and understand Rust.

Using supercharged enumerations in Rust

Some readers may have wondered why we didn't discuss enumerations earlier, when we were looking at the syntax of structures. The reason is that enumerations (hereafter *enums*) in Rust are significantly more powerful than those in C++.

At their simplest, Rust enums can easily duplicate the capabilities of C++:

simple_enum.rs

```
enum Numbers {
    Zero,
    One,
    Two,
}
```

simple_enum.cpp

```
enum class Number {
    Zero,
    One,
    Two
};
```

These two declarations and their semantics are almost identical. I've used `enum class` in the C++ example because this most closely matches the Rust usage. In other words, we must normally use `Number::Zero` or `Number::One` to use a specific value in both languages. Rust can import the value names directly into scope to get around this, similar to a `using namespace` declaration in C++, but this usually only happens for some common standard types.

Let's look at a more complicated Rust example now:

```
enum Result<T, E> {
    Ok(T),
    Err(E),
}
```

The `Result` type here actually comes directly out of the standard library. We can see that it's an enum with two generic types, but that might not make much sense if our intuitions are coming from C++. Why are we putting generic types next to each value?

Enums in Rust implement a very powerful abstraction called *tagged unions*. This can be implemented in C++ using an enum and a union, but more recently it's represented by the `std::variant` type. The general idea is that any variable with the type of `enum` can hold any of the values, as well as the value's associated data. But it can only represent one of the possible values at a time.

Coming back to `Result`, it's used to implement error handling in Rust. We'll see many more examples of this in later chapters, but for now, we'll play around with this type a little, just to examine the syntax and usage of Rust's enums:

```
impl Vector3 {
    fn divide(&self, value: f32)
        -> Result<Vector3, String> {
        if value == 0.0 {
            return Err("divide by zero!".to_string());
        }
```

```
        Ok(Vector3 {
            x: self.x / value,
            y: self.y / value,
            z: self.z / value,
        })
    }
}
```

This function can return either an error represented by the `Err` value or a normal return represented by the `Ok` value. But how can the caller tell which of the two states it might contain? That brings us to *pattern matching*.

Matching patterns

Pattern matching might be called *destructuring* in C++ parlance, but it doesn't show up often in historical C++ code. It's basically the process of taking a type that could potentially contain more than one state and making decisions based on the actual value it stores. Pattern matching in Rust starts with the `match` statement, which is a fancier version of C++'s `switch` statement:

```
let result = match vec.divide(divisor) {
    Ok(val) => val,
    Err(err) => {
        eprintln!("Error: {}", err);
        Vector3::new()
    }
};
```

The `match` statement takes an expression and carefully specifies the behavior for each possible value. In this code, we see that if `divide` returns a correct value using the `Ok` state, we will simply pull that value out of the `Result` type and assign it to a value. However, if `divide` returned an error, we instead print the error message to `stderr` and then provide some plausible fallback value for the rest of the program to use.

A `match` statement must be exhaustive, meaning that every possible value of the expression being passed must be handled in some way. Thankfully, we can use the `_` pattern to provide something like the `default` fallback case in a C++ `switch` statement, but in general, exhaustive matching is an important feature and removes the potential for bugs to creep in as code changes.

Rust provides a syntactical sugar for the common case where the programmer only cares about one possible state of an enum. It's called the `if let` operator, and it's most easily illustrated using the preceding `Result` type and its equivalent `match` statement.

if_let_statement.rs

```
if let Ok(val) = vec.divide(0.0) {
    println!("got val {}", val);
}
match vec.divide(0.0) {
    Ok(val) => println!("got val {}", val),
    _ => {}
}
```

The `if let` statement can be confusing at first, but it's used frequently in Rust code. Like a normal `if` statement, it can also have an `else` clause.

Summary

In this chapter, we learned how to declare and use variables, structures, and functions in Rust through direct comparisons to C++. Next, we briefly examined the core concepts around generic programming and pattern matching in Rust. Armed with this foundational knowledge, we should be able to understand many of the Rust programs we come across.

In the next chapter, we'll look at how exactly Rust implements its strong safety guarantees and how it affects us as programmers.

Get this book's PDF version and more

Scan the QR code (or go to `packtpub.com/unlock`). Search for this book by name, confirm the edition, and then follow the steps on the page.

UNLOCK NOW

Note: Keep your invoice handy. Purchases made directly from Packt don't require an invoice.

Get this book's PDF version and more

3

The Rust Safety Model

Now that we've explored the benefits of Rust and gotten a feel for its syntax, it's time to understand how exactly Rust enforces its safety checks. We'll take a deep dive into the compile-time and runtime restrictions Rust places on our programs and talk about how best to structure our code as a result. By the end of this chapter, we'll have an excellent understanding of Rust's safety model and how it helps us write correct programs through the concepts of ownership, borrowing, and lifetimes.

In this chapter, we're going to cover the following main topics:

- Tracking ownership
- Borrowing data
- Specifying lifetimes
- Understanding panics
- Changing how we write code

Technical requirements

The Rust examples in this chapter use version 1.82.0, but later versions of Rust will still work correctly. The Rust Playground at `https://play.rust-lang.org/` is an excellent way to experiment with the code examples.

The C++ code in this chapter uses C++11 concepts and must be compiled with C++11 or a more recent version.

Tracking ownership

To understand whether an operation on a piece of data is valid in a specific scope, the Rust compiler must first know who or what *owns* that data. Tracking the owners of every piece of data throughout the flow of a program could be a daunting task, but much of Rust's behavior is built around simplifying the job for the compiler. Once we learn and internalize these simplifications, they can reduce the cognitive load on us as programmers as well. In this section, we'll discover the rules of ownership in Rust and how they help prevent incorrect behavior from leaking into our programs.

The single ownership principle

Every value in Rust has only one owner at a time. This tends to lead to surprising behavior for programmers coming from C++. For instance, this code results in an error at compile time:

```
let data1 = String::from("Hello World!");
let data2 = data1;
println!("{}", data1);
```

In C++, the equivalent code would look something like this:

```
std::string data1 = "Hello World!"
std::string data2 = data1;
std::cout << data1 << std::endl;
```

Here, our C++ code works without a problem, with both the `data1` and `data2` variables containing their own complete copies of the string. But in Rust, we're violating one of the fundamental rules of the language.

In this example, a `String` structure is created with the `data1` variable having ownership of the data. In the second line, the ownership is transferred or *moved* to `data2`. Ownership is transferred through operations such as assignment, argument passing, and function returns. Since the string's data has been transferred to another owner, the `data1` variable can no longer be used by the program in any way, and attempting to print its contents will produce a compile error like this one:

```
error[E0382]: borrow of moved value: `data1`
```

This error probably won't make much sense without some additional background. To see why `data1` is no longer valid, we must understand that in Rust, transfer of ownership from `data1` to `data2` is implemented as a *move*. This makes the previous example much closer to this C++ code:

```
std::string data1 = "Hello World!";
std::string data2 = std::move( data1 );
std::cout << data1 << std::endl;
```

This code is likely buggy in C++. Moving `std::string` in C++ leaves the string in a *valid but unspecified* state, and printing the contents has no useful meaning. While this code will not work efficiently, it will still compile, leaving any potential errors for the programmer to find at runtime.

In Rust, a structure that is moved will be copied byte for byte into its new memory location. This is sometimes called a *shallow copy*, because it only copies the contents of the structure itself. In a shallow copy, the new structure receives direct copies of any pointers stored in the structure. Any heap allocations tracked by these internal pointers would not be copied.

In contrast, a *deep copy* not only copies the structure but also allocates new memory for any data referenced by pointers in the structure, and copies the pointed-to data into that memory. As a result, a deep copy creates a completely independent copy of the structure and all of its referenced data at another location in memory. A deep copy is called a *clone* in Rust.

In Rust, to clone our types, we must implement the `Clone` trait. This trait has a single function, `clone()`, that returns a deep copy of our structure. Many standard types have this trait implemented for us, most often by calling the `clone()` method on each member of the structure in turn. This implementation mirrors the recursive nature of a deep copy. Because the deep copy results in something completely independent of the original data, the Rust compiler recognizes it as a new piece of data with a completely different owner. As such, we can fix the previous Rust example using cloning like this:

```
let data1 = String::from("Hello World!");
let data2 = data1.clone();
println!("{}", data1);
```

Thinking about the internal data layout of the `String` type gives us a good example of the effects of moving versus cloning in Rust. A simplified version of this type could be implemented as a structure holding two member values: a pointer to a buffer of characters in heap memory and a value storing the size of the buffer. In Rust, when a structure such as this is moved, the result is a memory copy of 16 bytes for a 64-bit architecture, whereas a clone would copy both the structure and the entire buffer it holds into another newly allocated location in heap memory. In C++-style pseudocode, it might look like this:

```
struct String {
    const char* data;
    uint64_t size;
    void move(String& newLocation) {
        newLocation.data = data;
        newLocation.size = size;
    }
    void clone(String& newLocation) {
        newLocation.data = heap_allocate(size);
        newLocation.size = size;
        copy_bytes(newLocation.data, data, size);
    }
};
```

This example illustrates the concepts of moving, which happens automatically behind the scenes in our Rust code, and cloning, which we must explicitly request. It also gives us a hint as to why Rust must maintain only one owner for any given structure. After `newLocation.data = data` in the move function, we have two `String` structures, each pointing to the same piece of data on the heap. If we just made a shallow copy, we might have to decide which of the two structures is responsible for freeing that data. Rust's answer is simple because there is only ever one owner: when ownership is transferred, the responsibility for freeing data is transferred to the new owner as well.

Cleaning up old data

Deallocating the resources used by a structure, or what might be called *destruction* in C++, is called a *drop* in Rust. When dropping a structure, Rust will recursively run through all members and destroy them in the order in which they appear in the structure. Structures can add custom destruction code by implementing the `Drop` trait, which provides a `drop` function. If it is provided, the `drop` function will be called before the rest of the destruction process begins.

A Rust structure is dropped whenever its owner goes out of scope. Like C++, scope is often marked by a pair of braces enclosing one or more statements known collectively as a *block*. There is some nuance to scope in Rust, because ownership can be transferred to a higher scope through block expressions or function returns:

```
struct DropTest;
impl Drop for DropTest {
```

```
    fn drop(&mut self) {
        println!("drop");
    }
}
fn main() {
    {
        println!("checkpoint 1");
        let outer = {
            println!("checkpoint 2");
            let inner = DropTest;
            inner
        };
        println!("checkpoint 3");
    }
    println!("checkpoint 4");
}
```

The preceding code prints the following:

```
checkpoint 1
checkpoint 2
checkpoint 3
drop
checkpoint 4
```

In this example, we're transferring ownership from `inner` to `outer` using a block expression, so the drop does not occur until `outer` goes out of scope.

When shallow copies are enough

Occasionally, we might find dealing with Rust's ownership rules restrictive. Must we always worry about the owner of an integer or floating-point type? Consider the following code:

```
let data1 = 0u32;
let data2 = data1;
println!("{}", data1);
```

This example is nearly identical to the first code example in this chapter, except that we're using an integer suffix as a small syntactical convenience to change the type of our data from `String` to `u32`. Following that example, we should find that ownership was transferred from `data1` to `data2` and that the code produces a compile error when trying to access the previous owner. Yet unexpectedly, this code compiles and runs correctly, printing `0`.

What is going on here? The Rust developers recognized that the single ownership principle can be inconvenient for certain types of code and have provided a means to opt out of it when it can be done safely. In this case, being able to do it safely means that a shallow copy and a deep copy have identical behavior. For any structure meeting this requirement, we can opt out of the single ownership principle using a *marker trait* named `Copy`.

What exactly is a marker trait? We know that traits specify an interface that can be implemented for a structure, and we've seen a few examples already in this chapter, such as `Clone` and `Drop`. A marker trait is a trait with no functions associated with it. The trait only exists for the purpose of giving the compiler some specific piece of information about our type.

A marker trait can be implemented as follows:

```
impl Copy for MyStruct {}
```

However, a significantly more common way to define the `Copy` trait is to *derive* it. Deriving a trait in Rust is a way of letting the compiler implement the entire trait with no interaction from the programmer. This cuts down on a significant amount of boilerplate code when it can be used.

Deriving `Copy` for a structure looks like this:

```
#[derive(Copy, Clone)]
struct MyStruct;
```

It's not an accident that we also derived `Clone`. Rust requires `Clone` to be implemented for any structure that implements `Copy`. Code generated by deriving these traits will simply call the function provided by the trait on each member of the structure. Because of this, any type implementing `Clone` but not implementing `Copy` could block users from deriving `Clone` for types containing it.

For instance, if the `u32` type implemented `Copy` but not `Clone`, we would not be able to derive `Clone` for any structure containing a `u32` type. Since there would be no technical justification for this due to every copyable type being cloneable by definition, the Rust designers decided to sidestep the problem by requiring both traits to be implemented for copyable types.

Another restriction of structures implementing `Copy` is that they also must not implement `Drop`. Because `Copy` is only used for trivial types that contain no internal heap allocations, a user-defined destructor has no useful functionality to provide.

Now that we've covered the main concepts behind ownership and copying in Rust, we'll look at how to use references.

Borrowing data

A model that only allows a single owner at any given time could seem a bit restrictive, especially when it relies on shallow and deep data copies using moves and clones, respectively. Often, when passing parameters to functions, and sometimes even when storing data in structures, we just need to use a reference instead of passing the entire structure around. Fortunately, Rust allows us to produce a reference to a piece of data by *borrowing* it from the owner. Throughout this section, we'll refer to the act of creating a reference as a "borrow," and use "reference" to refer to the value produced by borrowing.

As with ownership, Rust puts additional rules on the use of references to make it easier to guarantee correct program behavior. The part of the compiler that enforces these rules is often referred to as the *borrow checker*.

Borrowing immutable data

An immutable reference is one that cannot cause the borrowed data to change, regardless of whether that data is mutable or not. To create an immutable reference, we prefix the data we wish to borrow with the & operator. This gives a variable containing a borrowed `String` the type `&String`, which we read as "a reference to `String`." As with C++ references, a reference in Rust internally functions as a pointer to the data with some additional rules placed around it to make access safer.

For immutable borrows, we have only one rule to follow: a piece of data can be borrowed immutably as many times in the same scope as needed, but none of the references can outlive the data that they are borrowing.

For instance, the following Rust code will fail to compile:

```
fn main() {
    let borrow_outer = {
        let data = 0u32;
        &data
    };
    println!("{}", borrow_outer);
}
```

Here, we're attempting to pass the reference to `data` to the outer scope through a block expression, but the data we're borrowing is dropped at the end of the scope. The compiler helpfully tells us that this is not allowed:

```
error[E0597]: `data` does not live long enough
 --> src/main.rs:4:9
  |
2 |     let borrow_outer = {
  |         ------------ borrow later stored here
3 |         let data = 0u32;
  |             ---- binding `data` declared here
4 |         &data
  |         ^^^^^ borrowed value does not live long enough
5 |     };
  |     - `data` dropped here while still borrowed
```

This checking is only possible because we have a single owner for every piece of data.

Borrowing mutable data

Borrowing data mutably complicates things significantly. As with other concepts in Rust, mutability must be specified explicitly when borrowing with the `&mut` operator, and a borrow of a `String` type is of the type `&mut String`.

The Rust compiler enforces the following three rules for mutable borrows to ensure they are safe:

- As with immutable references, a mutable reference cannot outlive its owned data.
- The data we're borrowing must be declared as mutable.
- Whenever we use a mutable borrow, we cannot use any other borrows, whether mutable or immutable, in the same scope.

Let's examine the compiler errors for these rules. We already saw an example of the first rule when learning about immutable borrows, so we'll start with the second rule. The following code will attempt to violate this rule by using a mutable borrow to create a mutable reference to an immutable piece of data:

```
let data = 0u32;
let borrow=&mutdata
```

The compiler rejects this immediately with a message like the following:

```
error[E0596]: cannot borrow `data` as mutable, as it is not declared as mutable
 --> src/main.rs:3:18
  |
3 | letborrow=&mutdata
  |                   ^^^^^^^^^ cannot borrow as mutable
```

This rule should make some sense, since the data is immutable, and a mutable reference would only be useful if we were trying to modify it. In C++, `const` is not as strict and could be removed with a `const_cast< >` or C-style cast, but Rust offers us no way in safe code to alter an immutable variable.

Let's examine some code that violates the third rule by attempting to borrow a piece of data while an immutable reference is already in use:

```
let mut data = 0u32;
let borrow=&data
let borrow_mut=&mutdata
println!("{}, {}", borrow, borrow_mut);
```

This produces the following error when compiled:

```
error[E0502]: cannot borrow `data` as mutable because it is also borrowed as
immutable
```

Similarly, if we attempt to borrow the same data mutably twice in the same scope, the compiler will also catch this problem:

```
let mut data = 0u32;
let borrow_mut_1=&mutdata
let borrow_mut_2=&mutdata
println!("{}, {}", borrow_mut_1, borrow_mut_2);
```

This results in a similar compiler error:

```
error[E0499]: cannot borrow `data` as mutable more than once at a time
```

These rules can make mutable references challenging to use correctly. In general, it is good practice to keep the scopes in which we use them as small as possible to prevent facing the compiler's wrath.

Dereferencing borrows

Dereferencing occurs when the * operator is used. The most common use of the dereference operator is to modify the data pointed to by a mutable borrow:

```
let mut owned = 0;
let borrowed=&mutowned
*borrowed = 1;
println!("{}", owned);
```

As expected, this code prints 1.

We can also use dereferencing to assign from a reference to another variable, but in general, this is of somewhat limited use since we are only able to assign types that implement Copy. Recall that the data is borrowed, after all. Just as your neighbor would be in the wrong to give a tool they borrowed from you to someone else, the compiler won't allow a borrower to transfer ownership of the data it's borrowing.

Just for fun, though, let's try it and see what the compiler says:

```
let data = String::new();
let borrow=&data
let stolen = *borrow;
```

As expected, the compiler is not happy about this situation:

```
error[E0507]: cannot move out of `*borrow` which is behind a shared reference
 --> src/main.rs:4:14
  |
4 | let stolen = *borrow;
  |              ^^^^^^^ move occurs because `*borrow` has type `String`, which
does not implement the `Copy` trait
  |
```

As the compiler hints, if we try this with a type that implements Copy, such as any integer type, the program will compile and function as we expect.

Borrowing with method calls

We recall from *Chapter 2* that methods in Rust are defined as associated functions that take an argument named `self` as their first parameter, most often as either `&self` or `&mut self`. We can now identify these as immutable and mutable references, respectively. The act of calling a method borrows the object on which we're calling the method, and these borrows must follow all the same rules that we've already discovered.

Let's see an example of trying to call a mutable method on an already-borrowed object. We would expect this to fail because a mutable borrow can only ever be the only active borrow in a scope:

```
let mut data = String::new();
let borrow=&data
data.push_str("Hello");
println!("{}", borrow);
```

Sure enough, this gives us a now-familiar error:

```
error[E0502]: cannot borrow `data` as mutable because it is also borrowed as
immutable
```

Rust's strict rules around borrows create programs that are easy for the compiler to validate, but when passing references to functions or storing them in structures, we need to give the compiler a little more help by providing it with extra information about how long our data is expected to live. That leads us to the third aspect of Rust's safety model: **lifetimes**.

Specifying lifetimes

To be able to validate our whole program, it's crucial for the compiler to always understand whether the owner of a borrowed piece of data remains alive and in scope. In some cases, this analysis is beyond the compiler's ability, and it leans on us to help it. This is where *lifetime annotations* come into play.

Understanding lifetime annotations

Every reference in Rust has a lifetime. Tracking these lifetimes is one of the most important jobs of the borrow checker. We've already seen how it works to prevent references from data that has been freed by going out of scope.

Most of the time, we don't need to be concerned about the lifetimes of these references. Either they're inferred or elided. Some code doesn't even allow us to specify them. Lifetime annotations are identifiable as lowercase identifiers preceded by a single quote and show up as part of either generic type parameters or a reference type:

```
fn print<'a>(s: &'a str) {
    println!("{}", s);
}
```

Here, the lifetime is a single letter, a. Most lifetimes in Rust code use the convention of a single letter, starting at "a" and moving to the next letter in the alphabet for each additional lifetime needed. But the lifetime name can be any identifier that is preceded by a single quote character. The portion enclosed in < > declares that the lifetime will be used for this function. Most often, we then put the lifetime directly after the & character, declaring a reference parameter to assign the lifetime to this reference.

Lifetimes in functions

It's easiest to talk about lifetimes in functions by talking first about when we do not need to specify them. When a function takes references as parameters but does not return a reference, we have no need to specify the lifetime of the parameters. In safe code, nothing can happen inside the function that will result in the owners of a reference being dropped.

Things start to get a little more complicated when our function returns a reference. The compiler infers that if there is only one reference parameter to the function, then the reference we're returning must have the same lifetime as that parameter. This is a good inference because the rules of safe Rust code would not let us produce a borrow to any other thing except a global variable.

But what if our function has two or more reference parameters? Now the compiler has no way of telling which of the reference parameters share a lifetime with the return value. Without a complicated static analysis of the function body, this isn't possible for the compiler to determine. In a less-strict programming language, it could even change based on the data passed into the function.

So, we must specify a lifetime annotation for any function with more than one reference parameter and one or more reference returns. Since they are a generic construct, the lifetime annotations for a function share syntactical space with any generic types used by the function. This can lead to an imposing syntactical explosion:

```
fn get_cmd<'a, 'b,T>(&'a mut self,param:&'bT)-> &'a mut Command;
```

No one would accuse this function definition of being pretty to look at, but if we break it down, it should quickly become understandable. The `get_cmd` function has two reference parameters with different lifetimes. We're not making any claims about how these two lifetimes relate to one another, only that they are allowed to differ. What this function does tell us is that the lifetime of the return value is identical to the lifetime of the object itself, likely because it is borrowing a part of the object. With this knowledge, the compiler can validate the lifetime of the references at all call sites using only the function signature.

Lifetimes in structures

In addition to understanding the lifetime of each function argument, the Rust compiler must also understand the lifetime of each structure.

Consider the following code:

```
let i = 0;
let holder=IntHolder{data:&i};
println!("{}", holder.data);
```

Without revealing the definition of `IntHolder` yet, we can see that it holds a reference to an integer type. How can the borrow checker validate that this reference does not outlive its owner? In order to help the compiler, we must annotate the lifetimes within the structure definition itself:

```
struct IntHolder<'a> {
    data: &'a i32,
}
```

With this annotation, we are telling the compiler that the lifetime of the object and its member are identical, which is to say that the reference held by the `data` member must be valid for the entire lifetime of the `IntHolder` object.

There is no lifetime inference or elision for references held by structures. Structures must explicitly specify a lifetime in these cases. One possible explanation for this is the special `static` lifetime. This is the lifetime given to static global data that will effectively never be destroyed as part of the program's normal execution. While the most common usage is to hold a reference to a literal string, instead, we'll make a change to our `IntHolder` structure to use a static lifetime:

```
struct IntHolder {
    data: &'static i32,
}
```

With this change, our original program no longer compiles:

```
error[E0597]: `i` does not live long enough
```

We've told the compiler that anything that can be dropped as part of the program's normal execution cannot be used with our structure. To make it compile again, we need to make the reference into a global:

```
static I: i32 = 0;
fn main() {
    let holder=IntHolder{data:&I};
    println!("{}", holder.data);
}
```

The rules for lifetime annotations aren't complicated, but they require some practice to use correctly. The part of the brain that deals with lifetimes isn't exercised as much by other programming languages, but this way of thinking eventually becomes second nature after writing enough code in Rust. Perhaps this is one of the reasons some programmers claim that learning Rust has helped them write and design better code in other languages.

Next, we'll examine the final piece of the Rust safety puzzle: handling critical runtime errors.

Understanding panics

While the Rust compiler works very hard to keep problems from occurring, a significant part of Rust's safety strategy is deciding what happens when something does go wrong. For time failures from which a program cannot reasonably recover, Rust uses *panics* as an error-handling method of last resort. In this section, we'll examine what panics do, what kinds of issues can cause them, and how we can write programs to avoid them.

Panicking as a safety mechanism

In *Chapter 1*, we talked about how the kinds of bugs caused by reading and writing outside of allocated memory have plagued C and C++ software. Buffer overruns are one of the most dangerous of all security issues. Let's see how Rust handles reading outside of an array:

```
fn main() {
    let values = [0; 10];
    let index = 11;
    println!("Element at index {} is: {}", index, values[index]);
}
```

When run, this program produces the following output:

```
thread 'main' panicked at src/main.rs:4:51:
index out of bounds: the len is 10 but the index is 11
note: run with `RUST_BACKTRACE=1` environment variable to display a backtrace
```

We've triggered our first panic! The program's runtime checks detected that our index was out of bounds, printed a useful error message including the line of source code that failed, and offered the option to produce a backtrace to help us narrow down the problem further.

Exiting the program is necessary to fulfill Rust's safety requirements. The reason that buffer overruns are such a danger is that they can be exploitable in such a way that allows an attacker to run their own malicious code remotely on an unsuspecting user's machine. Rather than allow this by continuing execution, Rust programs exit immediately.

If you've spent a lot of time tracking down bugs caused by memory overwrites in C++ code, this may seem like an amazing time saver. But if you're an end user, it might seem like a big hassle to have the program exit suddenly with a scary error message. It's important to avoid causing panics in our Rust code as often as possible.

Avoiding panics

The first step to avoiding a panic is to know what types of operations cause it. The Rust standard library documentation is excellent at calling out the conditions under which any function can panic. Third-party crate documentation does not always meet the same level of quality as the standard library, but when it is missing information the source is usually still available to check..

There are several common operations that will panic in Rust. Most obvious are a handful of macros that panic when the program calls them. The `unreachable!` macro is used to mark code that cannot be reached through the normal execution flow. The `todo!` and `unimplemented!` macros mark code that probably should be expected to be filled in later. The `assert!` macro and a handful of its variations will panic if an expected condition is not met. And, of course, the `panic!` macro will unconditionally generate a panic with a custom message.

The `Result` enum that we encountered in *Chapter 2* offers a function called `unwrap` that will return an `Ok` value if one is stored in the enum and panic if an `Err` value is stored instead. The `Option` type, which represents an optional value that is either `Some` or `None`, has a similar function. Because the `Result` and `Option` types are frequently used in APIs, programmers early in their Rust journey tend to use `unwrap` often.

We can see how this causes a panic in the following example:

```
let option_some: Option<u32> = Some(1);
let option_none: Option<u32> = None;
println!("unwrap some: {}", option_some.unwrap());
println!("unwrap none: {}", option_none.unwrap());
```

This produces the following output when run:

```
thread 'main' panicked at src/main.rs:5:41:
called `Option::unwrap()` on a `None` value
```

While `unwrap` is useful, calling it often risks creating a panic that will unceremoniously terminate your program. We can always use a `match` or `if let` statement to handle all the possible values of the `Result` and `Option` types, but these enums also have a series of variations of the `unwrap` function that do not panic. Be sure to check the documentation if you're thinking about using `unwrap`. Perhaps `unwrap_or` or one of its companion functions could be a better choice by giving the program a fallback value instead of panicking with an error.

We can use `unwrap_or` to fix the preceding example:

```
let option_some: Option<u32> = Some(1);
let option_none: Option<u32> = None;
println!("unwrap some: {}", option_some.unwrap_or(0));
println!("unwrap none: {}", option_none.unwrap_or(0));
```

The output of the program now looks like this, with no panic occurring:

```
unwrap some: 1
unwrap none: 0
```

There is one context where panics are always OK: tests. When a test encounters a panic, it will cause the test to fail rather than causing the test runner process to exit. This is almost always the desired behavior, and unit tests are one of the primary uses of the `assert` set of macros in Rust.

Now that we've got a complete picture of Rust's safety model, let's look at some of the implications it has on how we design our programs.

Changing how we write code

New Rust programmers, especially those coming from languages such as C++, often experience a season of frustration as they attempt to get their first programs to pass the compiler's strict validation. This experience is referred to as "fighting the borrow checker," and because of it, Rust is regarded by many to have a significant learning curve.

In this section, we'll look at some patterns that can lead to protracted arguments with the compiler, and how we can avoid them. This isn't to say that any of these patterns is inherently bad, only that it's best to be comfortable with the language before using them.

Avoiding references in structures

As we saw earlier, whenever a reference is used inside a structure, we must explicitly specify a lifetime annotation for it. Because the lifetime annotation is considered generic, it becomes part of that structure's type signature. This can lead to a cascading effect where adding a single reference to a structure can require adding lifetime annotations to several other structures and their usages.

The Rust developers may find a solution to this problem at some point, but until then, it's best to avoid storing references in a structure until you're very familiar with working with lifetimes. While this can slow down a program with needless copies, it's better for newer Rust programmers to get their programs working and compiling first to unlock the benefits of Rust's safety checking. In a second step, we can profile and make the program faster as needed.

Using copyable structures often

We should attempt to derive the `Copy` trait as much as possible. This allows us to move around the data more freely, but it must be done with some care. If we are too hasty with using `Copy`, we can get into a bad situation. If we have a simple structure that implements `Copy`, but later need to add a non-copyable member to it, it can result in a lot of fixups of existing code to conform to the single ownership principle.

To avoid this, it's best to use `Copy` for structures that are conceptually "plain old data," or **POD**. This is a technical term from C++ that has changed definitions throughout the various revisions of the C++ standard, but we can consider a less formal definition of the term for our purposes. We should consider a structure for `Copy` if none of its members require constructors or destructors, and we can be confident that they won't need to in the future.

Learning not to fear cloning

Borrowing helps us avoid unnecessary copies, but sometimes we can get into tricky situations in Rust code. This can happen especially often if we're attempting to translate existing code from another language. If you find yourself in an argument with the borrow checker, it can often be solved with a call to `clone()`.

The principle we examined earlier applies here too. We don't want to litter our code with needless copies, but we should make it safe first and fast second. The benefits of having a Rust program running for years in production without any crashes can often outweigh the small trade-offs in performance.

Using indices instead of references

One pattern that trips up beginners is creating structures that reference themselves. Even if it can be done in other languages, this is a non-starter in Rust because of its single ownership principle. For any references stored in the structure to remain valid, we must ensure that the data being borrowed outlives its owner, which isn't possible if the structure owning the data is the one being copied. If Rust did allow this, we would effectively be copying a pointer to the previous owner, which is no longer valid after the move.

Whenever we get into a situation where we want to create a self-referential structure, we must refactor it to use a different solution. One somewhat common attempt at doing this is to store a pool of items in a structure, as well as references in that pool. In this case, the easiest change to make is to use an index into the pool instead of a reference.

Using indices over borrows can help resolve other tricky ownership issues when referencing into array-like objects. If you get stuck and find yourself fighting with the compiler, consider whether you can change some of your accesses to use an index instead.

Summary

In this chapter, we examined the major aspects of Rust's safety strategy. We learned that data in Rust can only have one owner at a time, and how to transfer and borrow ownership as appropriate. We discussed how to provide lifetime annotations to help the compiler validate our code, and we looked at the nature of runtime panics to understand their proper use. Finally, we discussed how all of this can work together to change the way we write our code.

Next, we'll take a break from programming language theory to take an in-depth look at how to get the most out of Rust's build and packaging tooling.

Get this book's PDF version and more

Scan the QR code (or go to `packtpub.com/unlock`). Search for this book by name, confirm the edition, and then follow the steps on the page.

UNLOCK NOW

Note: Keep your invoice handy. Purchases made directly from Packt don't require an invoice.

4

Managing Rust Projects with Cargo

While the Rust safety model that we've been exploring gives us higher confidence in the correctness of our programs, one large reason that Rust is such a joy to use is its build and packaging tool, Cargo. By choosing "convention over configuration," Rust and Cargo make project creation, dependency management, and publishing straightforward and simple.

In this chapter, we're going to cover the following main topics:

- Structuring a Rust project
- Working with dependencies
- Publishing crates
- Exploring Cargo's capabilities

Technical requirements

The examples in this chapter use Rust 1.82.0, but they will also work using any newer version. If you need help installing Rust, please see the *Appendix*.

Structuring a Rust project

We've read that Rust projects use "convention over configuration," but what does this mean? In a C++ project, building requires a list of every individual file that must be compiled and a possibly different set of compile flags, include paths, and preprocessor defines for each one. This leads to configuration overload, and it has spawned several different build systems that attempt to manage the complexity around it in various ways.

In contrast, Rust keeps the build process simple by standardizing around a small amount of configuration and a set of conventions about the structure of the project that allow it to understand how to build each crate. In this section, we'll explore how Rust structures crates and how that structure affects what is built by the compiler.

Creating a basic project

We've seen in previous chapters that using Cargo to create a new Rust project from the command line is very simple:

```
$ cargo new my_bin_project
```

This will create a new binary crate in the `my_bin_project` directory underneath the current working directory. A binary crate represents a single native application.

Library crates, on the other hand, are intended to be used as dependencies of other crates, much like static libraries in C++. If we wish to create a library crate instead, we can use this command:

```
$ cargo new --lib my_lib_project
```

Whether you're making a binary or library crate, the `cargo new` command will create the minimum necessary file structure for you. For binary crates, it will create a small `main` function containing a `"Hello World"` example, and for library crates, it will create a simple passing unit test.

If we wish to use Git as our primary version control system, the `cargo new` command also creates a Git repository and a `.gitignore` file by default.

File structure of a crate

Looking at the files in `my_lib_project` created by the `cargo new` command, we see the following files for a simple library crate:

```
Cargo.toml
src/lib.rs
```

The `Cargo.toml` file specifies some metadata about our crate, including its name and version number. When we begin adding dependencies to our programs, they will be stored in this file as well. Cargo uses the **TOML** configuration language, which was designed to be lightweight and easy for humans to edit. A description of the TOML format can be found on its website: `https://toml.io/`.

Looking at the files in `my_bin_project`, we see a very similar structure:

```
Cargo.toml
src/main.rs
```

Here, we see our first example of Rust using the structure of a crate to make decisions about how to build it. There is no config in the `Cargo.toml` file indicating whether the crate is a binary or a library. The compiler decides which to build based on whether it encounters a `main.rs` or `lib.rs` file in the filesystem.

To perform a build, we can run the `cargo build` command from our shell. This command works from the root folder of any properly configured crate and will invoke the compiler to produce either a native binary or library in the project's `target` folder. This command also accepts various arguments, of which the most used is likely `--release` to instruct Cargo to perform an optimized build:

```
$ cargo build --release
```

While it may seem obvious to experienced engineers, be sure to use a release build whenever evaluating runtime performance. Rust discussion forums across the internet are filled with questions from users who did not realize that the default behavior of `cargo build` is to create an unoptimized binary!

Understanding modules

It would be inconvenient if Rust's build system only allowed us to have one source file for our entire project. Rust's strategy here is not a loosely connected set of source files stitched together at link time as in C++, but rather a more formally structured solution called **modules**.

The compiler always starts at the root file of the crate, whether it is `main.rs` or `lib.rs`. This root source file can add a module to the crate using the `mod` keyword. This keyword will cause the compiler to pull in a source file matching the module's name from a specific place in the crate's `src` folder.

Let's add a module to the `my_bin_project` crate that we created earlier in order to see an example. Modify the `src/main.rs` file to look like this:

```
mod greeting;
fn main() {
    println!("Hello, world!");
}
```

Of course, we haven't created any source files for `greeting`, so if we try to run the `cargo build` command, the compiler will unsurprisingly report an error. That error contains a very helpful message about what we'll need to do next:

```
help: to create the module `greeting`, create file "src/greeting.rs" or "src/
greeting/mod.rs"
```

As we can see, Rust allows two possible source locations for the module. Using the `src/greeting/mod.rs` file may make more sense if we intend to nest additional modules underneath `greeting`, but projects with simple organization can just use the `src/greeting.rs` file instead. We'll proceed by adding `src/greeting.rs` to our project with the following contents:

```
const GREETING: &str = "Hello World!";
```

We'll also change our `main` function as follows:

```
fn main() {
    println!("{}", greeting::GREETING);
}
```

We've scoped our new `GREETING` constant with the module name and used it to replace the hardcoded greeting. Are we done? Let's run `cargo build` to check:

```
error[E0603]: constant `GREETING` is private
```

We've discovered another property of Rust modules: they hide their contents from the other source files in the project by default. This is Rust's way of distinguishing between public and private interfaces. To allow an identifier to be accessed outside of our module, we must explicitly mark it with the `pub` keyword. Moving back to `src/greeting.rs`, we can make the required correction:

```
pub const GREETING: &str = "Hello World!";
```

With this change, our project now builds, runs, and prints `"Hello World!"` as expected.

As mentioned earlier, modules can be nested. As an exercise, try adding a submodule of `src/greeting.rs` by using the `mod` keyword inside it. Remember that the compiler's error messages can guide you at each step.

Working with binaries

Normally, a binary crate is built into a single executable that shares the same name as the crate. The `main` function is found in `src/main.rs`, and that serves as the entry point to the executable produced by the crates.

But there may be cases where we'd like to add one or more binaries to a library crate as well. Cargo exposes this by treating any file in the `src/bin/` directory as an independent binary. These programs can import our library crate and interact with it through its public API.

When we have any binary in our crate, we can use the `cargo run` command as a useful shortcut. This command will build the binary, if necessary, and then immediately invoke it with any arguments we provide. Just like `cargo build`, we must pass the `--release` flag to use an optimized binary. An example usage of `cargo run`, including arguments passed to the resulting program, could look like this:

```
$ cargo run --release -- --test
```

Anything after `--` is passed directly to the program being run, while anything before it is an argument to the `cargo run` command itself.

We saw that we can have more than one binary associated with our crate in the `src/bin/` directory. If we make use of this feature by putting a `test.rs` file into the `src/bin/` directory, it can put Cargo into a situation where it does not know which binary we intend for it to run. For this, Cargo provides a `--bin` option that can be passed to `cargo run` to specify which binary to run:

```
$ cargo run
error: `cargo run` could not determine which binary to
run. Use the `--bin` option to specify a binary, or the `default-run` manifest
key.
available binaries: hello_world, test
```

As we can see, Cargo's error message tells us the binaries we can specify, as well as how to specify a default binary in the `Cargo.toml` config file.

Now that we understand how Rust uses the structure of the files in our crate's folder to build, we'll look at another extremely important function of Cargo: **managing dependencies**.

Working with dependencies

Beyond its safety guarantees, one of Rust's primary strengths is a large, centralized repository of community-contributed crates accessible directly from Cargo. In this section, we'll learn how to locate interesting dependencies and import them into our projects with Cargo.

Exploring Rust's community crates

Crates contributed by the Rust community are indexed by a **registry**, with the default Rust registry residing at `https://crates.io/`. Whereas in C++ our dependencies could be scattered across tens of websites and use many different configurations, in Rust, this central registry hosts thousands of different crates, each of which can be imported into our project with a few simple commands.

Of course, we wouldn't want to import just any of them. We must locate a set of crates that meet our specific criteria around licensing, maturity, and functionality. Searching for the crates that meet our needs can be accomplished on the `crates.io` website, or it can be done through the `cargo search` command from the comfort of our terminal:

```
$ cargo search chess
```

When this command is run, Cargo outputs a list of several chess-related libraries.

The `cargo search` command is useful, but it only shows you the names of crates and a brief description. Using the website to search can be much more fruitful. For each crate indexed by `crates.io`, you can see its license, number of views and downloads, as well as links to documentation and the source repository.

Quickly locating and importing dependencies from the internet must be done with care, even when hosted by a trustworthy registry. Only packages with compatible licenses must be added to our projects, and each project may require a security review of the dependencies it uses. But for exploratory coding and casual work, the official Rust crate registry can usually provide something valuable in all but the most specialized of cases.

Managing dependencies with Cargo

Cargo provides several useful commands for managing dependencies. The `cargo add` and `cargo rm` functions are the easiest place to start. Let's say we wish to add `anyhow`, which is a popular error-handling crate. We can use a command like this:

```
$ cargo add anyhow
```

Cargo will search the registry for the latest version and add it as a dependency to our crate. It does this by editing the `dependencies` section of our `Cargo.toml` file. Looking at the file, we might see something like this:

```
[dependencies]
anyhow = "1.0.89"
```

The version of the dependency will likely be different depending on when the command was run, but the structure is the same. When we build our crate next, the `anyhow` crate and its dependencies will also be downloaded and compiled, and the `anyhow` public interface will be available to our crate.

Should we change our mind about needing this dependency in our project, we can run `cargo rm anyhow` to remove it from the `Cargo.toml`.

Configuring dependencies

When running the preceding commands, you may have seen an output like this:

```
Adding anyhow v1.0.89 to dependencies
       Features:
       + std
       - backtrace
```

Here, `cargo add` is displaying the features used by this crate. A **feature** represents some configurable aspect of the crate. Often, functionality is gated behind a feature if it represents advanced functionality not needed by all users, if it is experimental, or even if it is known to significantly affect compile times.

Documentation for each crate should be consulted to learn what each feature does and the consequences of enabling it. If you find that you wish to enable a feature, you can use the `--features` flag with the `cargo add` command like this:

```
$ cargo add anyhow --features backtrace
```

Examining `Cargo.toml`, we see that our dependency entry has changed to the following:

```
[dependencies]
anyhow = { version = "1.0.89", features = ["backtrace"] }
```

If we change our mind about the features we want to enable, we have several options, including manually editing the `Cargo.toml` file or using `cargo rm` before re-adding the dependency with a different set of features.

Adding non-Rust dependencies

Not all the complexity of any given build can be expressed with the small amount of information in `Cargo.toml` and the structure of the files provided in the crate. A frequent example is linking against dependencies not written in Rust. For example, linking to a library written in C may require compiling several individual C files with special compiler flags and then providing information to the linker that we require these files to be linked into our final binary.

The mechanism Rust uses to solve these challenges is called the `build.rs` file, which exists in the root directory of our crate. This file is essentially a program with the job of performing any custom build steps required for the program and notifying Cargo about any changes.

If the `build.rs` file exists in the root folder of our crate, Cargo will compile it into a binary and then run the resulting command. It will monitor both `stdout` and the build program's return code. If it panics or exits abnormally in any way, Cargo will halt the crate build. If the build program executes successfully, Cargo will examine the lines that it wrote to `stdout` to find any additional build instructions.

This mechanism is flexible, but it comes with some drawbacks. A build program that is not set up optimally can add a significant amount of time to each build. Additionally, the execution of the build program is not guarded in any way, making it a potential vector for malicious crates to exploit a user's system.

There are several crates that are designed specifically to be used inside a `build.rs` file, often for running compilation or preprocessing tasks. One of the more popular crates built for this purpose is the `cc` crate, which invokes a C or C++ compiler and notifies Cargo to link the resulting library into our crate.

To add it, we can use this command:

```
$ cargo add cc --build
```

By passing `--build`, we limit the crate to only be usable in development contexts such as the `build.rs` file. If we tried to use it in our crate directly, we would find that it was not available.

A simple `build.rs` file using `cc` might look like this:

```
fn main() {
    cc::Build::new()
        .file("src/hello.c")
        .compile("hello");
}
```

With this build program in place, we would be able to access the functions inside `hello.c` inside our crate by importing the `hello` library. While this small example gives us an idea of how to use Cargo to build C and C++ code, accessing the C and C++ functions from Rust is a larger topic that we'll explore fully in *Chapter 9*.

Having explored several aspects of managing and using dependencies in our crate, we'll now look at publishing our own dependencies for others to use.

Publishing crates

After making a useful library or program, we may wish to share it with the wider Rust community. We can do this by publishing it to a Cargo registry. Most often, we will be using the official Rust registry at `crates.io`, but internal registries may be available in some organizations.

Setting up an account

Each registry will have a different means of setting up an account. At the time of writing, the official Cargo registry only allows users to log in using a GitHub account. A GitHub account can be obtained by creating one on `https://github.com/`. Using GitHub is beyond the scope of this book, but it may also be able to provide hosting services for a Git repository containing our crate's source code.

Once an account has been created, we can use the `cargo login` command to obtain access to our chosen registry. Invoking it using the default configuration, we see the following:

```
$ cargo login
please paste the token found on https://crates.io/me below
```

Browsing to the link given, we'll be provided with an access token. After pasting it into our terminal, the key will be stored in the `~/.cargo/credentials.toml` folder, and we will be able to use privileged Cargo commands to interact with the registry.

Of course, it's important for this login token to be well-protected. If it were obtained by a malicious user, new versions of our crate could be published to our end users, containing backdoors or other security issues. We can use the `cargo logout` command to remove the local credentials file whenever needed, but if a token does become compromised, it should be revoked immediately from the registry's website.

Preparing a crate for publishing

The `cargo package` command can be used to prepare a crate for publishing. This command will ensure that all requirements are met, build the crate to ensure that it can be compiled, and create an archive file that will be pushed to the repository.

> **Note**
>
> If you are using Git for version control, it's important to ensure that all changes have been committed to the local repository before attempting to run the `cargo package` command.

To help others find and understand the purpose of our crate after it is published, several metadata tags may be added to `Cargo.toml`. The `cargo package` command will check for common ones and notify you if any are missing. Running it against `my_lib_project`, we see the following:

```
$ cargo package
warning: manifest has no description, license, license-file, documentation,
homepage or repository.
See https://doc.rust-lang.org/cargo/reference/manifest.html#package-metadata for
more info.
```

These metadata tags go in the `[package]` section of the `Cargo.toml` file. Each has a different expected format or version. For our `my_lib_project` crate, we might do something like the following:

```
[package]
name = "my_lib_project"
version = "0.1.0"
description = "Example of a library crate"
license = "MIT OR Apache-2.0"
```

We can add as many or as few metadata tags as needed, but we must keep in mind that these tags help others locate our crate in searches. Things like documentation, a home page, and a repository are all very helpful to the users of our crate. Documentation for these tags is available at the URL displayed by the `cargo package` command.

Understanding semantic versioning

If we've looked much at the version numbers of Rust dependencies, we'll see that they are all made up of three numbers separated by a period or decimal. Version numbers in Rust follow the concept of **semantic versioning**. This concept is explored in detail at `https://semver.org/`, but because of its importance to the Rust ecosystem, we'll cover the basics briefly here.

Semantic versioning starts with the three numbers we've observed, called the **major**, **minor**, and **patch** versions, when read from left to right. Every crate starts at `0.1.0` when it's created by Cargo, giving it a major version of `0`, a minor version of `1`, and a patch version of `0`. The version number should change whenever a new revision of the crate is published, and what it changes to is determined by the rules of semantic versioning.

The major version must be incremented whenever the public API of the crate is updated in a breaking way. This version number starts at `0` intentionally, implying that the crate has no stable public API and is still in development. But once it reaches `1.0.0`, the crate's public API is considered stable, and any backward-incompatible change must bump the major version and set the minor and patch versions back to `0`.

The minor version must be incremented when there are any backward-compatible additions to the public API. It may also be incremented when there are significant feature additions or improvements to the crate. When the minor version is incremented, the patch version must be set back to `0`.

This only leaves the patch version, which is incremented for bug fixes that do not alter the public API of the crate. This set of rules about what can and can't be updated with each version is used by Cargo to determine which version of the crate it should use when resolving dependencies. Closely following the semantic versioning rules should minimize hassle and breakage for projects choosing to use the crate as a dependency.

Now that we've successfully logged in to the repository, created a package using Cargo, and chosen the correct version number for our crate, it's time to send it to the repository for others to use.

Sending a crate to the repository

As we prepare to send our crate, we must do any final checks that are needed at this point to ensure that we're sending exactly what we intended. Once the crate is pushed to the repository, the files in our project are available to everyone on the internet, potentially indefinitely.

The `cargo package --list` command can be used to double-check which files are included in the package. It's good to check that no secret keys or any other sensitive data files were included at this point.

In the end, the actual publishing is a bit of an anticlimax after all the preparation. We simply run the `cargo publish` command, and our crate is sent to the repository and made available immediately for others to use.

In some emergency situations, a crate's author may wish to remove a broken version from the Cargo registry. This could include an accidentally published version, an unintentional breakage of semantic versioning rules, a licensing issue, or any emergency that must prevent other crates from using a specific published version as a dependency.

For **yanking** or removing a published version from the Cargo registry, the `cargo yank` command is provided. It's important to note that this does not remove any of the published files and does not prevent the distribution of anything that may have been put into the crate's package unintentionally. But yanking a crate does prevent new users from adding a dependency on it.

Now that we understand the publishing workflow, let's look at some helpful tools provided by Cargo that aren't directly related to building a project or its dependencies.

Exploring Cargo's capabilities

While Cargo makes building and dependency management easy, it also boasts many other capabilities that we can use to improve our Rust development experience. In this section, we'll explore several of Cargo's most useful features and examine how to extend it to provide even greater utility.

Using Cargo as a test runner

Cargo serves an important function as a test runner for Rust crates. Let's look briefly at how this works using the `my_lib_project` crate we created earlier:

```
$ cargo test
running 1 test
test tests::it_works ... ok
```

```
test result: ok. 1 passed; 0 failed; 0 ignored; 0 measured; 0 filtered out;
finished in 0.00s
```

This output is truncated to show the most important parts. We're running a test called `it_works`, which was generated for us by `cargo new`. Happily, it succeeds.

This is what we'll see if we open up `src/lib.rs` in the `my_lib_project` crate:

```
pub fn add(left: u64, right: u64) -> u64 {
    left + right
}

#[cfg(test)]
mod tests {
    use super::*;

    #[test]
    fn it_works() {
        let result = add(2, 2);
        assert_eq!(result, 4);
    }
}
```

What we are seeing is a common pattern used to include tests in the same source file as our code. We start by making an inline submodule named `tests` with the `mod` keyword. This module is marked with `#[cfg(test)]`, which tells the compiler to only compile it at all if we are running in the test config.

With `use super::*;`, we import theAPI of the parent module inside of our tests submodule so that we can call functions from it without any other adornment. Finally, we designate a function that serves as a test using the `#[test]` marker. While the submodule and config guard are convenient, the tests will not run without a `#[test]` marker.

Installing software with Cargo

In addition to *build* and *test* tasks, Cargo can also be used to install binary crates into the system path. Although it requires local compilation of the software, this can often be an easy way to install a wide array of useful programs on the local machine. It can also provide developers with a low-effort way to distribute their software, at least across the Rust community.

Cargo provides two subcommands to manage this feature: `cargo install` and `cargo uninstall`. As an example, we can use this command to install `ripgrep`, a highly regarded Rust program for searching within text files:

```
$ cargo install ripgrep
```

When passed only the name of a crate, the `install` command will search `crates.io` for a published crate, download it into a `temp` folder, compile it, and place the resulting binary in the same folder as the `cargo` executable itself, ensuring that it goes into the system path.

When the process is complete, we can execute the following command to display the full list of crates installed in this manner, their version numbers, and the names of the resulting executables:

```
$ cargo install --list
```

In the case of `ripgrep`, we'll find that the name of the command we've installed is `rg`, or `rg.exe` if we are using Windows.

The `cargo install` command can also install crates from a remote Git repository or even a local path if we pass the correct arguments. As with all of Cargo's subcommands, we can get detailed usage info through the `--help` flag:

```
$ cargo install --help
```

The `cargo uninstall` command is much simpler. Just pass the name of the crate you wish to uninstall, and Cargo will remove it from your path by deleting any associated binaries:

```
$ cargo uninstall ripgrep
```

This will, of course, only remove references to the copy of the software maintained by Cargo. If we have installed the same program redundantly through another program or installer, Cargo will leave those copies entirely alone.

Vendoring dependencies

In its default configuration, Cargo is configured to download dependencies from the internet into a local cache. Depending on the nature of our work, it may be more desirable to run Cargo in an offline mode and have it source all dependencies from a local directory on the filesystem instead of downloading them. This has the advantage of ensuring that neither the availability of external websites or services nor the whims of crate maintainers will ever result in an inability to build our project.

The practice of pre-downloading dependencies to provide a locked and always-available set is called **vendoring**, and Cargo has a `vendor` subcommand to assist with the process. Simply invoking the command from the shell is enough:

```
$ cargo vendor
```

This will download all dependencies our crate relies on into the `vendor/` folder underneath the crate's root folder. Cargo will ensure that the list of dependencies in that folder will exactly match the ones needed by our program, including removing any folders from previous runs of the `cargo vendor` command that are no longer needed due to changes that we have made.

Each time it's run, `cargo vendor` will also tell us that we need to add some configuration to a file named `.cargo/config.toml` file. This configuration is required to use the dependencies downloaded and organized by invoking the command. These lines only need to be added to this config once. If we no longer wish to use our vendored dependencies, we can simply delete the `vendor/` folder and remove the required lines from `config.toml` as well.

Extending Cargo with plugins

While commands such as `install` and `vendor` are built into the program directly, Cargo was designed to be extended by community-contributed subcommands referred to as **plugins**. Whenever Cargo encounters a subcommand it does not recognize, it will search for a binary matching that command's name in the system path. For instance, invoking `cargo plugin` on the command line would cause Cargo to search for an executable named `cargo-plugin` on the local system and execute it if found.

Authoring plugins is beyond the scope of this chapter, but it's important to know about this functionality of Cargo. Popular plugins can be found on `crates.io` either by searching using a web browser or by invoking a search with Cargo itself. All plugins start with the prefix `cargo-`, so they can be found with a command such as this one:

```
$ cargo search cargo-
```

There are many other interesting aspects of Cargo. In this chapter, we've only been able to explore the most common and useful ones. Passing the `--list` option to Cargo will show all the commands available to use, and the `cargo help` command can provide a great breakdown of each one. For online documentation, feel free to check out the Cargo book located at `https://doc.rust-lang.org/cargo/`.

Summary

In this chapter, we learned how to use Cargo to create new projects, add modules and dependencies to them, and publish our own code for Rust developers around the world to use. Then, we examined how Cargo can be used to test our crates and install new software on our machines. Finally, we saw how to use Cargo to vendor our dependencies and how to extend it to add further improvements.

In the next chapter, we'll examine how Rust's standard library implements common data structures and containers.

Part 2

Exploring the Rust Standard Library

In this second part of the book, we'll explore several topics related to the Rust standard library. We'll learn about the container, I/O, error handling, and iterator types provided by Rust and get extensive practice using them. Along the way, we'll learn about the conventions and vocabulary used by the standard library, and how each topic interacts with the Rust safety model. By the end of this part, you'll be comfortable working in Rust code and have an excellent understanding of its standard library and parts of the crate ecosystem.

This part of the book includes the following chapters:

5

Data Structures

Now that we understand Rust syntax and crate management, it's time to jump into the Rust standard library. We can think of this as Rust's version of the C++ **Standard Template Library** (**STL**). Despite some differences in approach, the C++ STL and Rust standard library provide much of the same functionality for working with different data structures, or **containers**, as C++ refers to them. In this chapter, we'll explore the most used containers in the Rust standard library and explain many Rust language and library concepts that help us use them more effectively.

In this chapter, we're going to cover the following main topics:

- Fundamentals of Rust data structures
- Working with indexed data
- Using dictionary types

Technical requirements

The examples in this chapter use Rust 1.82.0, but they will also work with any newer version.

If you need help installing Rust, please see the *Appendix*.

Fundamentals of Rust data structures

Many of the data structures and containers in Rust's standard library follow a consistent design and a similar set of rules. In this section, we'll explore these rules in the context of Rust's implementation of character strings. Strings in Rust are the subject of much confusion to new developers, partially due to the large number of purpose-built string types in the standard library and partially because they require a solid grounding in the fundamentals that we'll explore here. After this section, you should have a good understanding of the basic string types in Rust as well as the motifs used by other types of containers in the standard library, including how it deals with ownership and borrowing.

Properties of strings in Rust

New Rust developers are sometimes confused and overwhelmed by the number of different string types in the standard library, but each type serves a specific purpose.

The `String` and `str` types are the basic string types in Rust, and they are available to all programs using the standard library without any additional `use` statements. These two types represent a string encoded in UTF-8 format. Any attempt to construct a string with invalid UTF-8 data will result in an error.

Because these types represent a multi-byte character encoding, we cannot index into them directly to get to a specific character. Attempting to do so might put us in the middle of a multi-byte character, giving us indecipherable text. As such, indexing operations are not even provided on these types, but a wide variety of methods are provided for working with characters. A notable difference between C++ and Rust string types is that Rust has a rich API for string handling built directly into the member functions of its string types, while C++ occasionally relies on generic functionality in the `<algorithm>` header for manipulating strings.

As mentioned, there are many other string types throughout the Rust standard library. The `OsString` and `OsStr` types represent a platform-dependent string encoding. These are used to represent the `PathBuf` and `Path` types, which reside in `std::path` and provide an abstraction over OS-specific differences in file paths. Finally, the `CString` and `CStr` types in `std::ffi` represent zero-terminated C-style strings.

You may wonder why these types come in pairs. The reason is that the Rust standard library provides both **owned** and **borrowed** versions of many data structures to help us work with the borrow checker.

Owned and borrowed types

Most container types in the Rust standard library are owned, but these types are occasionally paired with a corresponding borrowed type. These paired types usually show up when we're dealing with string or string-like data such as filesystem paths. As we saw, most of the major string types in Rust work with an owned type paired with a borrowed type.

We can think about strings in C++ to understand owned and borrowed types better. After all, C++ itself also has multiple string types. The `std::string` type, which corresponds to the `String` type in Rust, is an owned type and manages its own memory that often resides on the heap. The `std::string_view` type acts more like a borrowed type and corresponds closely to the `str` type in Rust. String views do not own the memory they point to and, as a result, must be used with care, but they can perform several useful string manipulations cheaply.

> **Note**
>
> Borrowed types almost always show up as references in code. Thus, the `str` type is used as `&str` in practice. While discussing strings in this section, we'll use `str` as the type name when speaking about the structure itself. Whenever we speak about any instance of the structure, we'll use the `&str` type.

While `std::string_view` was added several years after `std::string` in C++, the `String` and `str` types in Rust were designed to work together from the start. We'll find that throughout the API exposed by these string types, Rust consistently returns a borrowed `&str` type for any operation that does not need new memory allocated and an owned `String` type for any operation that does.

For instance, the `str::trim` function, which removes whitespace from the start and end of the string, will return a new `&str` type. Just like `std::string_view`, there's no allocation required to perform this operation. We can think of both `std::string_view` and `&str` as a pointer to a buffer of bytes paired with an integer storing the string length. Trimming the string only requires incrementing the pointer and decrementing the length, as necessary.

In contrast, an operation such as `str::replace`, which replaces all occurrences of a pattern in an existing string with another string, must allocate memory to store its result. Accordingly, the `str::replace` function in Rust returns a `String` type. Let's look at an example. For extra clarity, the type annotations will be written out even though they are optional:

```
let literal: &'static str = "Hello world";
let owned: String = literal.replace("Hello", "Hi");
assert_eq!(owned, "Hi world");
```

A literal string has the `&'static str` type, where the `'static` lifetime means that the underlying data is never deallocated at any point in the program. When we replace data in the string, we have no choice but to allocate and copy the data into a new owned type and make the changes there.

Converting between owned and borrowed types

There are many ways to convert between a pair of owned and borrowed types in Rust. Some people might even say there are too many ways! The large number of options is because string types implement many different traits and, as such, allow the use of generic functions supplied by the trait implementations.

Our first option is to use member functions that are specific to each pair of types. The `String` type has an `as_str()` method to produce a `&str` type, which, of course, must be used according to Rust's borrowing rules. Similarly, `str` has a `to_string()` method to allocate a new `String` type out of a `&str`. Using these methods makes the intent explicit to readers of the code, but as these are not generic methods, they are tied specifically to the `String` and `str` types:

```
let owned: String = String::from("Hello world");
let borrowed: &str = owned.as_str();
```

If we wish to use generic methods, we can examine several choices among the traits that are implemented on our `String` and `str` types. The first is the `ToOwned` trait, which provides a `to_owned()` function. `ToOwned` is implemented by most borrowed types and returns a clone of the borrowed data. The return value of `to_owned()` depends on the class implementing it, but for `str`, it behaves identically to the `to_string()` function we've already discussed, which returns a `String`:

```
let literal: &'static str = "Hello world";
let owned: String = literal.to_owned();
```

Moving into more interesting territory, we find the `From` and `Into` traits. These traits expose an important mechanism in the Rust standard library for converting between types. The `From` trait provides the `from()` function, which takes a value as an argument and converts it into the structure we're expecting. The `From` trait for converting from `&str` to `String` looks like this:

```
impl From<&str> for String {
    fn from(s: &str) -> String {
        s.to_owned()
    }
}
```

With strings, this often shows up when constructing a `String` from a string literal, which, as we saw earlier, has the `&'static str` type:

```
let s: String = String::from("Hello World!");
```

The `Into` trait implements the `into()` function, which is called with no arguments. `Into` is implemented in terms of `From`, and implementing `From` provides an implementation of `Into` automatically. There is almost never a reason to explicitly implement `Into` in today's Rust versions.

Coming from C++, using `into()` can feel a bit magical. When we convert between types in C++, we're usually specifying the target type, but with `into()` in Rust, the target type is usually inferred from context:

```
let mut s: String = String::from("Hello");
s = "Goodbye".into();
```

We can see in this example that we didn't need to tell the compiler that we wanted to convert from `&str` to `String`. We just called `into()` and the compiler inferred from context that we need to convert to `String`. Because we have the appropriate `From` trait (and, therefore, `Into`) implemented for converting between `&str` and `String`, the compiler uses it to perform the conversion.

Lastly, we'll look at the `AsRef` trait and begin to see why having many ways of performing the same conversion makes sense. The `AsRef` trait is usually implemented by owned types with a corresponding borrowed type to return the borrowed type. As before with `String` and `str`, `as_ref()` will return a `&str` exactly as if the `as_str()` function discussed previously were called.

`AsRef` is most often used in generic functions as a trait bound. As we recall from *Chapter 2*, trait bounds both restrict the available types passed into a generic function and enable the generic functions to call trait methods on the generic parameters:

```
use std::path::Path;
fn use_a_path<T>(path: T)
where
    T: AsRef<Path>,
{
    let path:&Path=path.as_ref();
    todo!()
}
```

`AsRef<Path>` is implemented by several types, including `&str`, meaning that we can pass literal strings as paths when using this trait bound.

Customizing dereference behavior in Rust

Coming from C++, which is loaded with implicit conversions that can produce surprising results, we might appreciate Rust for its lack of implicit trickery. But dereferencing in Rust exposes an implicit behavior that becomes very important to understand to use the language well. That behavior is called **Deref coercion.**

`Deref` coercion centers around the `Deref` trait, which allows us to customize the behavior of the compiler when dereferencing occurs, often using the * operator. In practice, this is often used to cheaply coerce a reference from one type to another. Hopefully, this mention of converting types already conjures images of pairs of owned and borrowed types. Indeed, `String` implements `Deref` with the `str` type as a target, with the trait implementation in the standard library looking like this:

```
impl ops::Deref for String {
    type Target = str;
    fn deref(&self) -> &str {
        self.as_str()
    }
}
```

When a dereference of a `&String` type named `x` is performed in a context requiring a `&str`, the compiler calls `x.deref()` behind the scenes, which will, in turn, result in a call to `x.as_str()` per the trait implementation we just saw.

While we're concerned about the behavior of *dereferencing*, notice that the implementation of `Deref` converts from one reference to another. This is where `Deref` coercion comes into play: just as Rust will implicitly convert dereference operations using `*`, it will also implicitly convert from one type of reference to another in appropriate contexts.

In other words, whenever we use a `&String` reference, the Rust compiler will check whether we're expecting a `&String` type in the current context of the program. If we are, the type of the expression is `&String`, and we go on our merry way. But if the context expects a `&str` instead and the appropriate `Deref` trait is implemented for `String`, the compiler will implicitly coerce the type of the expression into a `&str` using the `deref()` function.

The effects of `Deref` coercion on the language and how we use it are wide-ranging and often surprising to new Rust programmers. There are two major effects that we run into in nearly every Rust program using string types.

The first effect is that values of the `String` type get access to almost all the functions implemented on the `str` type. In other words, the standard library doesn't need to provide an implementation of, say, `String::trim_end` to remove trailing whitespace because the `String` type has transparent access to `str::trim_end` thanks to `Deref` coercion.

Why does this happen? Recall that when we implement methods for a type, we most often give them a first parameter of `&self`. It's important to note that `self` is a reference type. When we call the member function, for example, `s.trim_end()`, the dot operator implicitly borrows `s` to provide `self` as a reference parameter. This triggers `Deref` coercion, meaning that if there is no `trim_end()` in `String`, it will look for one in `str` and call that transparently:

```
let literal = "Hello ";
let string = String::from(literal);
assert_eq!("Hello", literal.trim_end());
assert_eq!("Hello", string.trim_end());
```

In this small example, we're simply creating the same character string as both a `&'static str` literal and an owned `String` and demonstrating that we can call `str::trim_end` on each string with identical results. As before, the compiler inserts an implicit call to `deref()` to make this work, for example, `string.deref().trim_end()`. In practice, we never need to worry about this implicit call and can just think about `String` as inheriting the methods of `str`.

The second major effect of `Deref` coercion is most apparent when designing APIs. Sometimes we want to make a function that receives a string type, but we don't care whether it's `String` or `&str`. In these cases, we can take advantage of `Deref` coercion when crafting our function.

There are many possible solutions to this, including making users call `to_string()` or `as_str()` whenever they are faced with a function that takes the opposite type than we have. The solution that Rust programmers tend to choose most often is to make every immutable string parameter a `&str`. This allows strings that are already `&str` to be passed directly, and any `String` arguments can simply be borrowed with `&` to be passed using `Deref` coercion from `&String` to `&str`:

```
fn print_string(s: &str) {
    println!("{}", s);
}
fn main() {
    print_string("Hello");
    let owned: String = String::from("world");
    print_string(&owned);
}
```

In this case, we can pass the `"Hello"` literal string directly to the function because they both have the `&str` type. When we borrow the owned string, `"world"`, the compiler inserts an implicit call to `deref()` to convert the owned reference to `&str` rather than passing it as `&String`. This practice of using the borrowed type in function parameters is so commonplace that even the Rust linter Clippy will recommend it as a best practice. For more info about Clippy, see the *Appendix*.

Now that we've seen several examples of working with the various string types in Rust and explored fundamental concepts such as the `From`, `Into`, `AsRef`, and `Deref` traits, we'll begin to look at the standard library's support for containers that store contiguous, indexable data.

Working with indexed data

Just as C++ has `std::array`, `std::vector`, and `std::span` for storing contiguous elements that can be trivially indexed, Rust has arrays, vectors, and slices, respectively. In this section, we'll examine these elements of Rust and learn how they work together while preserving Rust's borrowing rules.

Using array types

We've already seen the syntax for declaring arrays in *Chapter 2*, and in *Chapter 3*, we learned that out-of-bounds access will cause a panic to enforce Rust's safety properties. Now, we'll focus on how to use Rust arrays in practice.

Arrays choose a fixed size at initialization that will never change during the runtime of a program. The size must also be known at compile time, meaning we can't, for instance, read a file of unknown size and then present the file's data to the rest of our program as an array.

Arrays are also a generic type, like all the indexed types we'll look at in this section. We can see both the type and initialization of an array here:

```
let my_array1: [u32; 5] = [0; 5];
let my_array2: [u32; 5] = [0, 1, 2, 3, 4];
```

The size, being fixed at compile time, is part of the type. In this case, we've initialized two different arrays of the same type with different values. As we saw in *Chapter 2*, the first line fills the array with five elements of a value of `0`, while the second line initializes each element individually.

We access an element of the array with the `[]` operator. If declared `mut`, we can assign to the elements of the array with the same syntax:

```
let mut my_array = [0u32, 1, 2, 3, 4];
assert_eq!(my_array[0], 0);
my_array[0] = 1;
assert_eq!(my_array[0], 1);
```

The elements of an array can also be iterated over with a `for` loop:

```
let my_array = [0u32, 1, 2, 3, 4];
for x in &my_array {
    println!("{}", x);
}
```

In this example, we have borrowed the array. When the array is borrowed, the loop variable becomes a reference. In this case, the `x` variable has the `&u32` type. Since the array was borrowed in this case, ownership was not transferred out of it. If we had passed `my_array` directly, ownership would be transferred by the looping operation, the `x` loop variable would contain owned values rather than borrowed ones, and the array would be unusable throughout the rest of the scope following Rust's ownership rules.

We can, of course, also borrow mutably as part of the loop:

```
let mut my_array = [0u32, 1, 2, 3, 4];
for i in &mut my_array {
```

```
    *i += 1;
}
println!("{:?}", my_array);
```

This program prints the following:

```
[1, 2, 3, 4, 5]
```

What's this odd `{:?}` sigil? This is one of many different modifiers accepted by the formatting macros in Rust. In this case, it tells the formatting machinery to make use of the `Debug` trait to format the string. Many types derive or implement the `Debug` trait to provide a visual representation of the type that would be relevant to a programmer rather than an end user.

Arrays inherit several common traits from their elements. That is, if an element type has the trait implemented for it, the array will as well. `Debug` is one of these traits, as well as `Copy` and `Clone`. This means we can use the *debug print* sigil in a format string to print any array, so long as its elements implement `Debug` as well. A full list of inherited traits can be found in the documentation for the array primitive type at `https://docs.rust-lang.org`.

Flexible runtime sizing with vectors

As with `std::vector` in C++, we use the `Vec` type in Rust to expose a runtime-sized array type. Vectors that are marked as mutable can grow and shrink at runtime as needed. This makes them a useful building block for many other data structures, including the `String` type we worked with earlier.

The `Vec` type is so important that it's included in Rust's *prelude*, which is the set of auto-imported symbols. This means that `Vec`, along with `String`, `Option`, `Result`, and several other common types, can be used in the program without an explicit `use` statement.

A vector can be constructed in place using the `vec!` macro:

```
let my_vec: Vec<u32> = vec![0, 1, 2, 3, 4];
```

This is like the syntax for initializing an array, but of course, we note that the length of the vector is no longer part of the type, as it was with the array. An immutable vector cannot be resized, but the fact that the type is the same as a vector with the same elements, but with any other length, is still an important property. This gives us the flexibility to write code that operates on any length.

There are other ways to initialize vectors as well. For instance, we can construct a mutable `Vec` type and push elements into it. Often, when doing this, we will let the compiler infer the type of the vector. While this is ultimately a stylistic choice, it's very common in Rust code to elide the types when they are not explicitly needed:

```
fn make_strings() -> Vec<String> {
    let mut ret = Vec::new();
    ret.push(String::from("Hello"));
    ret.push(String::from("World"));
    ret
}
```

In this function, the compiler has more than enough info to infer that we're constructing a `Vec<String>` when we call `Vec::new()`. It sees it not only from the fact that `ret` is used as the return type of the function, but also that we are pushing `String` types into the vector. If we still wanted to explicitly specify the type of the vector here, the most idiomatic way would be to give the `ret` variable an explicit type on initialization:

```
let mut ret: Vec<String> = Vec::new();
```

While `Vec::new` is used frequently, an alternative constructor you should know about is `Vec::with_capacity`. This constructor pre-allocates memory for the specified vector length. Like in C++, vector resizing is implemented by allocating new memory and copying every element into the new, often larger, internal buffer. This can be an expensive process, so we can use `with_capacity()` to avoid it when we know the exact or most likely size of our vector ahead of time. This constructor's behavior is similar to `std::vector::reserve()` in C++:

```
fn copy_vector(source: Vec<u32>) -> Vec<u32> {
    let mut ret = Vec::with_capacity(source.len());
    for i in source {
        ret.push(i);
    }
    ret
}
```

While the `copy_vector` function we see here has no real-world utility at all, it demonstrates a few different concepts. The first thing we notice is that `with_capacity()` is used since we know the size of the final vector ahead of time. Because of this, we know that the `push` function calls will not cause allocations, whereas they might in other cases.

The idea of pushing elements into a vector, potentially causing allocations, might raise thoughts of *iterator invalidation* in C++. When a vector is resized in C++, any stored iterators pointing into the vector become invalid. This situation is mostly unchecked by compilers and can be a source of bugs, but we are protected from errors like this in Rust. Recall that we must not have any other outstanding references when borrowing mutably due to borrowing rules. Therefore, there is no possibility of a dangling reference to memory that used to contain part of the vector.

Returning to the example, we also see that iterating over the elements of a vector with `for/in` is identical in syntax to iterating over the elements of an array. However, resizable type vectors offer more interesting manipulation options than just iteration. One of these is a specific method that can be very useful, called `Vec::retain()`. This method takes a closure (or "lambda" to C++ programmers) as an argument and uses it to filter the elements of the vector, keeping only those for which the closure returns `true`.

An example can be a call that filters out even numbers from a vector:

```
let mut v = vec![1, 2, 3, 4, 5];
v.retain(|x| x % 2 == 1);
println!("{:?}", v);
```

The `retain` function repeatedly calls the closure, passing the element into it as the `x` argument. We can see that our closure is set up to only return `true` for odd numbers, so all even numbers will be removed from the vector. As expected, the printed output will be as follows:

```
[1, 3, 5]
```

Working with borrowed data using slices

Of the categories we examined in the previous *Owned and borrowed types* section, the slice type in Rust is a borrowed type. Slices are closest to `std::span` in C++20, in that they represent a pointer-size pair that can be passed around cheaply. The pointer is always borrowed, making slices show up as a reference type in almost every context, much like `&str`. The slice type, `&[T]`, should not be confused with the array type, `[T; N]`. We don't read it as "array reference" as one might suspect, but "slice."

Slices are created by borrowing from a vector or array, but types can also provide a `Deref` implementation that allows them to coerce to a slice. As we may have expected, the `Vec<T>` vector and `[T; N]` array types provide exactly that `Deref` trait, providing them with access to all the methods attached to the slice type.

A slice can also be created from an array, vector, or slice by indexing using a *range*. Ranges are a first-class type in Rust representing a start and end index separated by the `..` operator. A range can omit the start or end index, meaning that the entire start or end of the container being indexed is included. This syntax is best seen in action:

```
let x = [0, 1, 2, 3, 4];
assert_eq!(&x[1..3], [1, 2]);
assert_eq!(&x[2..], [2, 3, 4]);
assert_eq!(&x[..2], [0, 1]);
```

Like `&str`, slices allow for many operations to be performed cheaply. These include partitioning into one or more slices and trimming from the beginning or end of the slice.

One operation implemented on slices that is of particular interest is sorting. As in the C++ STL, the Rust standard library provides two methods of sorting. The first, stable sorting, guarantees that elements that compare identically are still in the same relative order in the final sorted container. Unstable sorting, in contrast, makes no such guarantee. In Rust, the `sort()` method implements a stable sort, and unstable sorting must be specifically chosen with `sort_unstable()`. This is the opposite of the choice made by the C++ STL, where `std::sort` is an unstable sort, and `std::stable_sort` is used if stable sorting is required:

```
let mut x = [5, 4, 3, 2, 1];
x.sort_unstable();
assert_eq!(x, [1, 2, 3, 4, 5]);
```

Recall that due to `Deref` coercion, we can call slice methods on arrays and vectors. This is what allows us to call `sort_unstable()` on the array in this example.

For sorting functions to be called on a slice, the `T` type of the slice must implement the `Ord` trait, indicating that it is orderable. This trait implements a `cmp` method that compares `&self` and an `other` parameter of the same type and returns whether `self` is lower, equal, or higher than `other`. We'll look at implementing `Ord` for a custom type in the next section.

As with strings, we should take `Deref` coercion into account when designing APIs. When we need to pass data to a function, we'll want to use the `&[T]` or `&mut [T]` slice types as our arguments whenever possible. Because both arrays and vectors coerce into slices, this ensures that we'll allow the largest number of different types to be passed to our function.

Using dictionary types

Dictionary types, also referred to as *associative arrays* or simply *maps*, are an important data structure in many types of programs. Conceptually, they map a series of *keys* to a single *value* each, where the key and value may be different types. We'll examine how Rust implements maps in this section, and we'll also examine their close cousin, the set, which is a special case of a map with no values. Both map and set types will collectively be referred to as *dictionary types* throughout this section.

Flavors of map and set in Rust

Rust offers two "flavors" of map and set structures in its standard library. The first flavor is the *hash* flavor. The `HashMap` and `HashSet` types in the `std::collections` module store their data by creating a hash of the key and using that hash to pick a spot in memory to store the value. This means that the internal data is not sorted in any useful, human-interpretable way. The hash flavor roughly corresponds to the C++ `std::unordered_map` and `std::unordered_set` types, with one additional twist in that the hash is seeded differently every run of the program.

Seeding the hash can be thought of as adding a random, fixed prefix to each key before performing the hash. The effect of this is that the hash itself will not be determinable by the programmer ahead of time. This is done to close a potential security hole where an attacker makes use of internal knowledge of the hash to predict the memory locations of specific key-value pairs as they are added to the map or set. Because the hash flavor of `map` and `set` already defines the internal ordering to be of no use to a human, this behavior shouldn't cause many issues for programmers. However, it is still important to understand, since it is a major difference in behavior from the C++ standard library.

The other flavor of `map` and `set` structures is the `btree` flavor. The `BTreeMap` and `BTreeSet` structures also exist in `std::collections`. The `btree` prefix hints at an internal implementation, but the best way to think of these structures is that they are internally sorted in a deterministic and human-friendly way. These Rust types correspond almost directly to the `std::map` and `std::set` types in the C++ STL. Often, it's best to use the `btree` types in Rust when deterministic or sorted data will need to be produced by the program.

Basic map and set usage

At the most basic level, the `map` data structure requires only a way to add a key-value pair to itself and a way to query the stored value using only the key. Often, maps only allow a key to map to only one specific value, but whether they allow this value to be updated to a different value at a later point in the program is an implementation choice and differs from library to library.

To add a new key-value pair to our dictionary type, we can use the `insert()` function. This takes a key and a value as separate arguments for a map, while only taking one argument for a set. The `insert` function transfers ownership of its arguments to the internals of the dictionary type, which implies that we may need to clone the arguments if we wish to use them again later in the calling function. Let's look at an example:

```
use std::collections::HashMap;
fn main() {
    let mut map = HashMap::new();
    let key = String::from("greeting");
    let value = String::from("Hello World");
    map.insert(key, value);
    println!("{:?}", map);
}
```

In this example, `key` and `value` have their ownership transferred to the map and can no longer be used in the function after we call `insert`. The output of this program shows that the insertion happened as we expected:

```
{"greeting": "Hello World"}
```

The return value of `insert` will tell us whether the container was already storing an identical key in the case of a map, or value in the case of a set. In the case of a map, it will return an `Option<V>`, which is to say it will return either the previous value in the map or `None` if there was no previous value. For a set, it simply returns a `bool` telling us whether there was previously a value in the container.

> **Note**
>
> In Rust, using the `insert` function on a map will replace any value that is already mapped to that key. This is very different from the behavior of the C++ `std::map` and `std::unordered_map` insert functions. In C++, inserting will not replace an existing value but will instead return `std::pair<iterator, bool>`, where the Boolean tells the programmer whether an insertion was performed.

In order to retrieve the data from our map or set at a later point, we can call the `get()` or `get_mut()` functions on our dictionary type. These functions take a reference to the item we're looking for and return `Option` holding a reference to the value if one was in the map, or `None` otherwise. The reference returned is borrowed directly from the internals of the dictionary structure:

```
if let Some(value) = map.get("greeting") {
    println!("{}", value);
}
```

Recall that `if let` is syntactic sugar acting like a `match` statement with only one arm. In this example, we'll only print the value if one happened to already be in the map.

Using the entry API

Rust's `HashMap` and `BTreeMap` map types implement something called the *entry API* in the standard library. The entry API was designed to make it easier to perform conditional actions based on whether the key is already in the map or not. Depending on your task, this API can provide a more intuitive way of working with the data stored inside the map than the more traditional `insert`/`get` API we've just looked at.

The entry API is accessed through the `entry()` function, which takes an owned key type exactly like the `insert()` function, but does not take any value. The `entry()` function returns a special `Entry` type indicating whether the entry existed in the map or not. The `Entry` type has several helper functions on it for performing various tasks. Let's first look at an example:

```
use std::collections::HashMap;
fn main() {
    let s = "Hello World";
    let mut map = HashMap::new();
    for c in s.chars() {
        *map.entry(c).or_insert(0) += 1;
    }
    println!("{:?}", map);
}
```

This code implements a simple counter for how many times each character appears in a string using a `HashMap` type. We first must use the `HashMap` type from `std::collections` so that it's available in our program. Next, we declare our variables, including the string we're going to count and the map itself. In this case, the compiler fully infers the map's key and value types without us even bothering to write them out, but the full type is `HashMap<char, i32>`.

Next, we loop over each character in the string. Recall that in Rust, `char` is a UTF-8 code point and not a byte, as we might expect from C++. While we can't index into specific characters in multi-byte encoded strings, we can iterate through their characters efficiently.

When we call `entry()` for each character, we get back an `Entry` type that represents either an occupied or a vacant space in the map. If vacant, our only option is to insert, which we do with the `or_insert()` function. We set each missing value to zero, which transitions `Entry` to an occupied state. Finally, we add 1 to the value regardless of whether we just inserted it or if it was already in the map.

The resulting output will look a little bit like this:

```
{'e': 1, 'l': 3, 'r': 1, 'W': 1, 'd': 1, 'o': 2, ' ': 1, 'H': 1}
```

Since we're using `HashMap`, the output will be in a randomized order and will change from run to run, so running this code locally or in the Rust playground will give the same results printed in a different order.

One of the initially surprising things about the entry API is that the `or_insert` function can be a performance trap. Since `or_insert` only has an effect if there is nothing in the map at that entry already, we would expect it to only ever insert a value into the map once for each character, but our input string may have thousands of repeated characters in it. For most of those characters, we'd expect the function to do nothing, but the argument we pass to `or_insert` is always evaluated.

This means we can fall into a trap if the argument is not a simple value such as `0` but is instead a complicated object construction or other expensive operation. We would construct the object just to pass it to `or_insert` when, in most cases, it would be immediately discarded, causing us to waste a lot of work. For `Entry`, we have a workaround in the `or_insert_with` function. This function takes a closure as an argument, which is only called if an insert occurs.

We can change the preceding code to use `or_insert_with` like this:

```
*map.entry(c).or_insert_with(|| 0) += 1;
```

This change is only necessary when the initial value we wish to insert is complicated or expensive to compute. Clippy can warn when `or_insert` is used with an argument like this and recommend `or_insert_with` instead.

This is only a brief introduction to the entry API. For more information about its capabilities, see the `std::collections` documentation at `https://doc.rust-lang.org/`.

Enabling custom key types

Occasionally, we'll have a custom type that we'll want to use as a key for one of the dictionary types we've been discussing in this section. As usual, Rust relies on the trait system to signal that a type can be used as a key. The `HashMap` and `HashSet` containers require that the `Eq` and `Hash` traits must be implemented on their key types, while the `BTreeMap` and `BTreeSet` containers require that the type provide an ordering by specifying the `Ord` trait.

Let's start with the least complicated of the three traits in question: the `Hash` trait. In most cases, we can just derive this trait for our structure, like this:

```
#[derive(Hash)]
struct MyString {
    internal: String,
}
```

This works if all members of our structure have types that already implement `Hash`.

If we need a little more control over the eventual hash, we must manually implement the `Hash` trait. For the preceding structure, it'd look like this:

```
use std::hash::{Hash, Hasher};
impl Hash for MyString {
    fn hash<H: Hasher>(&self, state: &mut H) {
        self.internal.hash(state);
    }
}
```

This example produces basically the exact same result as the derive, but it can be extended or customized in cases where it is needed. If we need even further customization, documentation for the `Hasher` trait should be consulted. It implements a small API that allows us to write binary data to be hashed directly.

Our custom key must also implement the `Eq` trait, which represents the equality operation. Here, Rust declares a rare invariant that is not checked by the compiler in any way and is left entirely to the programmer to verify. The standard library requires that when the `Eq` trait implementation declares two objects as equal, their hashes, as produced by the `Hash` trait, must also be equal.

Understanding the `Eq` and `Ord` traits, oddly, requires understanding floating-point numbers. The `Eq` and `Ord` traits reflect a "total equality" and "total ordering," respectively, meaning that every value can be correctly compared with equality and ordered against every other value.

Floating-point numbers do not meet this criterion because of the behavior of the special `NaN` (*not-a-number*) value. NaN represents a specific bit pattern and is defined to not compare as equal to any other floating-point number, including itself. While many languages just ignore this property of floating-point numbers and leave handling it to the programmer, Rust encoded it into its type system by creating separate traits to represent "partial equality" and "partial ordering."

These two partial traits, `PartialEq` and `PartialOrd`, must be implemented for `Eq` and `Ord`, respectively, to be implemented. All the implementations of these traits need to be consistent with one another. That is, `partial_cmp` from `PartialOrd` needs to produce the same result as `cmp` from `Ord`, and so on. This is a good reason for us to use deriving as often as possible:

```
#[derive(PartialEq, Eq, PartialOrd, Ord)]
struct MyString {
    internal: String,
}
```

Deriving will always produce consistent results and present the easiest implementation of all options. Implementing these specific traits manually will be left to you, but the documentation for `PartialOrd` at `https://doc.rust-lang.org/` is an excellent place to start.

Summary

In this chapter, we dove into the most common containers in the standard library and examined their owned and borrowed versions. We learned what each container is for and saw examples of their use. Along the way, we learned about several important traits, including `Debug`, `From`, `Into`, `AsRef`, `Deref`, `Eq`, `Hash`, and `Ord`.

In the next chapter, we'll continue our journey into the Rust standard library as we take a look at Rust's approach to file I/O.

6

Reading and Writing Files

The set of topics around I/O and interacting with the filesystem often seems to be neglected in newer programming languages. More than once, I have sat down to try an experimental programming language just to find that the developers hadn't even implemented any means of opening a file.

Thankfully, this isn't the case with Rust, where the standard library is full of well-designed functionality for dealing with files and folders. In this chapter, we'll continue our exploration of the standard library with the goal of understanding how Rust exposes filesystem and I/O operations.

In this chapter, we're going to cover the following main topics:

- Working with files
- Exploring the Rust I/O API
- Simple serialization and deserialization

Technical requirements

Examples in this chapter use Rust 1.82.0, but they will also work with any newer version.

If you need help installing Rust, please see the *Appendix*.

You can find the code files for this chapter in this book's GitHub repository: `https://github.com/PacktPublishing/Rust-for-CPP-Developers`.

Working with files

Before getting into the meat of Rust's I/O handling, we're going to explore a few topics that will help lay the foundations needed for working with files. In this section, we'll investigate Rust's filesystem path abstraction, learn how to handle errors idiomatically, and discover a handful of useful functions that vastly simplify the task of reading files.

Using filesystem paths

Unfortunately, the most popular operating systems all have slight differences in the way they handle filesystem paths, meaning that we need an abstraction to handle those differences. Here, Rust has come to our rescue with the `std::path` module. This module implements a set of types and an API to deal with filesystem paths in a way that is as cross-platform as possible while being unobtrusive to the programmer.

What are the differences we're trying to abstract away? First, different platforms use different directory separators. Some platforms use a forward slash character, `/`, to separate them, while others use a backslash character, `\`. The second difference is character encoding. Windows specifies that filesystem paths are encoded in UTF-16, while Unix-like platforms don't tend to enforce any specific encoding.

As mentioned in *Chapter 5*, the Rust standard library contains two string-like types: `PathBuf` and `Path`. `Path` is a borrowed type, meaning that we'll commonly see it used as a reference. Underneath, these types are a thin API wrapper around the `OsString` and `OsStr` types, which are owned and borrowed types, respectively. The two types are responsible for abstracting away character encoding issues, while the methods of `Path` and `PathBuf` deal with abstracting away filesystem differences.

We usually construct a `PathBuf` type either by calling the `PathBuf::from` function with `String` or `&str`, or by pushing path elements individually into a mutable buffer constructed with `PathBuf::new`. Let's look at examples of both methods to construct the `src/main.rs` path:

```
let path1 = PathBuf::from("src/main.rs");
let mut path2 = PathBuf::new();
path2.push("src");
path2.push("main.rs");
assert_eq!(path1, path2);
```

If we type this code into the Rust Playground, we'll see that the assert passes. Even though we used a forward slash as our path separator, this code still passes on Windows platforms, since a forward slash is a valid path separator there. If we change the first path in the example to

`PathBuf::from("src\\main.rs")`, the assert will pass on Windows but not on Linux, where a backslash is not treated as a path separator. From this, we can see that it's best to use forward slashes if we are using literal paths for the most consistent cross-platform behavior.

Many Rust functions, including several functions for reading or writing files, choose to use `AsRef<Path>` as a generic type parameter describing the file's location on disk. In this case, we may not need to construct a `PathBuf` type at all. `AsRef<Path>` is implemented by both `String` and `&str`, meaning that we can pass normal, well-formatted Rust strings as paths to these functions.

Since we're able to pass normal strings to most functions that take paths as arguments, it may be tempting to just ignore Rust's path types altogether. However, the path manipulation functions in the standard library can still be very useful due to the extra operations they provide. For instance, we can easily strip file extensions, reference other files in the same directory, create a new absolute or relative path from an existing one, and canonicalize paths.

One extremely useful function of `Path` is its ability to directly query OS metadata. This functionality is exposed as the `stat` function in the C ecosystem. Calling the `metadata()` function gives us lots of useful info in the `Metadata` structure, including modification times and file size.

The `metadata()` function is interesting because it can return an error. But how should we handle this error? In the next section, we'll learn all about how to deal with functions like this one.

Handling errors in Rust

We can't talk about filesystem operations without talking about errors. Rust does not use exceptions for error handling like C++, but instead uses a combination of the generic `Result<T, E>` type and the `panic` mechanism. `Result` is a generic enum representing either an `Ok` variant holding a value of the `T` type or an `Err` variant holding a value of the `E` type. Whenever we have a function that can produce an error, we declare it to return `Result`. This encodes the fact that an error can be returned directly into the function's type signature.

In Rust, it's common for functions to immediately pass any errors to the calling function. This gives the caller the option to handle the error in some way, whether it be by recovering from it, logging it, or ignoring it. Many functions also choose to send the error to their own caller in turn, and this can continue all the way up to the `main` function of the program. If `main` returns an `Err` variant of `Result`, the program will exit and print the resulting error.

To some, the strategy of passing an error successively upward until the program exits might not seem like we're handling the error at all. But the end effect is somewhat close to exception handling in C++ in that the program can choose to handle the error at any point along the way. If no code specifically handles the error, the result will be a program exit. The advantages Rust's strategy provides are that the information about what can "throw" an error is encoded clearly in the type signature of each function, and that a returned `Result` cannot be ignored. To provide the latter behavior, Rust uses something similar in functionality to C++17's `[[nodiscard]]` attribute.

Other languages have used a similar mechanism for error handling as Rust, but they collect a lot of criticism because of the amount of work it takes to handle errors or pass them up the call stack. Is there a best of both worlds? The quest of the Rust designers, through a series of revisions after its initial stable release, was to minimize the amount of boilerplate with which programmers would have to contend. We'll examine their succession of solutions, starting with the most complicated and moving on to the most recent error handling idiom.

What does it look like to handle an error in Rust at the most basic level? As we saw, `Result<T, E>` is a generic enum that will hold one of two different variants. Recall that to interpret which value is held by an enum, we should use pattern matching. In this case, we'll look at what handling an error with a `match` statement looks like:

```
let value = match result {
    Ok(value) => value,
    Err(err) => return Err(err),
};
```

We can assume in this example that the `result` variable contains a `Result<T,E>` value returned by some function. Here, we wish to pull the value out of the result (or *unwrap* it) if there is no error. We want to do this so that the remainder of the function, which will presumably use the result, does not have to deal with the value being wrapped in the `Result` any longer. If the `Result` represented an error, we simply return the error to pass it further up the call stack.

Typing this verbose `match` statement every time we need to handle or pass along an error would be very inconvenient. One thing to note about the preceding block is that it works for any `Result<T,E>` type regardless of the types of `T` and `E`. Seeing this, the designers of Rust took the opportunity to improve the brevity of the code required to handle errors. This took the form of a macro called `try!` to wrap the behavior we've just seen:

```
let value = try!(result);
```

This cuts down the amount of work to handle errors considerably, but if we type out this example in the Rust Playground, we'll find that it doesn't even work anymore. This solution is deprecated, and the `try` identifier is repurposed since the 2018 edition of Rust. Still, the `try!` macro is a useful historical pit stop on Rust's road to concise error handling.

If `try!` is deprecated, that must mean that something even better has replaced it. And that better thing is what we call the question mark operator, `?`. It looks like this, in practice:

```
let value = result?;
```

The question mark operator provides the same functionality as the `match` statement we just saw. If the `Result` contains an `Ok` variant, it will unwrap the value and assign it to the `value` variable. If the `Result` contains an `Err` variant, it will return from the function immediately. Finally, we've arrived at a concise, yet syntactically distinctive way to handle errors.

Of course, because the preceding examples may all return an `Err` value, they can only be used from a function that itself returns `Result<T,E>`. This could mean that we must use the exact same type for `E` at each point in our call stack. But Rust provides a little help here by using the `From` trait. Recall that the `From` and `Into` traits can be used to convert between related types. This way, crates can provide their own error types that work seamlessly with the standard library ones.

It's worth noting that an error type is any type that implements the `std::error::Error` trait. This implementation is required for a type to be used as the `E` type in a `Result<T,E>` value. The standard library defines a handful of different error types, but the one we'll focus on most in this chapter is `std::io::Error`, which is used by most functions dealing with I/O of any kind. Most often in documentation and code, you'll see this type simplified as `std::io::Result<T>`, which is defined to be `Result<T,std::io::Error>`.

A `std::io::Error` provides us with a `kind()` function, returning a `std::io::ErrorKind` enum. This is helpful if you wish to handle specific errors without passing them up the call stack, such as perhaps the non-existence of a file. An example of using `ErrorKind` in this way might look like this:

```
if let Err(e) = std::fs::read_to_string("file.txt") {
    if e.kind() == std::io::ErrorKind::NotFound {
        eprintln!("File not found: {:?}", e);
    } else {
        return Err(e);
```

```
    }
}
```

Having explored Rust's error handling, we now have enough background to continue exploring I/O, but handling errors is a much larger topic than can be explained here. There are many popular crates that have been created to make it easier and more convenient. A good place to start looking for more information is the documentation for the anyhow and `thiserror` crates on `crates.io`. For now, we'll continue by looking at a few high-level abstractions Rust uses to read and write files.

Understanding high-level IO abstractions

Because reading and writing files is such a common operation, the Rust designers put a series of high-level abstractions into the `std::fs` module to make the process simple for many common use cases. These wrappers can read the entire contents of a file into a `String` or a `Vec<u8>` in one call. Similarly, they can write the entire contents of `&str` or `&[u8]` directly to disk in one call. We'll walk through examples of each function in turn.

First, we'll look at the `read_to_string` function. This takes in a generic `AsRef<Path>` parameter and returns a `std::io::Result<String>`:

```
let contents: String = std::fs::read_to_string("file.txt")?;
```

Following the behavior of the question mark operator, either the `contents` variable will contain a `String`, or we will return immediately, passing a `std::io::Error` to the caller. Recall that because we're using the question mark operator, this code must exist in a function returning `Result`.

The next helpful wrapper function is just called `read`. This function returns a `std::io::Result<Vec<u8>>`, where `Vec<u8>` is the best representation in Rust for an owned container of bytes:

```
let contents: Vec<u8> = std::fs::read("file.bin")?;
```

When writing files, we only have one wrapper function available to us, called `write`. This function takes two parameters, where the first argument is a generic `AsRef<Path>` representing a filename and the second is a generic `AsRef<[u8]>` representing the contents. Because `str` implements `AsRef<[u8]>`, we can pass a string or any type that can coerce to a byte slice to the `write` function, and it will end up in the file on disk as we expect:

```
std::fs::write("out.txt", "Hello World\n")?;
```

The `write` function returns `std::io::Result<()>`, where we may recall that `()` functions as a placeholder for "no type" in a similar way in Rust to the C++ `void` type. After handling the potential error using the question mark operator, there's nothing else for us to do with the function's return value, so we do not need to assign it to anything.

The `write` function will create the file if it does not exist, and it will overwrite any file that already exists at the same path on disk. On many platforms, this function will return an error if the file is already opened for writing by another process or marked as read-only by the filesystem.

While these high-level wrapper functions allow us to quickly write code for reading and writing files, they aren't powerful enough to meet the needs of every program. Next, we'll explore the full API that Rust exposes for I/O operations and see how these operations can be applied to various kinds of input and output sources.

Exploring the Rust I/O API

Now that we understand how to work with paths, handle errors, and perform simple reading and writing operations, we have yet to encounter the actual Rust IO API. First, we'll examine how to open files. Then, we'll dive into the fundamental I/O traits living in the `std::io` module that make up the API itself. We'll examine each of these traits in turn, and finally, we'll investigate ways that the Rust I/O API can be extended using the crate ecosystem.

Opening files for reading or writing

Before we can read or write any data, we need an input source or an output destination. While memory buffers or network sockets can all serve this purpose, files are the most common, so working with them is a natural place to begin.

Before a file can be read from or written to, it must be opened. Most operating systems expose different ways to open files. Usually, opening for reading and opening for writing are the most common methods, but depending on the filesystem, many more options could be available. In Rust, we can start with a handful of "easy" functions for more common file opening configurations, and then we'll move on to a more "advanced" API for a greater level of control when it is needed.

Perhaps the simplest case is opening an existing file for reading only. In the `std::fs` module, we find the `File` structure, which has an open method for this purpose. As with other functions we have worked with, `File::open` takes a generic `AsRef<Path>` parameter, meaning that we can specify the location of the file we're opening as either a `Path` reference or a string type:

```
let file = File::open("test.txt")?;
```

Because opening a file can fail for a number of reasons, `File::open` returns a `std::io::Result<File>`, and as such, we must handle it. As in other cases we've seen, this is usually done by passing the error to the caller, but occasionally it may be useful to specifically handle errors indicating that the file was not found on disk.

Recall that we can use the `kind()` function to handle situations like this one:

```
let file = match std::fs::File::open("test.txt") {
    Err(err) if err.kind() == ErrorKind::NotFound => {
        eprintln!("File not found!");
        return Err(err);
    }
    x => x?,
};
```

In this example, we're still just passing any `NotFound` error on to the caller, but we're also adding our own print before this occurs. Here, `x` is a pattern that matches any value not handled by the case. It is a named version of the `default _ catch-all` pattern and the `x` name was chosen arbitrarily.

When writing to a file, we can use the `File::create()` or `File::create_new()` functions. The `create()` function will open the file for writing, and will overwrite the file if it already exists on the system, while `create_new()` will return an error if the file already exists.

These functions are useful, but they don't provide us with the level of control needed to, for example, append to an existing file on disk. For that, we need to turn to `std::fs::OpenOptions`. This structure uses the *builder pattern*. A structure that is a builder exposes several functions returning the `&mut Self` type. The intent is that we can chain together as many methods as we need, each of which modifies some bit of state and then returns `self`. A final call then does the important work, using the accumulated state in the structure to determine its behavior.

The builder pattern is commonly used in Rust because the language does not support default function arguments or overloaded functions. It serves as an ergonomic way to accomplish complicated initialization that we might provide in C++ using a series of overloaded constructors or default arguments. Let's look at an example using `OpenOptions`:

```
let file = std::fs::OpenOptions::new()
    .append(true)
    .write(true)
    .create(true)
    .open("file.txt")?;
```

The `OpenOptions::new()` function creates a default set of options. The `append` and `write` methods then modify the default state to specify that we want to open a file for appending. Finally, we call the open method to perform the actual opening of the file using the options we specified. The return type of the open method is `std::io::Result<File>`, just like the `File::create` and `File::open` functions we saw earlier, which simply wrap `OpenOptions` themselves.

Now that we understand how to open files, we can begin to explore the I/O API itself.

Understanding fundamental I/O traits

In most language ecosystems, the fundamental operations of I/O are reading, writing, and seeking. Accordingly, Rust exposes these operations through the `std::io::Read`, `std::io::Write`, and `std::io::Seek` traits, respectively. As a convenience, the standard library offers the option to include all of these traits in a program at once with a `use std::io::prelude::*` statement.

Why are these operations implemented as traits rather than functions? The most important reason is that they expose a consistent interface across any number of different potential input sources or output destinations. The Rust standard library has many implementers of each of these traits, including files, memory buffers, and even network sockets.

However, one slight disadvantage of using traits for these APIs is that the trait designers must rely on implementations to follow the same behavior as the standard library types. The documentation for each trait specifies the exact behavior expected, but implementations outside of the standard library may or may not follow these recommendations. Using traits still wins over having disparate I/O APIs for each structure, but if we are relying on specific behavior from a third-party crate, we will need to validate that it matches our expectations.

We can begin examining the API with the `Read` trait. This exposes a handful of different functions for reading from the input source.

First is the `read_to_string` function, which reads the entire input buffer and appends it to `&mut String` that's passed as an argument to the function. This function returns a `std::io::Result<usize>` representing the number of bytes that were read. As with several functions that construct a `String` type in Rust, `read_to_string` will return an error if the data being read is not valid `UTF-8`. If this happens, the function is specified to leave the destination `String` unmodified.

With this knowledge, we can implement something similar to the `std::fs::read_to_string()` function we examined earlier:

```
let mut file = File::open("file.txt")?;
let mut buffer = String::new();
file.read_to_string(&mutbuffer)?;
```

One minor thing to note here is that we must declare the file as mutable, because `read_to_string()` needs to be able to modify the input source to advance the offset at which reading begins, sometimes called the *file pointer*.

The next function to examine is `read()`, which is actually the only function that implementers of the `Read` trait need to provide. The rest of the functions in the trait are written in terms of `read()` and are provided to all implementations automatically.

The `read()` function is similar to the `read_to_string()` interface in that it takes `&mut [u8]` as a parameter and returns a `std::io::Result<usize>`. Unlike `read_to_string()`, the slice passed in has a specific size. As a result, we're not reading to the end of the input and appending to the `u8` slice as we were with the dynamically sized `String` we worked with before. In fact, the slice can't be appended to at all. We're reading bytes directly into the slice, meaning that the most we can read from the input source is the number of bytes that can fit in the slice we've passed:

```
let mut f = File::open("file.txt")?;
let mut buf = [0; 10];
let bytes_read = f.read(&mutbuf)?;
```

This example reads, at most, 10 bytes from the file. What if the input source cannot provide enough bytes to fill the buffer? This is not an error. It's up to the caller to verify that the number of bytes read, as returned by an `Ok` result, is used properly. This can make `read()` somewhat unwieldy to use. If this causes a problem, the `Read` trait also provides the `read_exact()` function to guarantee that the buffer is filled. Since the `read_exact()` function implicitly specifies the number of bytes that will be read, there is no need to return `std::io::Result<usize>`, and instead this function returns `std::io::Result<()>`.

> **Note**
>
> If you intend to use several small reads to pull data from a file, you should wrap the input source in `BufReader`. This structure exposes the exact same `Read` interface, but behind the scenes, it reads from disk in larger chunks and caches them to memory for better performance. Many people attempting to benchmark Rust versus other languages have been tricked by the fact that they must opt into buffering.

Having covered the basics of reading, let's take a look at the `std::io::Write` trait. In some ways, writing is simpler to understand in Rust than reading because we're not dealing with any mutable buffers. Still, implementers of the `Write` trait must write two functions as opposed to one: `write()` and `flush()`.

The `write()` function takes a byte slice type, `&[u8]`, and returns `std::io::Result<usize>`, indicating the number of bytes written. Unfortunately, it is not considered an error if the returned `usize` indicating the number of bytes written is smaller than the size of the buffer that was passed. If this property is required, the `write_all()` method is provided, returning `std::io::Result<()>` just like its cousin, `read_exact()`:

```
let mut file = File::create("test.txt")?;
file.write_all("Hello World\n".as_bytes())?;
```

The other function in `Write` we need to examine is `flush()`. This ensures that written bytes are reflected by the I/O destination immediately. It's not unusual for I/O implementations to have some method of buffering writes between our program, which needs to run quickly, and our I/O destination, which may take a long time to process individual operations. Flushing is normally handled transparently by a well-behaved I/O implementation, but when we need to read data back immediately or ensure it's reflected immediately, we must call `flush()`.

Note that if we want to ensure that our writes are buffered, we can use the `BufWriter` structure to wrap our file. This mirrors the `BufReader` structure mentioned previously. We may want to use this if we're, for instance, making several small writes to a file.

Having explored writing, we'll look at the final trait in our exploration of the Rust I/O API. The `Seek` trait is used by the program to move around to different places in a file or buffer. Files and some other types of I/O streams maintain an internal pointer to decide where to begin the next read or write. This is often called the file pointer or cursor.

By default, the file pointer starts at the beginning of our input stream and continues moving through it linearly as we perform reads or writes. The functions provided by `Seek` allow us to manipulate this pointer to allow us to read from or write to arbitrary points in the file or buffer.

The primary method in the `Seek` trait that we'll use to accomplish this is the `seek()` function. This function takes a `SeekFrom` enum as a parameter, and returns the new offset of the file pointer as `std::io::Result<u64>`.

The `SeekFrom` enum gives us three potential ways to set the file pointer. Here, we're leveraging Rust's ability to store data along with an enum variant. `SeekFrom::Start` takes an unsigned offset from the start of the file, while `SeekFrom::End` and `SeekFrom::Current` take signed offsets from the end of the file and the current file pointer, respectively.

To read the last 10 bytes of a file, we can use code like this:

```
let mut file = File::open("test.txt")?;
file.seek(SeekFrom::End(-10))?;
let mut buf = vec![0; 10];
file.read_exact(&mutbuf)?;
```

To get the file pointer's current position in the file, we can also use `seek()`:

```
let pos = file.seek(SeekFrom::Current(0))?;
```

Seeking past the end of the stream may be allowed depending on the kind of I/O implementation we're using, but seeking to a location that's before the front of the file is disallowed and will always return an error.

Seeking isn't inherently supported by all types that implement `Read`. For instance, when reading directly from a `&[u8]` byte slice, reading is achieved by shrinking the slice to exclude the bytes already processed. When this happens, the original bounds of the slice are lost. Since we would not be able to expand the slice without risking out-of-bounds memory accesses, we cannot seek backward in a slice. However, the standard library offers a way around this for many types, including slices.

The `std::io` module has a type named `Cursor` that allows us to implement `Seek` for memory buffers. This can be useful for a variety of tasks. A common one is code that operates on a file in production but uses a memory buffer during unit testing. Wrapping our buffer in `Cursor` gives us a `File`-like behavior by providing `Read`, `Write`, and `Seek` traits.

Adapting the previous example to work with a cursor is straightforward:

```
let mut cursor = Cursor::new(b"test buffer");
cursor.seek(SeekFrom::End(-10))?;
let mut buf = vec![0; 10];
cursor.read_exact(&mutbuf)?;
```

With an understanding of the three fundamental Rust I/O traits, we can perform I/O operations across thousands of different kinds of streams. But these traits alone are not the full story, because the crate ecosystem can be used to add additional behavior to them.

Extending the I/O APIs

An advantage of the trait-based implementation of I/O behaviors in Rust is that traits can be extended. Extending a trait allows new methods to be added to every structure implementing that trait. Note that *extending* does not mean *overriding* in the C++ sense. The behavior of the original trait cannot be changed in any way by a trait that extends it. We can add methods that are identical to the ones in the original trait, but the compiler will require us to disambiguate between them when calling.

There are two steps required to extend a trait. First, we must declare our original `std::io::Read` trait as a *supertrait* of our extension trait:

```
pub trait ReadExt: std::io::Read {
    fn read_ext(&mut self, buf: &mut [u8])
      -> std::io::Result<usize> {
        self.read(buf)
    }
}
```

Here, we are just making a wrapper for the `read()` function. Notice that the syntax for specifying a supertrait is similar to the syntax for inheritance in C++. As with other contexts, we can use + to declare more than one trait as a supertrait. Notice as well that declaring a supertrait allows us to use methods from that trait in our implementations.

As the second step, we must tell the compiler that we wish to implement our new trait for every type that implements `Read`:

```
impl<T> ReadExt for T where T: Read {}
```

Now, so long as our `ReadExt` trait is imported with the `use` statement, we'll be able to call the `read_ext()` method that we've added to everything that implements `Read`, from `File` to

TcpStream. The ability to add behavior to standard types in this way adds an interesting dimension to the third-party crate ecosystem.

An extremely useful crate called byteorder uses this methodology to provide functions for reading and writing data using a specific endianness. While a full discussion of endianness is out of scope, recall that depending on the endianness of the architecture, integer and floating-point types stored to memory or the filesystem could have their bytes stored in reverse order. File formats storing data in this way usually specify an endianness for the data, which we must know and compensate for to read the data correctly across various architectures.

The byteorder crate provides ReadBytesExt and WriteBytesExt traits that extend the standard Read and Write traits, respectively. Each contains a full set of reading or writing functions for the various Rust integer and floating-point types, but the endianness of the data must be specified explicitly.

Let's look at an example. First, we'll want to import the parts of byteorder we wish to use:

```
use byteorder::{LittleEndian, BigEndian, ReadBytesExt};
```

Let's read a u32 from a byte buffer using each endianness and observe the result:

```
let mut cursor = Cursor::new([0xaa, 0xbb, 0xcc, 0xdd]);
println!("{:x}", cursor.read_u32::<LittleEndian>()?);
```

The {:x} format specifier used here tells Rust to print the results in hexadecimal. Treating the input data as little endian, we'd expect the bytes to be in reverse order from their in-memory representation. Indeed, our test prints the following when run:

```
ddccbbaa
```

Let's try again, but this time interpreting the data as big endian:

```
let mut cursor = Cursor::new([0xaa, 0xbb, 0xcc, 0xdd]);
println!("{:x}", cursor.read_u32::<BigEndian>()?);
```

The output again matches our expectations:

```
aabbccdd
```

Even the best API design can't anticipate all use cases. The byteorder crate demonstrates a large strength of Rust – holes in the standard library can be effectively covered by the crate ecosystem in a clean way. We'll examine another strong use of the crate ecosystem to provide a clean way to implement complicated behavior in the next section.

Simple serialization and deserialization

When working with structured text data in a format such as JSON, YAML, or TOML, we refer to **serialization** as the process of writing in-memory data out in the structured format, and to **deserialization** as the process of reading from the structured format and of producing a matching, in-memory copy of the data.

One of the most popular and useful crates in the Rust ecosystem is the `serde` crate. The name `serde` is a combination of "serialization" and "deserialization," and it provides a convenient interface for performing these important operations for a wide variety of structured file formats. In this section, we'll develop a simple application to load JSON data into Rust structures using `serde`, modify it, and write the results back into a new JSON file.

Reading a JSON file using serde

To begin, we will create a new Rust project locally to hold our work. A completed version of this project is available on GitHub, or you can follow along as we create it:

```
$ cargo new serde_test
$ cd serde_test
$ cargo add serde serde_derive serde_json
```

Here, we create the new project and add a few crates we'll need. The `serde` crate holds the basic generic interface that we will use for deserialization. The `serde_derive` crate allows us to use the derive attribute to create structures that can be constructed by `serde`. Lastly, the `serde_json` crate provides serialization and deserialization services specifically for the JSON format.

We'll also need to construct a JSON file to read. We'll use the following data as a test, saving it to a file named `pets.json`:

```
{
  "pets": [
    {
      "name": "Fluffy",
      "info": { "kind": "dog", "age": 3 }
    },
    {
      "name": "Princess",
```

```
            "info": { "kind": "cat", "age": 5 }
        }
    ]
}
```

This data isn't especially important by itself, but this format will at least force our serializer to deal with a reasonable subset of JSON features.

With our project created and our data ready to process, we'll construct a series of Rust structures that match the general format of the data we want to read. Each will derive the `Serialize` and `Deserialize` traits, which we'll need to import from `serde_derive` at the top of `main.rs`:

```
use serde_derive::{Deserialize, Serialize};
```

Let's begin working through the structure of our data, starting at the top level and working inward. First, we'll need a structure to hold our top-level object. We'll call this `PetFile`, and it will be the structure we pass to the `serde_json` crate when it's time to read in our data:

```
#[derive(Debug, Deserialize, Serialize)]
struct PetFile {
    pets: Vec<Pet>,
}
```

In addition to the two `serde_derive` traits, we're also deriving `Debug`. This will let our program print out the data more easily for inspection once we've read it in with `serde`. We can see how the structure itself matches the layout of our test data, which contains an array of objects. But we still need to define `Pet`, so let's do that now:

```
#[derive(Debug, Deserialize, Serialize)]
struct Pet {
    name: String,
    info: PetInfo,
}
```

The definition of `Pet` is beginning to show a bit of a pattern at this point. When we encounter an object in the JSON file, we make a new structure to represent that object. When we encounter an array in the JSON file, we add `Vec` to our structure. And finally, when we encounter any integer or string value, we can use a corresponding Rust type to represent it. At this point, the definition of `PetInfo` should hopefully be very predictable:

```
#[derive(Debug, Deserialize, Serialize)]
struct PetInfo {
    kind: String,
    age: usize,
}
```

Now that we've made structures to represent the test data and derived the proper traits, we're ready to begin working with `serde` itself. We'll start by reading the test data into the structures we just defined:

```
type AnyError = Box<dyn std::error::Error>;
fn read_pet_file(filename: &str)
    -> Result<PetFile, AnyError> {
    let data = std::fs::read_to_string(filename)?;
    let pets = serde_json::from_str::<PetFile>(&data)?;
    Ok(pets)
}
```

What's this strange-looking `AnyError` type alias? Aside from being a brief peek at Rust's take on runtime polymorphism, it's also a method of letting `Result` accept any error type. All types implementing the `Error` trait can convert to this type using the `From`/`Into` traits, which, as we noted earlier, are baked into the question mark operator's behavior. Normally, this behavior would be accomplished using a more advanced crate such as `anyhow`, but for our simple serialization example, this suffices.

The function itself reads the file we pass into a string, and then we pass the resulting data to the `from_str` function from the `serde_json` crate. This is a generic function, and we must tell the compiler which structure we wish to use to interpret the data. This results in us specifying our `PetFile` structure using the turbofish operator, `::< >`.

We lack only one thing to complete our example, which is our `main()` function:

```
fn main() -> Result<(), AnyError> {
    let pets = read_pet_file("pets.json")?;
    println!("{:#?}", pets);
    Ok(())
}
```

Our `main()` function reads the `pets.json` file and pretty-prints out the contents of our structures using the `Debug` trait we derived earlier. Note that in the format strings, the `{:#?}` format specifier means to pretty-print the debug representation, while the `{:?}` format specifier will just print the whole object on one line.

This is our first complete example of reading a file and parsing it with complete error handling. If you've been typing along, at this point, I recommend that you play with it. What does `cargo run` print with no changes? What happens if the file is missing? What happens if we change the format of the JSON file? Does the example still work if we add or remove properties in the data? What happens if we change the name of a key?

Some of the default `serde` behaviors might be unexpected or undesirable when encountering unknown or optional fields. Next, we'll take a look at how to alter the default behaviors for our structures.

Customizing serialization behavior

If you spent any time playing with the preceding example, you probably noticed that its behavior is very rigid. We're going to look now into how to customize `serde`'s behavior to get us closer to what we might want in a real program. When we derive the `Serialize` and `Deserialize` traits, the primary methods of configuration available to us are the Rust type system and custom attributes defined by `serde_derive`.

If you happened to try removing or renaming some of the data in our `pets.json` file, you probably saw an error from `serde` about a missing field. Every field we've declared in our Rust structures must be present in our data, or the program will return an error. But what if we want the program to cleanly handle both the existence and nonexistence of a field?

This problem is easy to solve using Rust's `Option<T>` type. By wrapping any type in `Option`, we tell `serde` to handle the non-existence of data cleanly by inserting a `None` value for any missing field. Fields that are not missing will, of course, be set to `Some(T)`.

To make the age field of our `PetInfo` structure optional, we could change the declaration in this way:

```
#[derive(Debug, Deserialize, Serialize)]
struct PetInfo {
    kind: String,
    age: Option<usize>,
}
```

Using `Option` can be a great solution, but it requires us to handle unwrapping `Option` when the value is used in our code. However, there is also another way to solve the problem of optional fields.

The solution lies in the power of `serde`'s custom attributes. The `#[serde(default)]` attribute can be used to place a default value (as defined by the implementation of the `Default` trait for that type) into our structure if the field is missing in our data. Most standard types define some sensible default value using the `Default` trait, and it can be derived or implemented explicitly for the types we use in our own programs.

If we wished to make the age field default to zero while also making it valid for it to be missing from our JSON file, we could use this syntax:

```
#[derive(Debug, Deserialize, Serialize)]
struct PetInfo {
    kind: String,
    #[serde(default)]
    age: usize,
}
```

There are other uses for `serde`'s custom attributes as well. Imagine that our data file contained a field that clashed with a reserved word in the Rust language, such as `type`. We can use an attribute to tell `serde` to use a specific JSON property name instead of the struct field name.

We could accomplish that using the `rename` attribute, like this:

```
#[derive(Debug, Deserialize)]
struct Data {
    #[serde(rename = "type")]
    type_: String,
}
```

We can also place different custom attributes on the structure itself. A useful example is the `rename_all` attribute. The Rust compiler is very strict about conforming to certain conventions for structure and variable names, but our JSON input files won't always conform to this standard. The `rename_all` attribute is used to provide a blanket transformation across all field names, so that we can happily use the Rust convention in our program while still reading the JSON convention correctly:

```
#[derive(Debug, Deserialize)]
#[serde(rename_all = "PascalCase")]
```

```
struct Data {
    test_field: String,
}
const INPUT: &str = "{ \"TestField\": \"test\" }";
fn main() {
    let data = serde_json::from_str::<Data>(INPUT).unwrap();
    println!("{:#?}", data);
}
```

In this example, we specified that all fields in the JSON were expected to be in the `PascalCase` convention. If we run this program, we'll see that the data is properly parsed and deserialized as we expect. The full list of available conventions can be found in the `serde` documentation.

Lastly, we'll highlight one final custom attribute. If you played around with the preceding working example, you might have noticed that `serde` does not mind at all if there are extra fields in the input that weren't specified in the Rust structure. These fields are simply ignored by default, but if we wish for their presence to instead raise a runtime error, we can simply add the `deny_unknown_fields` attribute to our structure:

```
#[derive(Debug, Deserialize)]
#[serde(rename_all = "PascalCase")]
#[serde(deny_unknown_fields)]
struct Data {
    test_field: String,
}
```

There are several more useful custom attributes in the documentation. If you feel like you've run up against a wall with `serde`, it is worth looking through them. For now, we'll continue our exploration of `serde` by adding support for serialization to our working example.

Writing out JSON

We've primarily explored deserialization, but now it's time to talk about serialization. This means that we need to examine how to transform the structures we've created in our program into a well-formatted JSON file representing the same data.

We'll work with the same `PetFile` structure as before. We could spend a lot of time constructing all of the various structures in Rust, but instead, let's just read it from the same file as before. This gives us some data as a starting point. Our program will increase the age of each pet by one and then write the data back out to the terminal.

Let's start with the modifications needed to our `main()` function:

```
fn main() -> Result<(), AnyError> {
    let mut pets = read_pet_file("pets.json")?;
    for pet in &mut pets.pets {
        pet.info.age += 1;
    }
    print_pet_data(&pets)?;
    Ok(())
}
```

This looks similar to our previous attempt, but this time, we've decided to modify our data. As such, we must declare the `pets` variable as `mut`. This allows us to iterate mutably over the values in `Vec<Pet>` with a `for pet in &mut pets.pets` loop. After incrementing the age of each pet by 1, we're calling a function to print the new data, which we'll define next:

```
fn print_pet_data(data:&PetFile)-> Result<(), AnyError> {
    let output = serde_json::to_string(data)?;
    println!("{}", output);
    Ok(())
}
```

This function calls the `to_string()` function from `serde_json` to serialize the structure back into JSON and create a `String` out of it.

Running this new version of our program with `cargo run`, we'll see the following output:

```
{"pets":[{"name":"Fluffy","info":{"kind":"dog","age":4}},
{"name":"Princess","info":{"kind":"cat","age":6}}]}
```

This is the correct data, but in an unfortunate format. JSON is often used as an interchange format that no humans are expected to consume, so the `to_string()` function does not bother formatting it in a human-friendly way. If we change the preceding code to use the `to_string_pretty()` function instead, we'll see much friendlier output. Feel free to try this, but for the purposes of demonstration, let's try outputting the data in a completely different structured format instead.

Back to our test program, let's add the `toml` crate into the mix:

```
$ cargo add toml
```

Changing our crate to use TOML as an output format is now as simple as changing one identifier in our `print_pet_data` function:

```
fn print_pet_data(data:&PetFile)-> Result<(), AnyError> {
    let output = toml::to_string(data)?;
    println!("{}", output);
    Ok(())
}
```

Running our program now results in a lovely TOML version of our input data, with our age modifications reflected:

```
[[pets]]
name = "Fluffy"

[pets.info]
kind = "dog"
age = 4

[[pets]]
name = "Princess"

[pets.info]
kind = "cat"
age = 6
```

This is only a brief tour of what `serde` can do, but I hope that it impresses upon you that complicated serialization can actually be simple to implement correctly in Rust. This is made possible by the amazing capabilities Rust offers to third-party crates to implement their own derive functionality and custom attributes, as well as a lot of clever software engineering from the Rust community.

Summary

In this chapter, we learned about working with the filesystem and handling errors. We dove into several different methods to read from and write to I/O streams with a special emphasis on using files. Finally, we concluded with how to use the `serde` crate to make working with structured text formats a breeze.

In the next chapter, we'll dive into another important part of the Rust standard library: **iterators**.

Get this book's PDF version and more

Scan the QR code (or go to `packtpub.com/unlock`). Search for this book by name, confirm the edition, and then follow the steps on the page.

UNLOCK NOW

Note: Keep your invoice handy. Purchases made directly from Packt don't require an invoice.

7

Understanding Iterators

The next stop on our tour of the Rust standard library is the iterator API. We know about iterators in C++ already, which we can use to *iterate*, or step one by one through the elements of the container, usually while performing an operation of some sort on them. While Rust iterators share the same name as C++ iterators, they end up being implemented quite differently. Rust's iterators are actually much closer to *ranges*, which were introduced in C++20.

In this chapter, we'll learn about the design of the Rust iterator library, the structures, functions, and traits that make up the iterator API, and how they compare to more traditional ways of looping through the elements of our containers.

In this chapter, we're going to cover the following main topics:

- Defining and creating iterators
- Consuming and composing iterators
- Examining iterator performance

Technical requirements

The examples in this chapter use Rust 1.82.0, but they will also work with any newer version.

If you need help with installing Rust, please see the *Appendix*.

Defining and creating iterators

At their core, iterators exist to make it easier to perform an operation or a series of operations on the items of a container. Behind this simple goal lies a lot of complexity. In this section, we'll examine what an iterator in Rust actually is, learn about the properties of iterators, and learn about ways to create them.

What is an iterator?

In Rust, an iterator is any structure that implements the `Iterator` trait from the `std::iter` module. The structure exists to hold the state required to produce the next value of the iteration. For instance, if we were iterating through the items of `Vec` or slice, the structure may store a reference to the slice and the index of the next element to visit.

The `Iterator` trait, on the other hand, exposes one required method that alone drives all iteration: the `next()` method. Iteration in Rust revolves around the simplicity of this one function, which returns an option containing the value of the next element of the container to visit. If there are no more elements in the container, the returned option holds a `None` variant.

A quick example may help to clarify this:

```
let v = vec![0, 1, 2];
let mut it = v.iter();
println!("{:?}", it.next());
println!("{:?}", it.next());
println!("{:?}", it.next());
println!("{:?}", it.next());
```

Here, we construct `Vec`, and then call `iter()` to return an iterator over this vector. We almost never think about the type of `it`, but it's a custom structure specifically for iterating over slices: `std::slice::Iter<'a, T>`. Recall that `Vec` will be coerced to a slice when needed, and in this case, the `iter()` method actually exists on the slice type. The `'a` lifetime in the `Iter<'a, T>` type implies that the structure will hold on to some part of our slice and thus cannot outlive it, while of course `T` is the generic type of the elements of our slice.

We then call the `Iterator` trait's `next()` method four times in a row. The output of this code will be as follows:

```
Some(0)
Some(1)
Some(2)
None
```

At this point, iterators in Rust may not seem especially compelling, but there is a lot more to the picture. In a real program, we wouldn't want to call `next()` over and over to accomplish anything, but it's important to understand that this is the basic building block of an iterator. With this in mind, let's move on to examine four important properties of Rust's iterators.

The properties of Rust iterators

Rust's iterators are lazy, unbounded, composable, and extensible. Let's examine each of these properties in turn.

When we called `iter()` earlier, what happened? We created a new structure and bound it to the mutable `it` variable. But no actual work happened until we began pulling values out of the iterator by calling `next()`. This is an example of what we call *lazy evaluation*. Rust's iterators do nothing by themselves and require something else to repeatedly call the `next()` method in order to do work.

Because iterators are evaluated lazily, they can also be ***unbounded***. While we'd never expect to have an infinitely sized container, not every iterator needs to be pointing to a container. We have seen that a `None` return from `next()` ends iteration, but there is nothing preventing us from making an iterator that never returns `None`, representing an infinite sequence.

In fact, we can easily make an iterator that does nothing but count up:

```
struct Counter {
    next_value: usize,
}

impl Iterator for Counter {
    type Item = usize;
    fn next(&mut self) -> Option<usize> {
        let value = self.next_value;
        self.next_value += 1;
        return Some(value);
    }
}
```

We won't make a program that keeps counting up infinitely, but we can see that this iterator works as expected with the following code:

```
let mut counter = Counter { next_value: 0 };
println!("{:?}", counter.next());
println!("{:?}", counter.next());
println!("{:?}", counter.next());
```

Similar to our earlier example, this prints the following:

```
Some(0)
Some(1)
Some(2)
```

But this time, since our iterator is unbounded, we can continue calling the `next()` function as many times as we need, and it will never stop iteration by returning a `None` value.

Iterators are also *composable*, which means that we can create a chain of iterators that pull from one another in sequence. In order to accomplish this, we must have a structure that holds one or more input iterators while also implementing the `Iterator` trait. Such a structure is called an *adapter* in the Rust standard library. We will see many examples of composition as we work through this chapter.

Finally, iterators are *extensible*. Because the iterator API relies heavily on the `Iterator` trait, we can extend this trait to add new functionality to it, just as we saw with the `byteorder` crate in the previous chapter. A third-party crate called `itertools` does exactly this, and provides a number of additional methods to anything implementing `Iterator`. While functionality provided by `itertools` has been added into the standard library proper over time, it's worth taking a look at it if you have a tricky iteration problem. It might just have the iterator or adapter you need.

Now that we understand these four properties, let's begin looking at iterators more deeply. We'll start with an examination of a number of different ways to create an iterator.

Creating iterators

There are several ways to create an iterator. We have already seen that one of them is to call `iter()` on a vector or slice. It's very common throughout the standard library to hide the creation of an iterator behind a convenience function like this one. While an `iter()` function is provided on many containers in the standard library, this is merely a convention; there is no specific trait providing this function.

When using `iter()`, convention dictates that we are creating an iterator that will return each value as an immutable reference as we iterate through the container. Many containers also offer an `iter_mut()` method, creating an iterator that functions similarly but returns mutable references. We can use it to edit values inside the container.

Here's an example that will add 1 to each element of a mutable vector:

```
let mut v = vec![0, 1, 2];
for value in v.iter_mut() {
    *value += 1;
}
```

Another way to create an iterator is using the `into_iter()` function provided by the `IntoIterator` trait. When called on an owned object, such as `Vec` or other container, this method will transfer ownership of the container to the iterator itself. When this happens, we will get owned rather than borrowed values out of the iterator, and the original container will no longer be accessible thanks to Rust's borrowing rules.

Let's look at the definition of `IntoIterator` to see why:

```
pub trait IntoIterator {
    type Item;
    type IntoIter: Iterator<Item = Self::Item>;

    fn into_iter(self) -> Self::IntoIter;
}
```

As we can see, the `into_iter()` function takes `self` as an argument, rather than the more common `&self` reference argument. This means that ownership of the object is transferred through the function call. This is the only way to get an iterator of owned values without cloning. Looking at one more example with type annotations, we can see the difference between `iter()` and `into_iter()`:

```
let v = vec![1, 2, 3];
for x in v.iter() {
    let _:&usize=x;
    println!("{}", x);
}
for x in v.into_iter() {
    let _: usize = x;
    println!("{}", x);
}
```

Here, `let _: &usize = x` is a small trick to annotate the type of `x`, because annotations are not allowed directly in the `for` loop. If the annotation and actual type do not match, the compiler will produce an error.

An important note is that if `into_iter()` is called on a borrowed value, its iterator will still return borrowed values. This is, of course, because the iterator cannot take ownership of the value in this case. But the most common explicit usage of `into_iter()` is to create an iterator that consumes the container and produces owned instead of borrowed values.

The last way we'll explore to create an iterator is to generate values directly. We saw this earlier with our `Counter` example, but there are a handful of utility iterators of this form in the standard library. There are `empty()` and `once()`, which yield zero and one value, respectively, as well as `repeat()`, which will yield a single value infinitely.

Possibly the most useful of the standalone iterators in the standard library is `zip()`, which takes two iterators as arguments and combines their values as a tuple to pass to later stages, stopping as soon as either iterator has no more values to produce:

```
let v1 = vec![1, 2, 3];
let v2 = vec!["one", "two", "three"];
let mut it = std::iter::zip(v1.into_iter(), v2.into_iter());
println!("{:?}", it.next());
println!("{:?}", it.next());
println!("{:?}", it.next());
```

This example will print the following:

```
Some((1, "one"))
Some((2, "two"))
Some((3, "three"))
```

We've looked at a handful of different ways to create iterators, but calling `next()` all of the time still seems pretty unappealing. So, in the following section, we'll look at different ways to pull values out of our iterators.

Consuming and composing iterators

As we've discussed, the least complicated way to consume an iterator is to call the `next()` method repeatedly to get each element until it returns `None`. While Rust has some syntax helpers, such as the `while let` loop, this can still be a cumbersome way to work with iterators. Surely it's not the only way? Let's take a look at the options provided by the language and standard library for consuming values from an iterator.

Looping through iterators

One of the most common and convenient ways to consume iterators ends up being the `for` loop that we've seen several times throughout the book. One surprising revelation might be that the `for` loop only exists to consume iterators. Now that we're working with iterators, we can fully explain the workings of this language construct.

The `for` loop is purely syntactic sugar, meaning that it hides a more complicated implementation that would be cumbersome to type out repeatedly. Say we do something like the following:

```
for x in v {
    println!("{}", x);
}
```

It actually expands to something like this:

```
let mut it = IntoIterator::into_iter(v);
while let Some(x) = it.next() {
    println!("{}", x);
}
```

The exact expansion is more complicated, but this simplified one gives us a general understanding of this language construct. The job of this construct is to turn the `in` expression into an iterator, and then consume the entire thing. The `for` loop relies heavily on the `IntoIterator` trait we encountered earlier.

In Rust, if we write `for x in v`, we'll get x as a series of owned values, but if we write `for x in &v`, we'll get x as a series of borrowed values or references. There's some subtlety to this that we can begin to understand as we investigate the expanded version of the `for` loop.

We know now that `for x in v` essentially equates to `for x in IntoIterator::into_iter(v)` and that `for x in &v` equates to `for x in`

`IntoIterator::into_iter(&v)`. We can also note that `for x in &mut v` equates to `for x in IntoIterator::into_iter(&mut v)`.

Each of these `IntoIterator` implementations (`T`, `&T`, and `&mut T`) need to be defined on our structure for this to work. Usually, `IntoIterator<&T>` and `IntoIterator<&mutT>` are implemented by calling `iter()` and `iter_mut()`, respectively, but this is a convention. Some containers choose not to define `iter_mut()` and `IntoIterator<&mutT>` at all, usually because correctness could be compromised by doing so.

Another important point about `for` loops is that `IntoIterator` has a blanket implementation for everything implementing `Iterator` that just returns `Iterator` with no change. This happens whenever we pass something that is already an iterator as the `in` expression of a `for` loop. For instance, when we call `for x in v.iter()`, it roughly expands to `for x in IntoIterator::into_iter(v.iter())`. The iterator we created with `iter()` is just passed through without any change, thanks to the blanket implementation.

Taken together, the following two loops end up being equivalent:

```
for x in v {}
for x in v.into_iter() {}
```

As do these loops:

```
for x in &v {}
for x in v.iter() {}
```

And these two loops:

```
for x in &mut v {}
for x in v.iter_mut() {}
```

Another implication of the expansion of `for` is that `IntoIterator` is implemented on a massive number of things in the standard library. These include both bounded and unbounded ranges, most container types, and several other things, which allows code like this:

```
for i in 0..10 {
    println!("{}", i);
}
```

We now know that this code expands to something closer to this:

```
let mut it = IntoIterator::into_iter(0..10);
while let Some(i) = it.next() {
    println!("{}", i);
}
```

Functions on the iterator trait

Of course, a `for` loop isn't the only way to consume an iterator. There are several functions on the iterator trait that consume the iterator as well. Many of these have useful secondary purposes. For instance, the `sum()` function on the iterator trait will consume an iterator of integer or floating-point values and return the sum of the values. Similarly, the `max()` and `min()` functions will return the highest or lowest element after consuming the iterator. These functions depend on the items we're iterating over being additive or comparable and are conditioned on the proper traits.

One of the most common and useful functions on the iterator trait for consuming iterators is `collect()`. The `collect()` function consumes the iterator and uses its values to create a new container. The container we are creating is a generic type, meaning that we often need to specify the type we're collecting into with a type annotation or with the turbofish operator, `::< >`.

Using our `Counter` iterator, we can demonstrate how to collect the values of an iterator into a new vector:

```
let counter = Counter { next_value: 0 };
let vector = counter.take(5).collect::<Vec<usize>>();
println!("{:?}", vector);
```

The `take()` function produces an adapter that yields at most the specified number of elements from the iterator before returning `None`. After this code is run, our vector contains the values `[0, 1, 2, 3, 4]`.

As in other situations, we do not need to use the turbofish operator (`::< >`) if we specify the type for the compiler in some other way. This can include using an annotation. Adjusting the previous example, we could elide the turbofish like this:

```
let vector: Vec<_> = counter.take(5).collect();
```

We do not need to specify the type of elements of the vector. Simply telling the compiler that we're collecting into `Vec` gives it enough information to infer the right choice. Whether we use an annotation or the turbofish is mostly a stylistic preference.

A special case occurs when the values produced by the iterator are of the `Result` type. Just to give us a contrived example to work with, I'll make `Vec` full of `Result` values for us to iterate over:

```
let v: Vec<Result<usize, String>> = vec![Ok(1), Ok(2), Ok(3), Ok(4)];
let result = v.into_iter().collect::<Result<Vec<_>, _>>()?;
println!("{:?}", result);
```

This example prints out a vector containing `[1, 2, 3, 4]`. What is happening here? When we have an iterator of `Result` values, the `collect()` function will check each of them in turn. If all values in the iterator are `Ok`, then the values held by each `Ok` result will be collected together and wrapped in an `Ok`. If any of the results are `Err`, the entire process stops and returns the first `Err` it encountered as the collected value.

While collecting into a `Result` value is a very powerful pattern, it can sometimes take some practice for engineers to fully understand it. I recommend setting up your own example on the Rust Playground and adjusting it until you have a great understanding of what is happening.

Now that we understand how to create and consume iterators, let's take a look at one of the most powerful features of iterators – chaining or combining them to perform complex operations efficiently.

Composing iterators with adapters

As mentioned earlier, an adapter is a special structure that both implements the iterator trait and also holds one or more iterators to pull from as input. Adapters provided by the standard library tend to be part of the iterator trait, and thus they can be used by every type implementing that trait.

A very simple example of an adapter is the `cloned()` function. This produces an iterator that takes the values of the input iterator, clones them, and then passes them on to the next iterator in the chain. We might want to use this when collecting from a reference:

```
let vector = v.iter().cloned().collect::<Vec<_>>();
```

This code will clone the values of an iterator one by one and then pass them to the `collect()` function to create a new vector. A simpler way to do this is just to call `v.clone()`, but this example hopefully shows how adapters can be used to chain together iterators.

Let's look closer at `cloned()` to understand what it's doing. Recall that this is a function implemented on the iterator trait, meaning that it has access to the iterator calling it as `self`. This creates a structure named `Cloned<I>`, where `I` is the type of the iterator. Because we're consuming the iterator, the `Cloned` structure just takes ownership of the iterator; there is no need to hold onto a lifetime.

The `next()` function of the `Iterator` implementation on `Cloned` simply makes use of the `cloned()` method on the `Option` type:

```
fn next(&mut self) -> Option<T> {
    self.it.next().cloned()
}
```

The `Option::cloned()` method works by returning a `Some` with a cloned value inside if `self` was `Some`, or `None` if the option was `None`. Whenever an adapter can be implemented with a method of `Option`, it's a useful shortcut due to the `next()` method of an iterator always returning an `Option` itself.

It's the large number of adapters available on the iterator trait that really makes the Rust iterator API shine. We'll go over a few common ones. First, we'll look at the `map()` adapter, which is probably one of the most frequently used adapters in the whole library. The term *map* is somewhat common in functional languages. For our purposes, we can think of it as applying a closure to each value returned by our iterator and, as an adapter, passing it along to the next iterator in the chain.

Here's an example of doubling the value of each number in a vector and collecting it into a new vector:

```
let v = vec![0, 1, 2, 3, 4];
let result = v.into_iter().map(|val| val * 2).collect::<Vec<_>>();
println!("{:?}", result);
```

The printed output from this program is as follows:

```
[0, 2, 4, 6, 8]
```

Another common adapter is `filter()`, which tests each element using a closure. Elements for which the closure returns `true` will be passed along, while elements for which it returns `false` will be skipped.

To keep only even numbers, we can use `filter()` to do something like this:

```
let v = vec![0, 1, 2, 3, 4];
let result = v.into_iter().filter(|val| val % 2 == 0).collect::<Vec<_>>();
println!("{:?}", result);
```

This example outputs the following:

```
[0, 2, 4]
```

And, of course, we can chain adapters together to express even complicated calculations as a series of small steps. Here is an example using both the `filter()` and `map()` adapters:

```
let v = vec![0, 1, 2, 3, 4];
let result = v
    .into_iter()
    .filter(|val| val % 2 == 0)
    .map(|val| val * 2)
    .collect::<Vec<_>>();
println!("{:?}", result);
```

This time, after filtering out the odd values and doubling the remaining ones, we see this output:

```
[0, 4, 8]
```

We've used `filter()` and `map()` together here, but the combination is so frequent that Rust provides a `filter_map()` adapter to do the same work. The `filter_map()` adapter returns an option, where a `Some` value is kept, and a `None` value is skipped. Our previous example rewritten with `filter_map()` looks like this:

```
let v = vec![0, 1, 2, 3, 4];
let result = v
    .into_iter()
    .filter_map(|val| if val % 2 == 0 { Some(val * 2) } else { None })
    .collect::<Vec<_>>();
println!("{:?}", result);
```

This has the same functionality and output as our previous example, but is often a more concise and direct way of accomplishing the work.

Take some time to look through the online Rust documentation for the iterator trait. There are several dozen useful methods available to produce adapters. We wouldn't expect to use more than a handful in any given program, but understanding the available options can help us make the most of the iterator API in our own programs.

Examining iterator performance

As C++ programmers, we must often deal with performance-sensitive code. It is natural for us to wonder about the runtime performance of these chains of potentially complicated iterator expressions. But as a result of lazy evaluation, generic function evaluation, and extensive inlining, performance in optimized builds ends up being quite good. In some tests, it has even been shown to outperform a hand-written loop. In this section, we'll examine how the Rust compiler can perform such a feat.

Dissecting an iterator expression

It might be hard to believe that iterator performance can beat a hand-written loop without seeing it in action, so let's go through a simple example. We'll dive deeply into an iterator expression, unrolling and inlining it by hand to get a sense of how the compiler will see it.

Our expression will be the relatively simple `v.into_iter().filter(|x| x % 2 == 0).map(|x| x * 2).sum()`, where `v` is a vector of `u32`. The first thing to know is that `sum()` is implemented with the `fold()` function on the `Iterator` trait. The `fold()` function repeatedly invokes a function on each element, passing along an accumulated value each time. If we unroll the `fold()` function as used in `sum()`, it looks like this:

```
let mut accum = 0;
while let Some(x) = self.next() {
    accum = accum + x;
}
accum
```

This looks a bit like what we'd normally write, but it's hard to see it as a compiler would with the syntactic sugar of the `while let` loop, so let's work on a more compiler-friendly representation that will allow us to see how the `next()` function is inlined:

```
let mut accum = 0;
loop {
    let x = self.next();
    if x.is_none() {
        break;
```

```
    }
    accum = accum + x.unwrap();
}
accum
```

Moving backward from `sum()`, the next thing in our target expression is `map(|x| x * 2)`. Because `map()` is an adapter, we can't expand it without understanding what is passed in. We'll use a placeholder value, `prev`, in this example. The `map()` adapter's `next()` function is just implemented by calling `Option::map`. But we'll skip a few steps here and inline that as well, leaving us with something like this:

```
let mut accum = 0;
loop {
    let prev = self.next();
    if prev.is_none() {
        break;
    }
    let x = prev.unwrap() * 2;
    accum = accum + x;
}
accum
```

Note that in this case, the `is_none()` check and `unwrap()` have moved up to happen on the result of `prev` instead of being part of `sum()`. This is a shortcut for the purposes of illustration, but in a real compile, the optimizer is able to understand that creating `Option` with `Some()` and then immediately unwrapping it is a no-op that can be elided.

Moving backward in the expression to `filter()`, we have a slightly more interesting implementation to consider, because `filter()` can skip values when the function passed to it returns `false`. The `filter()` adapter is implemented ultimately using the `try_fold()` function, which conceptually adds a nested loop to our manual inlining, but can be simplified as follows:

```
let mut accum = 0;
loop {
    let value = self.next();
    if value.is_none() {
        break;
    }
    if value.unwrap() % 2 == 0 {
```

```
        let x = value.unwrap() * 2;
        accum = accum + x;
    }
}
accum
```

Again, some liberties have been taken here for clarity. We might expect a more verbose inlining to contain an outer loop and an inner loop, but this has been simplified by hand for the purposes of illustration. The last step is to figure out what `v.into_iter()` actually does and add that into our unrolled loop.

It turns out that `into_iter()` on `Vec` yields a highly optimized implementation using raw pointers and unsafe blocks. It's too complicated to paste into our small example, so we'll just index the values with the `[]` operator. Keep in mind that while indexing would normally trigger a bounds check at runtime, in this example, we're using it as a stand-in for a more optimized implementation that does not execute the bounds check.

This makes our final, inlined loop look something like this:

```
let mut accum = 0;
let mut start_index = 0;
let end_index = v.len();
loop {
    if start_index == end_index {
        break;
    }
    let value = v[start_index];
    if value % 2 == 0 {
        let x = value * 2;
        accum = accum + x;
    }
    start_index += 1;
}
accum
```

Now, this might look similar to what we would write if we were trying to write the loop ourselves, and it seems like it might compile down to reasonable machine code. To check, we can compare the optimized assembly of this loop to the original iterator expression using a tool such as the **Rust Playground** or Matt Godbolt's **Compiler Explorer**. While there are some minor differences, the assembly for the inner loop is identical for this test.

Vectorization optimizations

One additional thing that the iterator API in Rust does well is preserve *vectorization* opportunities. Vectorization is a term for an optimization performed by LLVM and other compiler backends. The general idea is that if the compiler can prove certain properties of our loop, it can implement it using highly efficient **single instruction, multiple data (SIMD)** instructions on modern hardware. Often, this means that the loop can execute significantly faster for larger amounts of data.

Vectorization is notoriously tricky to get right because the restrictions the compiler has to work under to prove that vectorization on a specific loop is possible are hard to guarantee, and often the only way to check that you haven't violated any required conditions is to look at the generated assembly for a loop. Because of its functional design and careful implementation, the Rust iterator API is likely to construct most loops in such a way that the compiler's vectorization rules are met. This is why we sometimes see iterator expressions that outperform traditional loops.

Still, while Rust iterators may make it more likely that the compiler is able to perform this optimization, it's no guarantee. When maximum runtime performance is needed, be sure to run benchmarks or check the generated code locally. As we discussed earlier, online tools such as Matt Godbolt's Compiler Explorer (`https://rust.godbolt.org/`) or the Rust Playground can be very useful for this type of verification.

Summary

We've now learned a great deal about the Rust iterator API. We discovered that iterators are structures that implement the iterator trait and learned how to both write our own iterators and create them from existing containers. We then examined a number of ways to consume iterators, including collecting them into a new container. We also examined adapters and how they allow us to combine iterators to create powerful expressions. Then, we took an extensive tour through the implementation of an iterator expression to see why compilers are able to optimize them efficiently.

In the next chapter, we'll look into Rust's take on one of the most popular programming paradigms: **object orientation**.

Get this book's PDF version and more

Scan the QR code (or go to `packtpub.com/unlock`). Search for this book by name, confirm the edition, and then follow the steps on the page.

UNLOCK NOW

Note: Keep your invoice handy. Purchases made directly from Packt don't require an invoice.

8

Object-Oriented Programming

Object-oriented programming (**OOP**) has been a very popular paradigm in the programming community over the last few decades. Several popular languages either explicitly embrace the object-oriented paradigm or style themselves as "multi-paradigm" languages with some level of support for it.

Rust falls in the latter category, and in this chapter, we'll learn about Rust's unique take on object orientation, see how it contrasts with C++'s approach, and examine how it can be combined with Rust's functional influences.

In this chapter, we're going to cover the following main topics:

- Understanding object-oriented principles
- Examining object-oriented foundations in Rust
- Moving beyond object orientation

Technical requirements

The examples in this chapter use Rust 1.82.0, but they will also work with any newer version.

If you need help installing Rust, please see the *Appendix*.

Understanding object-oriented principles

While OOP is nearly ubiquitous in programming literature and discourse, it comes in many different styles and flavors. In this section, we'll briefly review the core principles of OOP in C++ so that we have a basis from which to examine Rust's implementation of these same principles.

The term *object-oriented programming* was coined by Alan Kay, designer of the Smalltalk programming language, in the 1960s. While the Smalltalk OOP model is of historical interest, it differs in several ways from the model chosen by C++ and many of its successors. As a result, OOP can be difficult to define precisely. Nevertheless, most modern discussions converge on a small set of core principles, which we'll examine in this section.

Abstracting behavior and encapsulating data

The focus of OOP is, of course, **objects**. An object is a collection of states that exposes a public interface to other objects in some form. Objects, in C++ and most other modern object-oriented languages, interact with each other by calling the **methods** or functions that make up an object's public **application programming interface (API)**.

An object is usually an **instance** of a **class**. It's here that most explanations break out the animal or shape examples. `Cat` might be a "class" of object, but the Russian Blue cat that just knocked over your coffee is a specific "instance" of the `Cat` class with its own state independent of every other object in the program.

Abstraction is a core OOP principle that states that objects should endeavor to expose only a small set of behaviors to other objects, and that they should always expose an API that focuses on *what* a class does rather than *how* it does it internally. This is an attempt at reducing complexity. The author of a class can focus solely on the implementation of its own functionality, while any users of the class in the program do not need to understand or focus on how it behaves at all. Abstraction is, of course, useful outside of OOP, but it's generally agreed upon as a core principle of OOP.

Aiding us in creating a simple, public API for our programs is the principle of **encapsulation**. This principle focuses on the mechanisms used to hide data and implementation details from other objects. In C++, this is accomplished by marking parts of the structure with access modifiers such as `public`, `private`, and `protected`. A strictly object-oriented approach may prefer to mark all data as private, but provide several accessors as part of the public API, perhaps something like this:

```
class Cat {
private:
      Color furColor;
public:
      void SetFurColor(Color color) { furColor = color; };
      Color GetFurColor() const { return furColor; }
};
```

First-time OOP learners often balk when seeing this. Isn't it just busywork? Why can't we just expose `furColor` directly without boilerplate accessor code? C++, after all, gives us the flexibility to mark everything as `public` and ignore the principle of encapsulation altogether.

The most commonly cited reason to go to the extra effort here is to protect users of your object from internal changes to the code. In theory, as long as the public interface does not change in its functionality, the underlying implementation of the object and the state it contains could change arbitrarily without breaking any code interacting with the object. Although there can be practical concerns with providing backward compatibility for long periods of time, providing a public API to interact with our object's private state is a useful technique to enhance code maintainability and understandability.

While abstraction and encapsulation make up the first half of OOP's core principles, they're also just good software engineering practices to many. To make a truly OOP language, we need to be able to allow programmers to model problems at different levels of abstraction, as we'll see in the next section.

Modeling problems with inheritance and polymorphism

In real programs, we might wish to deal with collections of objects. As an example, we can consider a ray-tracing program. We might want to trace a ray against a collection of objects in a scene, like in this highly simplified C++ example:

```
float min_distance = INFINITY;
for (const Object& object : sceneObjects) {
      float distance = object.intersects(ray);
      if (distance < min_distance) {
            min_distance = distance;
      }
}
```

In this case, we have a high-level piece of code that wants to treat every object in the scene identically, but in a scene, we may have several different kinds of objects that compute intersections against a ray in vastly different ways. For instance, the math for intersecting a ray with a triangle and intersecting a ray with a sphere are very different things.

In order to model problems in this way, an OOP language must allow us to refer to multiple specific types, such as `Sphere` or `Triangle`, with a common name and interface, such as `Shape` or `Object` in our example here. This capability in many OOP languages is called **inheritance**. In our ray-tracing example, we can use inheritance to create a hierarchy or tree out of our classes, with `Object` being the base or parent class for every entity in our scene. Inheritance is a natural way to model some problems, but it is not without its drawbacks. There are known inheritance problems with scary-sounding names, such as the *fragile base class problem* and the *diamond pattern*. We won't go into these problems here other than to note that they exist and that a lot of OOP best practices and even some language features are built around avoiding them.

In the case of our ray tracer, it isn't enough to simply define a hierarchy of object types for our scene. We also need to be able to specialize the behavior of each based on the specific type of the object (such as `Sphere` or `Triangle`). We also need this specialization to happen even if the compiler only knows that we're dealing with an `Object` class in the current context and has no knowledge of the specific type. This capability is called **polymorphism** in OOP literature.

In C++, inheritance and polymorphism are very tightly coupled. Without going too deeply into details that are already likely familiar to many C++ programmers, we might define our **base class** like this:

```
class Object {
public:
      virtual float intersects(const Ray& ray) const = 0;
};
```

This tells us that the `intersects` method is *pure virtual* in C++ terms, meaning that no implementation exists in the base class. A `virtual` method in C++ is one we're allowed or even expected to override with a more specific implementation.

The derived or child `Triangle` class might look like this:

```
class Triangle : public Object {
public:
      float intersects(const Ray& ray) const override;
};
```

Polymorphism in this setup is achieved by a runtime table of function pointers called the **virtual table**. On construction, each object stores a pointer to that class's virtual table. When we call the `intersect` method using `Object`, the compiler will generate code to look into the virtual table of the object and pull out a pointer to the `Triangle::intersect()` method if our `Object` happens to be a `Triangle`, or the `Sphere::intersect` method if our object is a `Sphere`, and so on with all other child types.

This functionality is often referred to as **dynamic dispatch**. "Dispatch" here simply means calling a function. Dynamic dispatch requires that the function's address be looked up at runtime at a small performance cost, while **static dispatch** refers to the much more common case where the compiler knows the address of the function call at compile time.

The four principles we've looked at here – abstraction, encapsulation, inheritance, and polymorphism – make up the core of the OOP methodology. With these four principles in mind, we'll begin to look at Rust's take on object orientation and how it differs from C++.

Examining object-oriented foundations in Rust

Rust's take on object orientation can be seen as very nontraditional. Rather than creating a direct reimplementation of C++'s flavor of object orientation with small tweaks, Rust's designers chose to rethink object-oriented concepts in the context of the core safety and performance goals of the language.

In this section, we'll take a deeper look at what object orientation means in Rust and how familiar object-oriented concepts are expressed using its language features.

Implementation and data visibility

As described earlier, abstraction and encapsulation are good, general software engineering principles in addition to being core tenets of OOP. Rust has support for data hiding and specifying a public API, but this works differently than you might expect coming from C++.

In Rust, everything is private by default, but it's not private to the structure as it might be in a C++ class. Rather, it's private to the *module* in which we're working. That means that any other functions or structures in the module can see and potentially manipulate the fields of our structures directly in a way that typically requires the `friend` keyword in C++.

OOP purists might be surprised at this, but it represents a balance between purity and practicality. Modules in Rust are used to group together related code and data rather than to represent one specific structure. If we want to aim for strict purity, it is always possible to use one module per structure.

Making things public involves the `pub` keyword in Rust. This can show up in various contexts.

To make a structure visible outside the module, we put the `pub` keyword on it:

```
#[derive(Copy, Default)]
struct Color(u32);
pub struct Cat {
      fur_color: Color,
}
```

We can also make individual members of the structure public using a similar technique:

```
pub struct Cat {
      pub fur_color: Color,
}
```

This will allow code outside the module to see the fur_color member and read or modify it directly. It is possible to make fur_color public without making Cat itself public. This can be useful in cases where access is needed from submodules or tests without exposing the type as part of the module's public API.

Of course, we can also make methods and functions public as well, thus exposing them outside the module. We'll look at a method to do that here, but the usage is identical for free functions:

```
impl Cat {
    pub fn get_fur_color(&self) -> Color {
        self.fur_color
    }
}
```

Methods can be public even when the overall structure is not, for the same reasons related to testing and submodules described previously. Let's see an example in action with a typical test setup:

```
#[derive(Default)]
struct Cat {
    pub fur_color: Color,
}

#[cfg(test)]
mod tests {
    use super::*;
    #[test]
    fn default_color_is_black() {
        let cat = Cat::default();
        assert_eq!(cat.fur_color.0, 0);
    }
}
```

In this case, we were able to access fur_color directly from the test due to it being marked as pub. But we did not mark the Cat structure as public, preventing it from being visible outside of the module.

Trait definitions can also be made public to ensure that they are visible outside the current module. Note that associated functions that are part of the trait are considered public if the trait is public, without any additional markup required. Items in a trait always share the visibility of their trait:

```
pub trait Meows {
    fn say_meow();
}
```

Finally, a last use of the pub keyword is to declare a module itself public, making all of its public items visible in turn:

```
mod a {
    pub mod b {
        pub fn c() {
        }
    }
}
```

By declaring module b as public, we can then access it in code that has module a imported. We could call function c like this, for instance: `a::b::c()`.

Rust's visibility and module systems provide enough flexibility to implement strong data hiding guarantees and thus meet the abstraction and encapsulation goals of traditional OOP. In the next section, we'll examine how Rust treats inheritance.

Composition over inheritance

We've said that Rust's design is a reimagining of core OOP principles rather than a copy and paste of C++'s specific interpretation of them. Nothing embodies this more than Rust's take on inheritance. Basically, there is no inheritance in Rust. Can we still call Rust an OOP language? Let's examine how inheritance is actually used before drawing a conclusion.

Traditional inheritance defines an *is a* relationship, where we're moving from a less-specific thing to a more-specific thing. A rectangle *is a* shape, or a cat *is an* animal. The more specific types inherit all the properties of their more general counterparts, while also adding specific properties that reflect their own uniqueness. A principle called the **Liskov substitution principle** formalizes this idea, stating that a program using the less-specific parent type should be able to substitute in any of its more-specific child types without changing the program's behavior.

In addition to *is a* relationships, inheritance in C++ is also used to specify a common interface for several different classes to follow. Each child type inherits from the class that defines the interface, as we saw earlier in our ray-tracing example. This is more often an exercise in practicality than in strict OOP design. We'd be more likely to say that the child class *implements* the parent class's interface than to say that the child class *is a* type of the parent class.

So, how do we express these concepts in Rust if we don't have inheritance? It's hard to avoid the phrase "composition over inheritance" in Rust literature. Rust wants our structures to be "composed of" their parts, meaning each part is explicitly added as a member of the structure. By taking this stance, Rust avoids several traditional inheritance problems, such as the fragile base class and diamond problems of multiple inheritance, while keeping the state held by each structure explicit.

Rust encourages us not to think about problems in terms of inheritance relationships, but rather in terms of state and behavior. We can generalize the preceding uses for inheritance into two categories. An *is a* relationship may require us to consider state and behavior, while an *implements* relationship only requires us to consider behavior. When following the principle of composition over inheritance, we want the base type's state to be exposed as a structure, and we want shared behavior to be separate as a trait. An example is needed to see this clearly, so let's go back to the classic OOP example of animals.

An `Animal` base class in C++ might look something like this:

```
class Animal {
      std::string m_name;
public:
      const std::string& GetName() const { return m_name; }
      void SetName(const std::string& name) { m_name = name; }
};
```

Depending on our program, we might want to add other states here as well, but we'll just use the name to keep things simple.

In translating this design to Rust, we want to consider the state and the behavior separately. As a direct translation, we might make an `AnimalState` structure to hold the data, and an `AnimalBehavior` trait to define the behavior. That would look like this:

```
struct AnimalState {
      name: String,
}

trait AnimalBehavior {
      fn get_name(&self)-> &str;
      fn set_name(&mut self,name:&str);
}
```

If we wish to implement Dog or some other type of animal, it might look like this:

```
struct Dog {
    animal_state: AnimalState,
}

impl AnimalBehavior for Dog {
    fn get_name(&self) -> &str {
        &self.animal_state.name
    }
    fn set_name(&mut self, name: &str) {
        self.animal_state.name = name.to_string();
    }
}
```

We might look at the preceding design and think that it's a lot of boilerplate. Rust does offer mechanisms to reduce this overhead. In particular, traits allow us to specify default implementations for the functions implemented by the trait. For a large interface, we could implement most of the functionality in terms of only one or two methods to get our state structure. An example may look like this:

```
trait AnimalBehavior {
    fn get_animal_state(&self)-> &AnimalState
    fn get_animal_state_mut(&mut self)-> &mut AnimalState;

    fn get_name(&self)-> &str {
        &self.get_animal_state().name
    }
    fn set_name(&mut self, name: &str) {
        self.get_animal_state_mut().name = name.to_string();
    }
}
```

This simplifies the trait implementation for each type implementing the trait significantly because it only needs to implement two functions to have access to the entire interface:

```
impl AnimalBehavior for Dog {
    fn get_animal_state(&self) -> &AnimalState {
        &self.animal_state
    }
    fn get_animal_state_mut(&mut self) -> &mut AnimalState {
```

```
            &mut self.animal_state
        }
}
```

It's worth noting that you're not likely to see much Rust code written this way in the wild. While still supporting the OOP style, Rust naturally biases away from it as a means of representing problems due to its module-based concept of data visibility and its stricter separation of state and behavior. Rust encourages us to think of traits as collections of related behaviors rather than being tied directly to specific kinds of objects. The examples here are mostly to show that it's possible to write in a more object-oriented style in Rust, not to suggest it as a best practice.

Nevertheless, we're still missing one key part of the OOP equation. How do we handle polymorphic types in Rust?

Dynamic dispatch in Rust

Coming from C++-style OOP, it might be tempting to think that because Rust doesn't support inheritance, it must not support polymorphism, but this isn't true. The concepts of inheritance and polymorphism are often conflated due to being artificially tied together in several modern OOP languages, but they can be implemented independently, as Rust shows.

As we've seen, Rust's take on OOP focuses on what things *do* instead of what things *are*, which means that solutions are often based around traits rather than structures. Polymorphism is no exception. The key to achieving polymorphism in Rust is something called a **trait object**. If we have several different structures that implement the same trait, we can place them in containers as trait objects and then use dynamic dispatch to call the trait's functions at runtime.

To make this clearer, let's design an imaginary GUI library. Every widget in our library will implement the `Widget` trait. In the interest of simplicity, we'll just say that the `Widget` trait only contains a single function to return the two-dimensional size of the widget:

```
trait Widget {
    fn compute_size(&self) -> (u32, u32);
}
```

We'll now want to define a `Container` widget that allows us to hold one or more other widgets inside of it. Here, we've uncovered a case where we need to refer to perhaps many different widgets without needing to understand exactly what they are. Trait objects come to our rescue here:

```
struct Container {
        children: Vec<Box<dyn Widget>>,
}

impl Widget for Container {
        fn compute_size(&self) -> (u32, u32) {
                let mut size = (0, 0);
                for child in &self.children {
                        let (w, h) = child.compute_size();
                        size.0 += w;
                        size.1 += h;
                }
            return size;
    }
}
```

Here, we've specified that the `children` member of our `Container` structure takes a vector of trait objects. We can create a trait object with either `&dyn Trait` or `Box<dyn Trait>`. The `Box` type is a standard library type used to allocate objects on the heap, and is somewhat analogous to `std::unique_ptr` in C++. As in C++, we must use references or pointers to take advantage of polymorphism in Rust.

Internally, a trait object is a **wide pointer** comprised of a pointer to the object itself and a pointer to a lookup table of functions similar to a C++ virtual table. When our trait method is called on the object with `child.compute_size()`, the lookup table is referenced to find a pointer to the correct implementation of the function to be called. We then dispatch the function call using the dynamically determined address. The layout algorithm used by our container is nonsensical, but it works well as an example.

In order to see our GUI library in action, let's first create another type of widget:

```
struct Label {
        text: String,
}

impl Widget for Label {
        fn compute_size(&self) -> (u32, u32) {
                (10 * self.text.len() as u32, 10)
```

```
    }
}
```

Again, we've chosen a simplified size computation for the purposes of the example, but now that we have more than one widget, we can construct a reasonable working example:

```
fn main() {
        let hello = Label { text: "Hello World!".to_string() };
        let welcome = Label { text: "Welcome to Rust!".to_string() };
        let mut outer = Container { children: Vec::new() };
        let mut inner = Container { children: Vec::new() };

        inner.children.push( Box::new(welcome) );
        outer.children.push( Box::new(inner) );
        outer.children.push( Box::new(hello) );

        println!("Final size: {:?}", outer.compute_size());
}
```

When we call `outer.compute_size()`, the function will traverse the hierarchy of objects we've created in a depth-first manner computing sizes, dynamically dispatching the `compute_size` trait method each time.

Limitations of dynamic dispatch

There's one final nuance to trait objects, which is the concept of **dyn compatibility**, formerly called **object safety**. Rust disallows using traits as trait objects under certain conditions. The full list of these conditions is available in the Rust documentation, but there are a few that frequent users of trait objects are likely to run into.

First, functions associated with the trait can be broken down into *dispatchable* and *non-dispatchable* categories. Dispatchable means that the compiler will allow us to call the function through a trait object, while non-dispatchable means that it will not. To ensure `dyn` compatibility, every function in the trait must either be dispatchable or explicitly non-dispatchable.

A dispatchable function must be a method. That is, it must have `&self` or some variant of `self` as the first argument. It also must not have any generic type parameters or return `Self`. All other functions in a trait are non-dispatchable, because the compiler would run into problems with dynamically dispatching them. For instance, a function with generic type parameters could have several different implementations depending on the types for which it was generated, but we only have one spot in our virtual table for each function in the trait.

We said that for every function, the trait must be dispatchable or "explicitly" non-dispatchable. What does it mean to be explicit here? Rust offers an escape hatch to programmers who want to retain dyn compatibility while still keeping non-dispatchable functions in the trait. A function can be made explicitly non-dispatchable by adding the special `where Self: Sized` bound.

The following trait would normally not be dyn-compatible, because it mixes dispatchable and implicitly non-dispatchable functions:

```
trait DynCompatibilityTest {
      fn dispatchable(&self);
      fn non_dispatchable<T>(&self,value:T);
}
```

Say you attempted to use it as a trait object with some code like this:

```
let v: Vec<Box<dyn DynCompatibilityTest>> = Vec::new();
```

You would get an error from the compiler:

```
error[E0038]: the trait `DynCompatibilityTest` is not dyn compatible
```

To make the trait dyn-compatible, we can explicitly add the `where Self: Sized` bound to the non-dispatchable function:

```
trait DynCompatibilityTest {
      fn dispatchable(&self);
      fn non_dispatchable<T>(&self, value: T) where Self: Sized;
}
```

Compiling our test vector again, we see that the compiler now succeeds. The trade-off, of course, is that we cannot call the `non_dispatchable` method through a trait object. By explicitly marking it, we've told the compiler that its implementation is known only at compile time and that it should not have an entry in the virtual table. Despite this, we can attempt to call it through a trait object with some simple code.

```
let v: Vec<Box<dyn DynCompatibilityTest>> = Vec::new();
for obj in &v {
      obj.non_dispatchable(0);
}
```

This yields the following compiler error:

```
error: the `non_dispatchable` method cannot be invoked on a trait object
```

The topic of dyn compatibility is more advanced than this simple introduction, and I recommend reading the Rust documentation (`https://doc.rust-lang.org/`) for more information. While it can be a confusing topic, this short introduction should help you avoid most of the issues that newer Rust programmers run into with it.

Having discussed data visibility, composition, and dynamic dispatch, we've now covered how each of the core principles of OOP maps to Rust. In the next section, we'll examine how to mix Rust's functional and OOP techniques.

Moving beyond object orientation

We've learned that Rust is a multi-paradigm language. While providing the ability to implement object-oriented designs, it is also strongly influenced by functional programming languages. In this section, we'll first look into modeling problems using Rust enums, and then we'll dive into ways that we can mix the functional and object-oriented styles to take advantage of Rust's multi-paradigm capabilities.

Modeling problems with Rust enums

A very similar way to achieve a type of polymorphic behavior is to use Rust enums. Because enums in Rust can contain different states for each variant, they create a natural representation for certain types of problems. Often, in functional languages, we see this technique praised as an excellent way to represent **abstract syntax trees (ASTs)** in compilers and other tree-based data structures.

While Rust enums specify different states for each variant, it is pattern matching that helps us differentiate the behaviors. Say we have an enum representing a simple structured text format such as this one:

```
enum StructuredText {
    Paragraph(Vec<StructuredText>),
    Heading(String),
    Line(String),
}
```

Then, we could perhaps write a function to render the structured text using pattern matching:

```
fn render_plain(structured_text: &[StructuredText]) {
    for st in structured_text {
        match st {
            StructuredText::Paragraph(children) => {
                print!("    ");
                render_plain(&children);
                println!();
            }
            StructuredText::Heading(text) => {
                println!("\n{}\n", text);
            }
            StructuredText::Line(text) => {
                println!("{}", text);
            }
        }
    }
}
```

Given some structured text, this code will render it to our standard output stream. Here, we choose to indent paragraphs and place an extra newline between headings and paragraphs.

This example highlights some key ideas when working with Rust enums. Rather than implementing the behavior of each variant separately behind a common interface, we're implementing the behavior for each variant in a single function. Because pattern matching is exhaustive in Rust, states that we skip in any function implementation will be raised as a compiler error. You can perhaps see the pros and cons between the functional style and OOP-style polymorphism with dynamic dispatch already. In the OOP style, our different enum variants would each be independent structures, all likely implementing a `Render` trait. We'd then use the `Render` trait as a trait object to enable us to dynamically jump into the correct implementation for each structure at a small runtime performance cost.

Even if there are many variants, using the enum style helps keep the implementation closer together if each variant can be implemented with a relatively small amount of code. If the number of variants is small but the code required to implement each is complex, maybe then the OOP style wins out. In the end, the enum style makes it a small change to add new behaviors but a large change to add new variants, and the object-oriented style makes it a small change to add new variants but a large change to add new behaviors. Thankfully, there's no reason we can't mix the enum and OOP styles together.

Combining functional and object-oriented styles

Let's imagine that we want to write our structured text data to many different output formats. We'll use the functional style as before for outputting the text itself, but we can use trait objects to output our data in several different forms. We start by defining a trait interface that generalizes our `render` function:

```
trait StructuredTextRenderer {
      fn render(&self, structured_text:&[StructuredText]);
}
```

Now we can make other output formats, such as `XMLStructuredTextRenderer`:

```
struct XMLStructuredTextRenderer;

impl StructuredTextRenderer for XMLStructuredTextRenderer {
      fn render(&self, structured_text: &[StructuredText]) {
            for st in structured_text {
                  match st {
                        StructuredText::Paragraph(children) => {
                              println!("<p>");
                              render(children);
                              println!("</p>");
                        }
                        StructuredText::Heading(text) => {
                              println!("<h1>{}</h1>", text);
                        }
                        StructuredText::Line(text) => {
                              println!("{}", text);
                        }
                  }
            }
      }
}
```

We'll also wrap our previous `render_plain` function in a trait implementation:

```
struct PlainStructuredTextRenderer;

impl StructuredTextRenderer for PlainStructuredTextRenderer {
      fn render(&self, structured_text: &[StructuredText]) {
```

```
            render_plain(structured_text);
        }
}
```

With our trait implementations set up, we can create an array of boxed trait objects to dispatch to the appropriate renderers:

```
fn render_all(structured_text: &[StructuredText]) {
        let renderers: Vec<Box<dynStructuredTextRenderer>> = vec![
                Box::new(XMLStructuredTextRenderer),
                Box::new(PlainStructuredTextRenderer),
        ];
        for r in renderers {
                r.render(structured_text);
        }
}

fn main() {
        let structured_text = vec![
                StructuredText::Heading("Hello".to_string()),
                StructuredText::Paragraph(vec![
                        StructuredText::Line("This is the first line".to_string()),
                        StructuredText::Line("This is the second line".to_string()),
                ]),
        ];
        render_all(&structured_text);
}
```

Again, the functional and object-oriented methods each have different strengths. While you may naturally gravitate toward one solution or the other, always remember that they can work together in a complementary way should the situation call for it.

Summary

In this chapter, we've briefly reviewed the core principles of OOP. We then saw how Rust implements and sometimes reinterprets those principles. Finally, we saw examples of how to mix object-oriented techniques with other aspects of the Rust language.

In the next chapter, we'll explore ways that Rust can interoperate with C and C++.

9

Working with C++ in Rust

We've been focusing specifically on Rust for a few chapters, but now it's time to delve back into C++. While ideally, all our software would be able to benefit from Rust's safety guarantees, the reality remains that there are many libraries written in C and C++ that we may wish to use as part of our Rust programs. Or, perhaps we want to leverage Rust inside a completely different programming language ecosystem. Whether we're replacing an older system with Rust piece by piece or creating extensions for a third language such as Python, understanding how to use Rust to interact with other languages is an essential skill.

In this chapter, we'll discover Rust's **Foreign Function Interface** (**FFI**). The FFI refers to the set of language features that allow us to call functions from other languages in our Rust code and to make our Rust functions and data types available to other languages.

In this chapter, we're going to cover the following main topics:

- Communicating between Rust and C
- Generating and updating bindings
- Strategies for C++ binding
- Using bindings effectively

Technical requirements

Examples in this chapter use Rust 1.82.0, but they will also work with any newer version. If you need help installing Rust, please see the *Appendix*.

Some examples in this chapter require the SDL2 development library to be installed on your system.

You can find the code files for this chapter in this book's GitHub repository: `https://github.com/PacktPublishing/Rust-for-CPP-Developers`.

Communicating between Rust and C

While we've been discussing Rust in the context of C++, communication between the two languages happens only through the C **application binary interface** (**ABI**). In this section, we'll learn what an ABI is and how the C ABI serves as the common glue between many different languages, including Rust and C++.

Understanding the C ABI

In C and C++, we often compile source files into object files independently and link them all together into an executable as a post-process. To be linked together properly to create a working program, a function's implementation and every call to it must agree on an architecture-specific convention for how parameters are passed and values are returned. This must happen reliably, even if the function implementation and calls to the function are spread out across different object files created by entirely separate compiler invocations.

A similar problem arises whenever the compiler wishes to generate code to access a member of a structure. The C compiler usually inserts padding into different parts of the structure to keep accesses to each member aligned. Each invocation of the compiler must understand how to lay out each structure's data and padding bytes in memory so that it can generate reads and writes to each member consistently.

The *calling convention* and *structure layout* used by the compiler are two major aspects of an ABI. The C ABI is not standardized and varies across CPU architectures and operating systems, but it is stable, simple, and ubiquitous enough for most cross-language communication needs. For these reasons, it has become a kind of universal vocabulary used by several different programming languages when they need to communicate with one another.

Like C++, Rust's compiler includes built-in support for communicating using the C ABI. This allows it to not only communicate bidirectionally with C code but also produce extensions and modules for other language ecosystems such as Python and JavaScript. While Rust does not natively support the *C++ ABI*, we can make use of the fact that both Rust and C++ support the *C ABI* to communicate between the two languages.

Declaring C-compatible structures in Rust

Rust's default structure layout rules differ significantly from C's. Where C is focused on allowing the programmer to control memory as directly as possible, Rust will sometimes choose more efficient memory layouts behind the scenes for safety and performance reasons. When we want to declare a Rust structure that's usable with the C ABI, we must mark it explicitly to prevent the compiler from making these types of optimizations.

Rust provides the `repr` attribute to specify the memory layout of a structure. For an FFI-compatible structure, we can use the `repr(C)` attribute:

```
#[repr(C)]
struct Vec3 {
    x: f32,
    y: f32,
    z: f32,
}
```

While `repr(C)` will cause the structure's layout to match the C ABI, it does not mean that every structure using this attribute will work correctly across languages. Many Rust data types, such as `String` or `Vec<T>`, will not make any sense when passed to a C library, and the compiler will not warn you about using many of these features.

The reason the compiler is uncharacteristically loose with the behavior of these structures is that `repr(C)` has two uses in Rust. The first use is FFI, which is our primary interest in this chapter. But `repr(C)` can also be used to tell the Rust compiler to preserve the order of members in memory. Because there are multiple uses for this feature, the compiler cannot warn or error just because FFI-incompatible patterns are used in the structure.

Calling C functions from Rust

To enable communication between Rust and C, both sides must understand the functions and structures we are trying to use in terms of the C ABI. We often call definitions that can be used to call across different languages *bindings* because they bind the two languages together. In the next few sections, we'll explore the process of creating bindings for a popular C library, SDL2, which is used for graphics and window management tasks in many games. If you are unfamiliar with SDL2, you can learn more at `https://www.libsdl.org/`.

To make a C function available for Rust code to call, we declare it with an `unsafe extern` block. Here, we will create bindings for initializing and shutting down SDL2. Let's start by making a new crate:

```
$ cargo new bind_c_manual
$ cd bind_c_manual
```

The C definitions for the SDL2 functions we wish to bind are here:

```
int SDL_Init(Uint32 flags);
void SDL_Quit(void);
```

Our corresponding Rust bindings in `src/main.rs` will look like this:

```
#[link(name = "SDL2")]
unsafe extern "C" {
    fn SDL_Init(_: u32) -> i32;
    fn SDL_Quit();
}
```

Before we can successfully call any foreign functions, we must in some way tell the linker to import the library in which they exist. That's exactly what the `#[link(name = "SDL2")]` attribute is doing. This tells Rust to add the SDL2 library during the `link` phase so that its functions are available when creating the final executable.

> **Note**
>
> Successfully using the `link` attribute requires the development libraries to be installed globally on the user's system. Because of this, it may not provide the best experience for all users of your crate and may not work at all on platforms like Windows. We'll examine other options for linking later in the chapter.

Looking at our code example again, the `unsafe extern "C"` block tells the Rust compiler that function definitions inside of it must use a calling convention that conforms to the C ABI for our target. In this case, the `unsafe` part of `unsafe extern` means that the compiler cannot guarantee that the definitions we type in will match the library we're trying to work with or work correctly at runtime. The functions inside this block also default to `unsafe`, meaning that they require special `unsafe` markup to call.

Let's call SDL's startup and shutdown functions in our `main` function just to observe if we are able to call into C code:

```
fn main() {
    unsafe { SDL_Init(0) };
    unsafe { SDL_Quit() };
}
```

If linking to the SDL library was successful, our program will build and run without error. Unfortunately, this program doesn't do anything interesting yet. Let's expand our example to bind enough SDL functionality to create a window:

```
use std::ffi::c_char;
#[repr(C)]
struct SDL_Window([u8; 0]);

unsafe extern "C" {
    fn SDL_CreateWindow(
        title: *const c_char,
        x: i32, y: i32,
        w: i32, h: i32,
        flags: u32,
    ) -> *mut SDL_Window;
    fn SDL_Delay(ms: u32);
    fn SDL_DestroyWindow(window: *mut SDL_Window);
}
```

The definition of `SDL_Window` here is a zero-sized type in Rust. This only works because `SDL_Window` is an *opaque type*, meaning its contents are obscured by design in the original C library. The `window` handle is only used by passing it around as a pointer, so we can use a zero-sized array to designate it as an opaque type in our Rust bindings.

Note that we were able to pull in the helper `c_char` type from the `std::ffi` module. This module contains several Rust types that directly match their corresponding C types. While we can also use the corresponding Rust types in many cases, the types in `std::ffi` are more portable in cases where we can't assume a consistent bit width across all architectures.

With these bindings available to us, we can now do something interesting with our program. Let's replace our `main()` function with this code:

```
let name = c"Hello World";
unsafe {
    SDL_Init(0);
    let window = SDL_CreateWindow(name.as_ptr(), 0, 0, 320, 200, 0);
    SDL_Delay(2000);
    SDL_DestroyWindow(window);
    SDL_Quit();
}
```

Rust conveniently provides the `c""` syntax to create a C-compatible, zero-terminated string of the `&std::ffi::CStr` type. We must pass a pointer to this string to the foreign function, so we call `.as_ptr()` to turn our `CStr` reference into a pointer. Since our foreign functions are unsafe, we can call them all in a single `unsafe` block.

Assuming that SDL2 works correctly with our system, the resulting program pops up a small window on our desktop for two seconds before exiting. Of course, there are many more interesting things that can be done with SDL if we choose to bind more functions, but it would be tedious and error-prone to continue manually as we have been. Thankfully, there are other options, but first, let's look at the case of linking a Rust function into a C program.

Exposing Rust functions to C

Until now, we have focused on how to call a C function from Rust, but we are also able to call a Rust function from C programs. Let's start by creating a new library project with Cargo:

```
$ cargo new --lib from_c
$ cd from_c
```

We can now make some edits to the default `add` function created by Cargo to expose it to a C program:

```
#[unsafe(no_mangle)]
pub extern "C" fn add(left: u64, right: u64) -> u64 {
    left + right
}
```

Much like C++, the Rust compiler by default produces *mangled* symbol names that contain encoded information about the definition. These definitions are incompatible with C, so we must turn them off with the `#[unsafe(no_mangle)]` attribute for our symbols to be found when linked to a C program. By using `extern "C"`, we tell the compiler that our function uses the C calling convention.

Rust library crates by default create a special kind of static library called `rlib` when building. The `rlib` format contains extra information used for linking between Rust crates, but it is not understood by C tooling. To link our function into a C program, we must direct the linker to create a C-compatible static or dynamic library instead. To do this, we must add a `[lib]` section to `Cargo.toml`:

```
[lib]
crate-type = ["cdylib"]
```

This produces a shared library that we can then link to C. If we wish to use a static library, we can set the crate type to `staticlib` instead. Note that `crate-type` is an array. Specifying multiple values will cause the linker to produce one output of each type.

Lastly, we'll need to create a header containing our function definitions for the C side to consume. This needs to reside somewhere that the C compiler can see it. Let's call it `from_c.h` and put it in the root folder of our crate:

```
#include "stdint.h"
extern uint64_t add(uint64_t left, uint64_t right);
```

Now, we can also place a C program in the root of our crate to test that everything worked. Let's call it `test.c`:

```
#include <stdio.h>
#include "from_c.h"
int main() {
  uint64_t sum = add(5, 6);
  printf("sum is: %zu\n", sum);
  return 0;
}
```

Compile using the compiler of your choice. On Linux, using `clang`, this command will compile our test program:

```
$ clang -o test -L ./target/debug/ -lfrom_c -Wl,-rpath=target/debug test.c
```

On Windows, using the MSVC target, we'll need to link in a few system libraries and add the `.exe` extension:

```
$ clang -o test.exe -L .\target\debug\ from_c.dll.lib -lws2_32 -luserenv -lntdll
test.c
```

When running the resulting C program, we see the expected output:

```
sum is: 11
```

One thing we see in all the examples so far is that to link the two languages together, there must be two separate copies of each function or structure's definition. Since both the C and Rust copies of each definition must match exactly, we are faced with the undesirable, error-prone task of manually updating both definitions if any changes are made. In the next section, we'll investigate ways to resolve this challenge by creating the Rust bindings automatically from the C source code.

Generating and updating bindings

In *Chapter 4,* we learned that crates can specify a `build.rs` file to support build operations not normally covered by Cargo. This might include generating Rust code, compiling non-Rust code, or linking additional libraries into our Rust program. We'll need to lean on these capabilities as we discover how to generate bindings to C code automatically.

Using bindgen to keep bindings up to date

When a C library and Rust bindings cease to match each other for any reason, our Rust program will begin to display errors or crashes. These issues can be frustrating to track down if you're not aware of the problem. For this reason, it's usually best not to hardcode bindings like we did in the previous section. Instead, we can generate the bindings automatically from a C header file to ensure that they match correctly.

Fortunately, there are crates that can help us with this task. In particular, the `bindgen` crate was designed to be used from `build.rs` to generate Rust bindings to C code. When we include a crate in our project specifically to use in `build.rs`, it is called a **build dependency**. Let's make a new crate and add `bindgen` as a build dependency with `cargo add` like this:

```
$ cargo new bind_c_bindgen
$ cd bind_c_bindgen
$ cargo add bindgen --build
```

It's common for crates that provide bindings to embed the target library directly into their tree. This makes building the bindings and the library itself much easier and more reliable from system to system. We can embed the SDL2 source tree into our crate in one step with the following command:

```
$ curl -L https://github.com/libsdl-org/SDL/releases/download/release-2.30.9/
SDL2-2.30.9.tar.gz | tar xz
```

This gives us a folder named `SDL2-2.30.9` in our crate's root folder.

To use `bindgen`, we typically start by making a C header file local to our crate that will include the headers for which we want to generate bindings. It's not a requirement to make our own local header file, but it can simplify the management of the bindings and the build script. We'll call this header `wrapper.h`, and it goes into the root of our crate as well. Our initial `wrapper.h` file is quite simple:

```
#include "SDL2-2.30.9/include/SDL.h"
```

With our wrapper in place, the `build.rs` script in our crate's root then looks like this:

```
use std::path::PathBuf;
fn main() {
    let bindings = bindgen::Builder::default()
        .header("wrapper.h")
        .parse_callbacks(
            Box::new(bindgen::CargoCallbacks::new()))
        .generate()
        .expect("Unable to generate bindings");

    let out_path = PathBuf::from(
        std::env::var("OUT_DIR").unwrap());
    bindings
        .write_to_file(out_path.join("bindings.rs"))
        .expect("Couldn't write bindings");
}
```

This creates a `bindgen::Builder` instance, specifying our wrapper header as the input. Behind the scenes, the `parse_callbacks` function also configures Cargo to regenerate the bindings if our `wrapper.h` file changes.

With our bindings successfully generated, we query the `OUT_DIR` environment variable that is automatically defined by Cargo to determine where our bindings should be placed on disk. If writing the bindings succeeds, our build script concludes successfully.

We can now run `cargo build` to create our bindings. You can inspect the generated `bindings.rs` file in the target folder if you wish to examine it. But at this point, the bindings are just a loose Rust source file sitting on our filesystem. We need to import them into our crate in some way. What we're looking for is Rust's `include!` macro, which just inserts one source file into another, much the same as C++'s #include. In src/main.rs we can add the following lines:

```
#![allow(non_upper_case_globals)]
#![allow(non_camel_case_types)]
#![allow(non_snake_case)]include!(concat!(env!("OUT_DIR"), "/bindings.rs"));
```

Rust, by default, is very particular about casing conventions for types, variables, and functions, but there is very little C code that will follow these conventions. Therefore, we use attributes to disable these compiler warnings for our crate. While attributes using the #[] syntax will apply to the next item in the source file, attributes using the #![] syntax affect the entire crate.

The include itself uses the concat! and env! helper macros. These concatenate a string and look up an environment variable at compile time, respectively. Just as Cargo defines the OUT_DIR environment variable when compiling our build script, it is defined while compiling the rest of our crate as well.

Now, our bindings are fully available in our crate. But to use them, we must first re-examine linking the C library into our crate.

Compiling and linking C libraries

When we were creating bindings manually, we used the #[link] attribute to bring in system libraries. This has a few downsides for users of the crate because it requires the development libraries to be installed on the system. This means that developers attempting to use our crate may run into confusing build errors if they do not happen to meet these requirements. Additionally, on platforms such as Windows, there is no central location for development libraries, making a crate that relies on the #[link] attribute unusable for many developers.

We've already taken the first step toward solving this problem, which is embedding the source of the library we wish to bind into our crate directly. We were able to generate bindings from the C headers this way, but what about linking the library itself?

In *Chapter 4*, we looked briefly at how to use the cc crate through build.rs to link C code into our program. This is great for small libraries, but SDL2 is a complex library comprised of several C source files. It might be tedious to list them all individually, and we risk it breaking whenever we upgrade the C library we're binding.

The Rust community has created several crates to try to alleviate these problems, available for browsing in the **Build Utils** section of the crates.io website. There are many different build and package management tools supported by the Rust community, but since SDL provides configuration for the CMake build generation program, we'll begin by looking at the `cmake` crate. As with our other build dependencies, it can be added to our crate like this:

```
$ cargo add cmake --build
```

In our `build.rs` file, we can then add these lines to compile the library so long as CMake is installed on our development system:

```
let dst = cmake::Config::new("SDL2-2.30.9")
    .profile("Release")
    .define("SDL_SHARED", "OFF")
    .define("SDL_STATIC", "ON")
    .define("SDL_MAIN_HANDLED", "ON")
    .build();
println!(
    "cargo:rustc-link-search=native={}",
    dst.join("lib").display()
);
if cfg!(target_os = "windows") {
    println!("cargo:rustc-link-lib=static=SDL2main");
    println!("cargo:rustc-link-lib=static=SDL2-static");
} else {
    println!("cargo:rustc-link-lib=static=SDL2");
}
```

We first pass the name of the folder containing our SDL2 source to `Config::new` and then begin passing various configuration options. In this case, we're selecting to build a release version of the SDL2 library regardless of whether we're building our crate in `Debug` or `Release` mode. The remaining preprocessor definitions are needed to link SDL2 as a static library so that users of our crate are not reliant on a dynamic library to be installed on their system to run their programs.

It may seem odd that we're printing strings from our build script, but this is how we communicate information to Cargo that it might need to configure the build properly. When Cargo executes the build script, it will search its output for a few specific strings. In this case, we're adding the output folder of the CMake build step to the linker's library search path and requesting that additional libraries be linked depending on the target OS. Usually, these prints are done by the crate itself, and we don't have to worry about them, but the `cmake` crate does not choose to do this and instead requires us to specify what we wish to link manually.

The specific configuration passed to the cmake crate will be different for each library and often will need to change depending on which platform we're building against. Creating a robust set of bindings that works easily for all users and platforms can require a significant amount of work. For many platforms, the small amount of code we've examined here will not provide a complete working crate. A complete example can be found in the `sdl2` crate on `crates.io`.

This brings up a final point about creating C bindings: while it's important to understand how to create bindings when needed, always look around to see whether appropriate bindings for the C library you are working with already exist. The community often follows a convention of distributing raw bindings as a library with the `-sys` suffix, while higher-level APIs constructed on top of those bindings often lack this suffix.

At this point, we should be very familiar with using the C ABI, but expanding our program to use C++ presents even more challenges. In the next section, we'll begin to examine how to work with foreign C++ functions and classes.

Strategies for C++ binding

While there are several useful libraries in C, we are also likely to encounter C++ code that we would like to use in our Rust programs. This is especially true if we're trying to convert a C++ program to Rust piece by piece. Unfortunately, the C++ ABI is not directly supported by Rust, so we must look for strategies to redirect our C++ code through the C ABI to create bindings. Thankfully, a lot of thought has gone into this problem in the Rust community, giving us several options to explore.

Throughout this section, we'll use the `toml++` library to demonstrate different options for creating C++ bindings. While Rust has an excellent crate for parsing the TOML format available already, this library makes a good example because it is a single header and can be easily added to our example projects. The library can be found at `https://github.com/marzer/tomlplusplus`.

Manually creating bindings

If we are binding a small amount of relatively simple C++ code, it can be straightforward to create the bindings manually.

To set up for this, we'll create a new crate and download the `toml++` header file:

```
$ cargo new bind_cpp_manual
$ cd bind_cpp_manual
$ curl -O https://raw.githubusercontent.com/marzer/tomlplusplus/v3.4.0/toml.hpp
```

The manual binding strategy revolves around creating a C API for our C++ code using C++'s `extern "C"` functionality. For this example, we'll only create bindings for just enough of the library to parse a TOML file. To do this, we create an `api.cpp` file in the root of our crate that looks like this:

```
#include "toml.hpp"
extern "C" void *toml_parse_file(const char *path) {
    toml::parse_result result = toml::parse_file(path);
    if (result) {
        return new toml::table(std::move(result).table());
    } else {
        return nullptr;
    }
}
extern "C" void toml_free_table(void *tbl) {
    delete static_cast<toml::table*>(tbl);
}
```

To compile this code, we must next add the `cc` crate as a `build` dependency:

```
$ cargo add cc --build
```

Then, we add the following to our `build.rs` file:

```
fn main() {
    cc::Build::new()
        .cpp(true)
        .std("c++17")
        .define("TOML_EXCEPTIONS", "0")
        .file("api.cpp")
        .compile("api");
}
```

This compiles our `api.cpp` file with the appropriate flags and generates the necessary Cargo annotations to link the resulting library `api` into our crate.

Now, the only remaining step is to create the C API on the Rust side and begin using our functions. Since we have a TOML file readily available in our crate's `Cargo.toml` file, we'll parse this file to test that everything works. Our crate's `main.rs` file ends up looking like this:

```
use std::ffi::{c_char, c_void};
unsafe extern "C" {
    fn toml_parse_file(path: *const c_char) -> *mut c_void;
    fn toml_free_table(tbl: *const c_void);
}
fn main() {
    unsafe {
        let table = toml_parse_file(c"Cargo.toml".as_ptr());
        if table.is_null() {
            println!("Failed to parse TOML");
        } else {
            println!("Parsed TOML successfully");
        }
        toml_free_table(table);
    }
}
```

Running our program, we see the output `Parsed TOML successfully` as expected.

There are several disadvantages to this approach, as you might see from this example. Not only are we writing a lot of code in C++ when we'd rather write it in Rust, but we're also contorting the semantics of C++ into a C API. This includes using heap allocations where normally we would not need any, discarding type information by passing through `void` pointers, and compressing error-handling information into `nullptr`.

Because of these downsides, this approach is only useful for quickly creating bindings for a very small number of functions. We'd generally want to replace it with a more robust approach as soon as possible.

Calling C++ directly from a Rust program

The cpp crate provides a way to use Rust macros and a build script to generate the C ABI bindings between Rust and C++ automatically. This has the interesting effect of combining the two languages in the same source file. Let's start by making a new crate:

```
$ cargo new bind_cpp_macros
$ cd bind_cpp_macros
$ cargo add cpp
```

```
$ cargo add cpp_build --build
$ curl -O https://raw.githubusercontent.com/marzer/tomlplusplus/v3.4.0/toml.hpp
```

This sets up the cpp crate and its build dependency, then downloads the toml.hpp header directly into our crate's root folder, as in our previous example.

Let's look at the required setup in build.rs first:

```
fn main() {
    cpp_build::Config::new()
        .flag_if_supported("-std=c++17")
        .flag_if_supported("/std:c++17")
        .define("TOML_EXCEPTIONS", Some("0"))
        .build("src/main.rs");
}
```

This looks similar to the configuration we used in the manual binding example. We pass our chosen C++ standard in two different formats to ensure that it works on GCC, Clang, and MSVC build environments. The cpp_build crate will scan our main.rs file for any cpp! macros and automatically generate whatever *glue code* is needed to sit between the Rust and C++ code we write.

The technique of mixing C++ and Rust in a single source file probably doesn't make much sense until we see an example, so let's look at our new main.rs file:

```
use cpp::cpp;
cpp! {{
    #include <iostream>
    #include "toml.hpp"
}}
fn main() {
    let path = c"Cargo.toml";
    let path_ptr = path.as_ptr();
    unsafe {
        cpp!([path_ptr as "const char *"] {
            toml::parse_result result =
                toml::parse_file(path_ptr);
            if (result) {
                std::cout << result << std::endl;
            } else {
                std::cout
```

```
                << "Error reading TOML file"
                << std::endl;
            }
        })
    };
}
```

The format used by the cpp! macro resembles a Rust closure in some ways, but we must explicitly specify the C++ types we're using. Despite the syntax, we've successfully embedded C++ into our Rust crate. The resulting C++ code looks very much like our previous example, although instead of maintaining a C API in both the Rust and C++ code, we have the bindings generated for us by our build script.

The cpp crate is not the only option we have for creating C++ bindings. The bindgen crate we used for binding C also supports a limited subset of C++. The popular cxx and autocxx crates also allow us to create glue code between Rust and C++. In addition to these existing crates, there are new approaches popping up frequently. If one specific crate does not meet the needs of your projects, it's likely that one of the others will.

Having explored strategies to bind C++, we'll now look at how to make the most out of our bindings.

Using bindings effectively

Calling foreign functions requires the use of the unsafe keyword because there is no way the Rust compiler can guarantee that they follow Rust's safety rules. This introduces potential risks such as memory corruption or undefined behavior, which could lead to crashes or other bugs. To manage this, we need a strategy to mitigate the risks and dangers that can be posed by unsafe code while still benefiting from FFI.

Unsafe Rust code allows operations that normally wouldn't be allowed in Rust code, including the ability to dereference raw pointers and access the fields of unions. While these operations can be essential for dealing with foreign code, we often want to hide them behind safe interfaces to ensure that anyone using our bindings is able to benefit from Rust's compile-time checking in their own code.

How do we create a safe interface to an unsafe library? The answer is more art than science, so different solutions will look good to different programmers. Mostly, we'll be replacing C or C++ patterns with safe Rust patterns. This means replacing pointers with references or slices, replacing null pointers with Option, and replacing error handling with Result. But even within this framework, there is a lot of potential variation.

If we take the `SDL_CreateWindow` call we observed earlier, we can look at several potential ways to create a safe wrapper for it. First, let's create a Rust type that our safe wrapper can use:

```
struct Window(*mut SDL_Window);
impl Drop for Window {
    fn drop(&mut self) {
        unsafe {
            SDL_DestroyWindow(self.0);
        }
    }
}
```

We've created a `Window` wrapper structure to hold the `SDL_Window` pointer returned by SDL2. This allows us to restrict access to the pointer. Unless we mark the pointer as `pub`, access to it will be restricted outside of our module, preventing it from being exposed directly to users of our code.

The wrapper structure also gives us the option of using an `impl Window` block to create a convenient interface for the various functions using a Window. We've also implemented the `Drop` trait for this structure, giving us a way to ensure that its resources are cleaned up when the last owner goes out of scope.

We'll implement the actual call to `SDL_CreateWindow` as a function inside our `impl Window` block as `new`. Per the SDL2 documentation, window creation can return `NULL`, upon which the programmer must call `SDL_GetError` to determine the source of the error. This behavior suggests that we should use `Result` as our return value, giving us the following function skeleton:

```
impl Window {
    fn new(title: &str, x: i32, y: i32, w: i32, h: i32, flags: u32) ->
Result<Window, String> {
        todo!();
    }
}
```

We know from our earlier example that `SDL_CreateWindow` takes the window title as a C-style string, but here in our safe interface, we're exposing it as a Rust `&str` type. This requires us to perform some internal conversions as part of our function, but presents a safe and familiar API to Rust users.

The implementation of our function ends up mostly being string conversions:

```
let title = CString::new(title).unwrap();
let window_ptr = unsafe {
    SDL_CreateWindow(title.as_ptr(), x, y, w, h, flags)
};
if window_ptr.is_null() {
    let err = unsafe {
        CStr::from_ptr(SDL_GetError()).to_bytes()
    };
    let err = unsafe {
        String::from_utf8_unchecked(err.to_vec())
    };
    return Err(err);
}
Ok(Window(window_ptr))
```

When going from a Rust string to a C string, we'll most likely have to use `std::ffi::CString`, while going from a C string to a Rust string, we can often use `std::ffi::CStr`. These roughly correspond to C-style versions of the Rust `String` and `&str` types, respectively, in that `CString` behaves as an owned type, and `CStr` behaves as a borrowed type. When moving from a Rust string type to a C-style string type, we must allocate a new buffer that contains a trailing zero byte. However, when moving from a C-style string to a Rust one, we need to merely locate the trailing zero byte and treat everything up to that as a slice.

Aside from the string conversions, the rest of this function should be straightforward. We're simply calling `SDL_CreateWindow` with the passed-in values, checking for `null`, and either returning an error containing the value of `SDL_GetError` as a Rust `String` type or returning an instance of our `Window` wrapper structure.

With our safe interface in hand, we can re-implement one of our earlier examples in safe, idiomatic Rust:

```
let w = Window::new("Hello World", 50, 50, 320, 200, 0);
if let Err(err) = w {
    eprintln!("Error creating window: {}", err);
} else {
    unsafe { SDL_Delay(2000) };
}
```

We still haven't wrapped the call to `SDL_Delay`, but if we were endeavoring to create safe, high-level bindings for the entire SDL2 library, we'd likely follow the same process with this and other functions.

Summary

In this chapter, we examined the basics of exposing both C and C++ code to our Rust programs and exposing Rust programs back to them. We've seen both how to create bindings for C and C++ manually and how to make use of some of the many approaches provided by the Rust community to produce more complete and reliable bindings.

In the next chapter, we'll dive into optimizing our Rust programs.

Part 3

Moving into Advanced Rust

In this third part of the book, we'll look at more advanced topics such as optimization and multithreading, and macro development. We'll explore where these topics overlap with C++ and where Rust presents something completely different. By the end of this part, you'll be confident in your ability to work in Rust, and we'll explore several possible next steps for your Rust journey.

This part of the book includes the following chapters:

- *Chapter 10, Optimization in Rust*
- *Chapter 11, Multithreading in Rust*
- *Chapter 12, Metaprogramming with Macros*
- *Chapter 13, Continuing with Rust*

10

Optimization in Rust

Rust's baseline performance tends to be similar to that of modern C++, but no matter how fast our programs run, there will always be ways to squeeze a little more speed out of them. In this chapter, we'll examine the topic of optimizing performance in Rust programs.

Our ability to optimize depends heavily on the tooling we're using to identify bottlenecks. While several high-quality commercial performance analysis tools exist, we'll be focusing primarily on tools that are free of cost and work across many different platforms.

In this chapter, we're going to cover the following main topics:

- Understanding the performance of safe Rust
- Measuring the performance of Rust programs
- Improving performance using unsafe Rust code
- Optimizing with SIMD instructions

Technical requirements

Examples in this chapter use Rust 1.82.0, but they will also work with any newer version.

If you need help installing Rust, please see the *Appendix*.

You can find the code files for this chapter in this book's GitHub repository: `https://github.com/PacktPublishing/Rust-for-CPP-Developers`.

Understanding the performance of safe Rust

Rust programs often perform well even without any special attention paid to their behavior. Many teams have found that they get performance improvements just from rewriting their code in Rust. However, others have found the Rust version of their code to be slightly slower than its C or C++ counterpart. How can we reason about this?

In this section, we'll examine both positive and negative consequences of using Rust when our programs need the best performance attainable. By understanding the major performance differences between Rust and C++, we should be able to develop an intuition for the expected performance of the code that we're writing.

Aliasing

C++ programs frequently fall victim to the performance hazard of *aliasing*. When two pointers point to the same location in memory, they are said to *alias* one another. If a pointer, `x`, can alias a pointer, `y`, then a write to `x` can potentially change the value of the memory pointed to by `y`. A compiler must account for this by loading `y` from memory after any write to `x`, or vice versa. While these loads and reloads are unnecessary if the pointers do not indeed point to the same location in memory, the compiler often cannot verify this at compile-time and must generate the most conservative code possible. This can result in poor performance when aliasing occurs in a tight loop or other performance-critical context.

Compiler writers and language designers alike recognize this problem and attempt to find ways to mitigate it. For instance, the C++ standard declares that two pointers of different types cannot alias. The compiler can assume, for instance, that an `int*` type and a `float*` type will never point to the same location in memory, meaning it can omit all unnecessary loads and reloads of memory when dealing with those two pointers. This optimization is called *type-based alias analysis* or *strict aliasing*, but again, it can only be employed when two pointers are of different types.

Type-based alias analysis is a brilliant optimization that makes a lot of sense in practice. After all, it's going to be very rare for valid code to treat `int*` and `float*` types as aliasing. In general, the memory could only hold one of the two types at a time, since they have different bit patterns and interpretations. Of course, if the programmer does go out of their way to violate this rule and alias two pointers of different types, the compiler will produce undefined behavior and, often, incorrect code generation.

In situations where the programmer is working with two pointers of the same type, we cannot rely on type-based alias analysis to save us from unnecessary reloads. For this case, many compilers provide a keyword that the programmer can use to promise the compiler that two pointers do not alias. This is often some variant of the keyword `restrict`, which was standardized for C in the C99 spec. The `restrict` keyword in all its compiler-specific variations can be necessary for optimal performance, but it implies a contract between the programmer and the compiler that is difficult to verify statically. If the `restrict` keyword is used but the program's behavior changes or a programmer misuses the function, the compiler will happily produce undefined behavior and, again, incorrect code without any warning.

The Rust compiler, on the other hand, will not compile programs that fall foul of the aliasing problem, so long as they are using the safe subset of Rust. Recall that any object borrowed mutably must have only one reference at a time. The static guarantees of safe Rust prohibit us from creating situations where two separate mutable references could point to the same location in memory. The Rust compiler communicates that we have no aliasing to its compiler backend, LLVM, which then generates machine code that contains no redundant loads from memory.

Because Rust's safety rules are precisely tuned to avoid aliasing, we get this optimization for "free" from Rust, while many C++ programs still suffer from excess reloads from memory that should be unnecessary. Between strict aliasing optimizations and `restrict`, carefully written C++ programs can often match the code generation of the Rust compiler. But in Rust, these guarantees are part of the language semantics, while in C++, they require extreme care to achieve and maintain.

Initialization and bounds checking

One aspect of safe Rust that is relevant to code performance is that the compiler will disallow reading of uninitialized memory. For arrays, for instance, this can imply that the entire range of memory is initialized even if it is ultimately unused. When an array is used as a byte buffer, it can be the case that the array's contents will be completely overwritten with new data immediately after being initialized. In this case, any time spent initializing the buffer is effectively wasted.

We also saw in previous chapters that a large part of Rust's safety contract involves runtime enforcement of memory bounds. This is especially relevant for slices, arrays, and vectors. Each indexing operation must not only read memory and return the value at that part of the buffer, but it must also check to be sure that the index being used is not past the end of the buffer. In a tight loop, these checks can take a noticeable amount of time. While understanding that safety is beneficial, if we could get rid of some or all of these boundary checks, we might find our tight loops running a lot faster.

Initialization and bounds checking overhead isn't just theory. It occasionally shows up in real situations. A team porting the Brotli compression algorithm from C to Rust in 2016 noted that the Rust version performed more slowly than the original C version. After they removed expensive initialization and bounds checking, their performance improved by over 10%. While the overhead of initialization and bounds checking normally results in a great trade-off, in tight loops, it can have a large effect on program performance.

Both initialization and bounds checking are important safety devices, and they keep our programs predictable and free from several classes of errors. But the trade-offs chosen by safe Rust and older C and C++ styles, for example, lead to very different performance considerations. C++ is much closer to both the behavior and performance of Rust when using modern containers such as `std::array` and `std::vector` than when using C-style idioms.

Moving and cloning

The performance cost of heap allocations at the wrong time and place can quickly add up. While this is a possible pitfall in almost every programming language, Rust is affected by it in a unique way. The limitations of safe Rust can often lead newer programmers into inefficient cloning just to ensure that their programs pass the compiler's strict borrow checking conventions. When this happens, it can severely degrade a program's performance.

But a potential increase in heap allocation from inefficient cloning isn't the whole story. As we saw when learning about the borrow checker, a deep copy or clone that might result in heap allocation is explicitly accomplished by calling `.clone()`. All other copies are shallow and have `move` semantics, which never result in a heap allocation. Pervasive use of `move` semantics can be a significant optimization, especially for types using growable, heap-allocated buffers such as `String` and `Vec`.

C++ also has `move` semantics as an optimization since C++11. We should expect that C++11 code using `move` correctly and pervasively would perform very similarly to a Rust program. But there are a couple of complicating factors in C++. First, `move` constructors can be provided by the programmer and thus could be inefficiently implemented. And second, explicitly calling the `std::move` function is required to opt into `move` semantics in some contexts. Forgetting to use it often results in a slower path.

The choices around `move` semantics made by the two languages are interesting because they followed different paths but ended up in a similar place. Rust made these choices not just because of performance concerns but to implement its safety model. C++, on the other hand, has added `move` semantics into the language after several years, specifically to improve performance. In both languages, we should attempt to avoid copies and heap allocations in performance-sensitive code, but when we cannot, we should ensure that we're using `move` appropriately.

These differences between Rust and C++ are important to understand because they give us an intuition for the performance of our code. But when working to improve that performance, we can never rely on intuition alone. We must always begin with performance measurement.

Measuring the performance of Rust programs

Before we can understand how to improve the performance of our programs, we must understand exactly which part of the program is slow. The process of figuring out which parts of a program are running slowly is called *profiling*. In this section, we'll look at several common approaches to profiling and see how the Rust ecosystem supports them.

Every profiling method adds some cost to the runtime of your program. There's a general trade-off we make when profiling: the usefulness of the information we are gathering becomes greater as the overhead of profiling and, consequently, the runtime of our program grows worse. In this section, we'll examine various methods of profiling in order from least intrusive to most intrusive. But first, we need something to measure.

Producing a test case

We'll use the same test case for each method of performance measurement. An interesting and realistic test case with which to start our optimization journey is matrix multiplication. This is a common operation across many different applications, isn't bound by disk or network bandwidth, and has enough depth to give us an interesting optimization challenge.

We'll start by making a library crate to hold our example:

```
$ cargo new --lib performance_test
```

In the `src/lib.rs` file, we'll add the following function that will be the primary focus of our performance measurement and improvement efforts:

```
type Matrix = Vec<Vec<f32>>;
 pub fn matrix_multiply_original(a: Matrix, b: Matrix) -> Matrix {
    let a_rows = a.len();
    let a_cols = a[0].len();
    let b_cols = b[0].len();
    let mut out = vec![vec![0.0; b_cols]; a_rows];

    for i in 0..a_rows {
        for j in 0..b_cols {
            for k in 0..a_cols {
                out[i][j] += a[i][k] * b[k][j];
            }
```

```
        }
    }
    out
}
```

While we won't discuss the mathematics of the operation we're implementing here, the code itself is rather straightforward. We declare a type alias for `Matrix` for brevity, but underlying each matrix is just a vector of vectors. We are making a handful of assumptions about the validity of the matrices passed in that we would need to enforce if this were a real program. First, the number of columns in matrix `a` must be equal to the number of rows in matrix `b`. Second, every column vector must be the same size as the first column vector in each matrix. And finally, no matrix can have a dimension of `0`. Aside from that, performing `multiply` is simply a matter of initializing a new output matrix and filling in the values correctly.

Since we'll be improving this example as we go, this specific one is named `matrix_multiply_original`. We'll keep each revision around as a new function to aid comparison between them later. We'll expose the function we're interested in measuring at the time as `matrix_multiply` using an alias in `src/lib.rs`:

```
pub use matrix_multiply_original as matrix_multiply;
```

This will allow us to keep track of our progress by giving a way easily switch between different implementations of the algorithm.

To create a meaningful test case for our matrix multiplication, we need to add a means to configure the size of the matrices being multiplied, fill the matrices with random values, and finally, perform the actual multiplication. Let's start by writing a utility function that creates a matrix filled with random values. We'll need to install the `rand` crate for this to work:

```
$ cargo add rand
```

Then, we can add this function to `lib.rs`:

```
fn make_random(rows: usize, columns: usize) -> Matrix {
    let rng_iter = &mut rand::rng().random_iter();
    (0..rows).map(|_| Vec::from_iter(rng_iter.take(columns))).collect()
}
```

This function uses the `rand` crate to create an iterator we can repeatedly call to get random numbers. We then individually create a set of vectors of a length of `column` using the range iterator, `(0..rows)`, and finally, collect all of our `column` vectors into a single vector of rows.

Now, we'll begin working on a command-line interface to configure our test program. To add a command-line interface to our library crate, we'll create a file named `src/bin/cli.rs` in our crate. Since this will be the only binary associated with our crate, it will run automatically when we use `cargo run`. Let's create the directory and the source file:

```
$ mkdir src/bin
$ echo "" > src/bin/cli.rs
```

Inside `cli.rs`, we'll first import the functions we'll need from our crate:

```
use performance_test::{make_random, matrix_multiply};
```

Following this, we will make a small utility function to deal with command-line arguments. Our program will accept three command-line arguments representing, respectively, the number of rows, `m`, in matrix `a`, the shared number of columns in matrix `a` and rows in matrix `b` as `k`, and the number of columns in matrix `b` as `n`:

```
fn get_args() -> Vec<usize> {
    let mut ret = Vec::new();
    for arg in std::env::args().skip(1).take(3) {
        if let Ok(val) = arg.parse::<usize>() {
            ret.push(val);
        }
    }
    ret
}
```

This function uses several tricks to turn our command-line arguments into a `Vec` containing three elements. The `std::env::args()` function returns an iterator of the command-line arguments. We skip the first argument, which, like `argv[0]` in C++, contains the program name. We then call the `parse` function to convert all three of our command-line arguments from text to `usize`. This operation can, of course, fail if we were to pass anything that's not a valid textual representation of a number, so we ensure that we only push to the output vector if the operation succeeded. Importantly, the `Vec` we return can only ever hold three elements if all three of our arguments both existed and were properly convertible to `usize`.

Having finished our small collection of utility functions, our `main` function in `src/bin/cli.rs` can now look like this:

```
fn main() {
    let args = get_args();
    if args.len() != 3 {
        eprintln!("Usage: m k n");
        return;
    }
    let (m, k, n) = (args[0], args[1], args[2]);
    let a = make_random(m, k);
    let b = make_random(k, n);
    let _c = matrix_multiply(a, b);
}
```

We first get the arguments as `Vec<usize>` from our helper function, `get_args`. The only valid value is three arguments, so if we don't have this exact number, then it means that someone omitted or passed something invalid for one of them. We print a brief usage message and exit in this case. Following that, we construct our `a` and `b` matrices and perform the multiplication. Since this is just a test program for analyzing performance, we have no actual use for the returned C matrix and prefix it with _ to inform the compiler that it may be unused.

We'll be working with and improving the `matrix_multiply` function throughout the chapter, but at the moment, we have a working test program to which we can pass different parameters and see their effects on performance. Things should proceed more or less as we expect, with larger values taking noticeably more time than smaller ones.

Despite having written and typed it out, we don't actually know that much about this program's performance yet. For instance, what's the overhead of the argument parsing and initialization of the multiplicands versus the cost of the multiplication itself? We can make guesses to answer this, but when it comes to serious performance work, there is no substitute for direct measurement.

Annotating blocks of code

The simplest and often least intrusive means of profiling is to manually annotate sections of the program. This generally involves finding an appropriate library and placing a structure instance within a scope that we wish to be measured. The structure will log the current execution time on both construction and destruction, and log the difference between the two. This difference represents the amount of time taken by the code executed between the two timestamps.

A very simple example is to use the `elapsed` crate to annotate our test program. We first must add it to our project:

```
$ cargo add elapsed
```

This crate provides a `measure_time` function. It takes the code to measure in a closure and returns a tuple containing the elapsed time and the closure's return value. This provides an easy way to get a high-level understanding of the different parts of your program. First, we'll import the `measure_time` function at the top of `src/bin/cli.rs`:

```
use elapsed::measure_time;
```

Then, we can use it to time our matrix multiplication:

```
let (elapsed, _c) = measure_time(|| matrix_multiply(a, b));
    println!("Multiply took {}", elapsed);
```

The time returned by the function, which we've called `elapsed` in this example, is a small wrapper around the `std::time::Duration` type that implements the `std::fmt::Display` trait. This allows us to print the time taken in a very user-friendly way. Try a few different arguments on our test program to see the difference:

```
$ cargo run --release -- 4 4 4
     Finished `release` profile [optimized] target(s) in 0.03s
      Running `target/release/cli 4 4 4`
 Multiply took 917.00 ns

 $ cargo run --release -- 400 400 400
     Finished `release` profile [optimized] target(s) in 0.00s
      Running `target/release/cli 400 400 400`
 Multiply took 199.89 ms
```

We can see that the runtime increases as the work increases, which is obvious, but also that the `elapsed` crate has given us a very friendly and precise way to describe exactly how much time our multiplication is taking.

The `elapsed` crate is great for getting a quick understanding of the performance of small programs, but for more complicated cases, the amount of data needed to identify bottlenecks can be onerous to gather and analyze using this method. For this reason, a preferred method among many programmers is to generate a *flame graph*.

A flame graph is a visual representation of the runtime of a program. This type of graph displays several nested *spans*, which track annotated sections of code, or *samples* that track discrete points in program execution. The term *flame graph* comes from the way this information is displayed, with spans often creating a series of peaks resembling flames rising out of a fire. If your program is annotated well, a flame graph can be a quick and useful way to understand its performance.

Flame graphs are a very popular representation of program performance, so there are several tools available for creating and viewing them. Viewers are built into browsers such as Chrome, but there are also web-based viewers, such as **Firefox Profiler** or **SpeedScope**, available. Before we can dive any deeper into flame graphs, however, we should create one using our matrix multiplication example.

One way to create a flame graph from spans in the Rust ecosystem is to use the popular `tracing` crate along with its companion crate, `tracing-flame`. These crates produce output that must be processed by the `inferno` tool to produce a loadable flame graph. For a large application, this might be a good way to go, but to keep our example simple, we'll use the `flame` crate instead. This crate exposes a straightforward API and can directly produce flame graphs without other tooling.

To make our example a little more interesting, we can change the `main` function to generate 50 multiples at our target size. We'll annotate both the initialization phase, where we fill the matrices with random values, and the multiplication. This will give us a great idea of the relative costs of each. First, though, we'll add the `flame` crate:

```
$ cargo add flame
```

After this, we can add the loop and our annotations:

```
for _ in 0..50 {
        flame::start("initialization");
        let a = make_random(m, k);
        let b = make_random(k, n);
        flame::end("initialization");

        flame::start("multiply");
        let _c = matrix_multiply(a, b);
        flame::end("multiply");
    }
```

```
let f = std::fs::File::create("perf.html").unwrap();
flame::dump_html(f).unwrap();
```

The `flame` crate's `start` and `end` functions delineate our spans, and the `dump_html` function renders the performance information into an HTML file that can be loaded in any browser. This type of flame graph does not need any special viewer, but it can still provide us with enough information about the runtime of our program to be interesting.

If you've been following along, try generating the flame graph now. Play around with different matrix sizes to see how the relative cost of initialization and multiplication changes. Perhaps try putting a span inside `matrix_multiply_original` to see whether it gives different results than the one we've placed outside the function.

Manually annotated spans can be extremely useful when placed judiciously. Their runtime overhead is often low enough that they can stay in the code indefinitely, providing the ability to catch unexpected slowdowns that would otherwise go unidentified. But they have limitations, the most obvious of which is that they can only measure the things that are annotated.

To get a better understanding of our program's performance, we need an even better tool. We need to move beyond manual annotation to something that can tell us even more information about how our code is executing, ideally without us having to change our program at all.

Sampling profilers

A sampling profiler works by taking snapshots or samples of your program's call stack at fixed intervals. Sampling profilers often take samples hundreds or thousands of times a second. When placed together in a viewer, probable hot spots in the program show up as the places that collect the most samples. As the sampling rate increases, both the accuracy of the data collected and the runtime overhead of the sampling process increase. The sample rate is often defaulted to something that tries to manage the balance between those two factors, giving us enough info to make decisions while not affecting the runtime in an adverse way.

Sampling profilers often provide instrumentation libraries that programs can use to add high-level annotations to the profiles as well as the call stacks, so we can mix the two together in the same visualization. This gives us a great mix of high- and low-level information, making sampling profilers one of the most powerful tools in the performance investigation toolbox.

There are a variety of commercial options for sampling profilers. Many are tuned to one platform or the other, since the process of sampling often involves interaction with the OS or system-level libraries. In this chapter, we'll demonstrate a cross-platform, open source tool called `samply` that exists in the Rust crate ecosystem.

We can install `samply` using `cargo`:

```
$ cargo install --locked samply
```

Before going further, we need to add one bit of configuration to the `Cargo.toml` file of our `performance_test` crate:

```
[profile.release]
debug = true
```

We must set `debug = true` for our release build configuration. It may sound like an odd setting, but doing this does not alter the runtime performance of the release build. Instead, it instructs the compiler to include full debugging information, which is required for `samply` to be able to resolve call stacks to lines of source code.

After adding this info, we'll rebuild our performance test, being sure to build it in `release` mode to enable compiler optimizations:

```
$ cargo build --release
```

Now, we're finally ready to begin profiling. Using `samply` is straightforward. From our `performance_test` crate, we can run the `cli` binary using the `samply record` command. Let's pass it some large matrix sizes in order to get a useful profile:

```
$ samply record target/release/cli 500 500 500
```

The syntax of this command is simple. `samply record` first takes the path of the program we want to run, followed by any arguments we want to pass to it. If you're using Windows, you'll need to run `target/release/cli.exe`. If everything works as expected, `samply` will open the profile in your default browser automatically when the program has finished running.

> **Note**
>
> At the time of writing, the web tooling used by `samply` cannot load profiles in the Safari browser. If Safari is your default browser, you can set the `BROWSER` environment variable to a different browser's executable when running `samply` to allow it to load the profile correctly.

After `samply` opens the profile in a browser, it keeps a local web server running in the background. This server is used to send source code and symbol resolution information to the web tooling used to view the profile. If you cancel the web server and need to reload the profile, you can use `samply load profile.json.gz` to start a new server and reopen the web tooling.

The specific information the sampling profile tells us will potentially be different depending on the machine on which it's run and the arguments passed to the program. It's very important at this point to take some time to examine the profile produced by `samply` yourself, especially if you're new to performance investigation or the tooling involved.

On my machine, the process takes around 17 seconds to execute 50 multiplications of two random 500x500 matrices, and the sampling profile shows that about 40% of the time is spent in or around an `index` function. Additionally, about 16% of the time is spent in a similar `index_mut` function. We can guess that these are the functions called when we index into a vector for reading or writing, respectively, which is a very common operation in our matrix multiplication code.

At this point, we should start following the scientific method to improve our code. We'll make a theory and test it. One theory could be that the overhead of Rust's bounds checking could be causing significant slowdowns in the indexing operations. Another could be that it's just down to the cost of memory access or cache usage patterns.

These are great theories, but we need a way to test them. We could use our sampling profiler to observe how the time taken moves around as we make changes. Often this is a great strategy, but there can be times when the performance bound we're investigating is part of a very long process or hard to capture. In those cases, we can look into another useful performance analysis tool to test our theories: benchmarking.

Benchmarking

Benchmarking is the practice of taking small parts of a program and measuring their performance in isolation. The unit of code being benchmarked is often just a single function. Rather than acting as a tool to discover where the program is spending its time, benchmarking is designed to allow us to compare two implementations of the same code and answer the surprisingly difficult questions of which implementation is faster and by how much. This gives us a tool that allows us to verify that our optimizations are effective and to test theories about the performance of a given piece of code.

Benchmarking can have surprising complexity. The largest issue a benchmarking suite must deal with is variance. The messy realities of operating systems and hardware can make the same code take different amounts of time depending on what else is going on at the time it runs.

Benchmarking suites usually deal with this problem by running the code in two phases. The first is the *warm-up* phase. This runs the code a few times, often without measuring its performance. The goal of the warm-up phase is to ensure that any caches that might affect the code, either in the code itself or at the operating system level, are fully populated and stable before we start running our performance tests.

The second phase runs the code several times and measures each run. It then uses statistical metrics such as mean and standard deviation to provide a probabilistic analysis of the code's runtime performance. This strategy not only gives us high confidence in the results of the analysis, but it also means that we can measure improvements over much smaller pieces of code than would be practical otherwise. A good benchmarking suite will try to interpret this analysis for you into a single number: how much faster or slower the code is than the last time it was run.

Cargo has built-in support for benchmarking through its `cargo bench` command, but it requires us to supply a *harness* that will actually run the benchmarks. There is a built-in harness in the works, but at the time of writing, it's not part of the stable Rust distribution. So, in order to run our benchmarks, we must use a crate from the wider Rust ecosystem while the official benchmarking features are being stabilized. The most frequently used crate for this purpose is `criterion`. To get started, we must first add `criterion` as a `dev` dependency to our project:

```
$ cargo add --dev criterion
```

Next, we must add a Rust source file to the `benches/` folder underneath our crate's root folder:

```
$ mkdir benches
```

The `benches/` folder is understood by `cargo bench` as the correct place to look for benchmarks that the user might want to execute.

Now, let's create the benchmark itself in the `benches/multiply.rs` file:

```
use criterion::{Criterion, criterion_group, criterion_main};
use performance_test::{make_random, matrix_multiply};
use std::hint::black_box;

fn criterion_benchmark(c: &mut Criterion) {
    let x = make_random(100, 100);
    let y = make_random(100, 100);
    c.bench_function("multiply 100x100", |b| {
```

```
        b.iter(|| matrix_multiply(
            black_box(x.clone()),
            black_box(y.clone())
        ))
    });
}

criterion_group!(benches, criterion_benchmark);
criterion_main!(benches);
```

At a high level, our `criterion_benchmark` function is creating some input and passing it a closure that executes our aliased `matrix_multiply` function several times. Because our closure will be called multiple times, we need to clone the inputs each time since our function takes ownership of its arguments. We could avoid this by changing the parameters to be references if we thought that this cloning was slowing down our benchmark.

The `black_box` hint function is used to inhibit compiler optimizations that might otherwise impact the runtime of the benchmark. A benchmark intentionally does not look much like any usage of our function in a real program, and we want to ensure that the compiler doesn't remove any computation that might be important to timing our code. For instance, an aggressive compiler might optimize the code in such a way as to cache the computation, causing our function to only run once while the harness expects it to run many times.

The `criterion_group!` and `criterion_main!` macros complete the boilerplate necessary to run our benchmark. But first, we must add a section to `Cargo.toml`:

```
[[bench]]
name = "multiply"
harness = false
```

This tells Cargo about our benchmark in the `multiply.rs` file and turns off the built-in benchmarking harness. We disable this because we are using Criterion's harness, and we don't want the two to conflict in any way.

Now, we can finally run `cargo bench` to execute our benchmark. On my system, the report shows that our 100x100 matrix multiply runs in about 2.2 **milliseconds (ms)** per iteration:

```
multiply 100x100        time:   [2.2395 ms 2.2412 ms 2.2429 ms]
```

In each run of `cargo bench` from here on out, `criterion` will compare the benchmark to previous results and tell us whether the benchmark got faster, slower, or stayed the same. Now is a great time to use the information we got from `samply` to attempt to improve our function's performance.

We recall that the major issue exposed by our sampling profile was that the function is spending a lot of its time inside the standard library functions that perform indexing into `Vec`. We weren't sure whether this was just the cost of accessing memory or whether it was the cost of overhead related to bounds checking. But if we take a closer look at our function, maybe we can make an improvement in both.

This inner loop of our `matrix_multiply` function could possibly be inefficient, because it's repeatedly executing a load from memory, modifying it, and storing it back to the same location:

```
for k in 0..a_cols {
    out[i][j] += a[i][k] * b[k][j];
}
```

But we don't modify `i` or `j` at all in this loop, meaning that we're storing to the same location for each iteration of the loop. We could change this to modify a single `f32` instead and only write it to memory at the end of the program. Let's copy our `matrix_multiply_original` function into a new function named `matrix_multiply_indexing_opt` to give it a try:

```
let mut sum = 0.0;
for k in 0..a_cols {
    sum += a[i][k] * b[k][j];
}
out[i][j] = sum;
```

The code now looks much better, and we can guess that it will be an improvement based on the information we have. Now, the calculation should occur in a register, and we only need to check the bounds of the `out` vector once. But we must measure to be sure that we've improved performance. First, let's update our `matrix_multiply` alias to point to our new function:

```
pub use matrix_multiply_indexing_opt as matrix_multiply;
```

Now, we can run `cargo bench` to see the improvement versus `matrix_multiply_original`:

```
multiply 100x100        time:   [540.10 µs 540.25 µs 540.39 µs]
                        change: [-75.920% -75.897% -75.874%] (p = 0.00 < 0.05)
                        Performance has improved.
```

Wow! A 75% improvement just from this simple change. Of course, this result is just on my specific machine and will be different from other hardware, but this seems like an excellent change. At this point, we might want to take another look at a sampling profiler to see whether there's any more obvious low-hanging fruit, but this is a great win for now. We'll continue investigating other potential improvements in the next section, but let's take a moment to reflect on what we've learned here.

The most important part of performance work is measurement. The complexities of hardware, operating systems, compilers, and our own code all contribute to creating a situation where guessing about what slows down a program or algorithm is rarely fruitful.

We've seen that performance measurement techniques exist on a spectrum where runtime overhead and information gained increase relative to one another, leading us to employ several different techniques to get the best info for any given situation. High-level annotation, sampling profilers, and benchmarking all exist at different points in this spectrum and shine at different times. Whatever methods we have available to us, profiling our code is a requirement to help us make decisions about how to improve it.

In our next section, we'll take a look at the forbidden art of unsafe Rust code and how we can use it to continue improving our matrix multiply example.

Improving performance using unsafe Rust code

While we should prefer safe Rust code whenever possible, some optimizations may only present themselves in an unsafe context. Unsafe Rust code is exactly what it sounds like... unsafe. There are many challenges to working with unsafe Rust, and it requires a much greater understanding of the language to use it correctly. We'll only be examining some small parts of the unsafe Rust universe in this section. For a much larger treatment of the subject, the best source of reference is *The Rustnomicon*, available at `https://doc.rust-lang.org/nomicon/`.

Dropping into unsafe code to improve performance is not always necessary, but there are a handful of times when it can help push us over the line for a really critical section of code. Armed with our benchmarking setup and matrix multiplication example from the previous section, let's dive into the world of unsafe Rust and examine two specific ways it can help us optimize our code.

Removing bounds checks

Earlier, we speculated that bounds checking overhead was wasting a lot of our program's time. Now, it's time to check. Even though the compiler may be able to remove bounds checks in safe code under some conditions, Rust allows you to remove them unconditionally as an unsafe operation.

While we normally index using the indexing operator, `[]`, we can also call the `get()` function, which returns `Option<T>`. The `get()` function is part of the `slice` type, meaning it is implemented on other types such as `Vec` and arrays that can incorporate `Deref` into a slice. This function allows us to react to the results of the bounds check by handling the `Some(T)` and `None` cases of `Option`. When we're using the indexing operator, `[]`, an out-of-bounds index will simply panic, so `get()` is a good choice for programs that want to eliminate as many potential panics as possible.

Along with `get()`, the `slice` type also provides `get_unchecked()`. This unsafe function returns the results of the indexing operation, whether the index was in bounds or not. We can elide our bounds check using this function, but we must, of course, be very careful that our index is actually within the proper bounds of the matrix to avoid undefined behavior. In our matrix multiplication example, we know that this is true because we specifically constrained the loop indices based on the sizes of our matrices.

Let's begin with `matrix_multiply_indexing_opt` and copy it into a new function, `matrix_multiply_unsafe_indexing`. We'll then change the inner loop to use `get_unchecked`:

```
let mut sum = 0.0;
for p in 0..a_cols {
    sum += unsafe {
        a.get_unchecked(i).get_unchecked(p) *
        b.get_unchecked(p).get_unchecked(j)
    };
}
unsafe { *out.get_unchecked_mut(i).get_unchecked_mut(j) = sum };
```

All `unsafe` Rust code needs to be inside an `unsafe` block or function. We usually want to keep our `unsafe` blocks small rather than enclosing an entire function. Remember, `unsafe` is an auditing tool in Rust. We only have to look at the code in the `unsafe` blocks when determining whether a program upholds Rust's safety guarantees.

In this example, we've also used the mutable version of `get_unchecked` for writing out the final result. We should expect a performance gain from these changes, but it's unclear how much improvement we should expect. Again, we must update our `matrix_multiply` alias:

```
pub use matrix_multiply_unsafe_indexing as matrix_multiply;
```

Now, let's try running `cargo bench` to see what `criterion` says about our new code:

```
multiply 100x100        time:   [358.54 µs 358.75 µs 359.05 µs]
                        change: [-33.740% -33.696% -33.643%] (p = 0.00 < 0.05)
                        Performance has improved.
```

Another great improvement! In this case, `unsafe` bought us a significant win, and we have high confidence that the code won't overrun our buffers due to the structure of our code.

Avoiding expensive initialization

Frequent initialization of buffers can be a hidden performance hazard. When we detect this with a profiler, we should look for ways to minimize it. Some of those ways may end up using unsafe Rust.

An important thing to understand is that Rust only initializes the memory that we use. For instance, let's look at `Vec::with_capacity()`. This function is similar conceptually to the `reserve()` function of `std::vector` in C++. When a `Vec` is created with `with_capacity()`, the standard library will allocate as much space as needed to hold the number of elements that we specify, but will leave this memory uninitialized. This makes sense and is still safe because the memory is inaccessible due to bounds checking on the `Vec` indexing operator inherited from `std::slice`. The memory is only initialized when we call `push()` on the vector to add an element.

We can make use of this information to reduce the initialization cost of arrays, for example, by converting them to `Vec` and using `with_capacity()`. This works very well whenever the buffer is filled linearly, because it's a solution that still makes use of entirely safe Rust. It turns out that our `matrix_multiply` example follows this pattern, so we can reduce initialization costs using safe Rust only.

Let's copy `matrix_multiply_unsafe_indexing` into a new function, `matrix_multiply_init_opt`, and update our type alias. Then, we can make the following changes:

```
let mut out = Vec::with_capacity(a_rows);

 for i in 0..a_rows {
        let mut row = Vec::with_capacity(b_cols);
        for j in 0..b_cols {
               let mut sum = 0.0;
               for p in 0..a_cols {
                      sum += unsafe {
```

```
                    a.get_unchecked(i).get_unchecked(p) *
b.get_unchecked(p).get_unchecked(j)
                };
            }
            row.push(sum);
        }
        out.push(row);
    }
```

Benchmarking this change, however, results in a slight performance decrease on my machine. This is disappointing, but still valuable to understand. The cost of our initialization is a minimal part of the function's runtime, because it happens once, whereas the inner loop runs several times. The slowdown itself is likely because we moved an allocation into an inner loop. I encourage you to attempt to fix this by initializing the rows upfront. For the purposes of this chapter, we'll switch back to `matrix_multiply_unsafe_indexing` as our fastest example thus far.

It's nice when we are able to fill a buffer linearly, but this is not always practical. When we need to fill the buffer in a non-linear order, we may need to start using `unsafe` blocks. The easiest way to do this again involves `Vec::with_capacity()`, followed by the unsafe `Vec::set_len()` call. The `set_len()` call simply resets the size of the `Vec` without pushing any elements into it. When we set the length to the amount reserved with `with_capacity()`, we are given an entirely uninitialized buffer and are free to write into any element. This is a very useful trick when calling into C APIs that we know fill the entire buffer, but we must be very careful not to read any of the uninitialized elements in the vector before they have been written.

Moving into more complicated uses of uninitialized memory, Rust provides the `std::mem::MaybeUninit` type. At its simplest, `MaybeUninit` is a wrapper type around whatever we want to remain uninitialized. Let's look at an example of using it on a simple copyable type:

```
let mut my_usize_wrapper = MaybeUninit::<usize>::uninit();
```

This creates a wrapper around an uninitialized `usize` value. The programmer is expected to write a value into the wrapper at some point using the `MaybeUninit::write()` function:

```
my_usize_wrapper.write(0);
```

At this point, the value held by `MaybeUninit` is initialized, but the compiler doesn't have any way to verify this. It's trusting us to make the right choices because we're in `unsafe` land.

To get our value back out of the wrapper type, we call `MaybeUninit::assume_init()`:

```
let my_usize = unsafe { my_usize_wrapper.assume_init() };
```

This little dance with the wrapper type allows us to tell the compiler not to worry about initialization and just trust that we've done it correctly. `MaybeUninit` is a complicated type, and a full explanation of it isn't appropriate here. Please check the Rust documentation if you have a need to use it.

As always, unsafe code is very tricky to use and should be avoided if possible. Always try to optimize using safe alternatives first. In this section, we've shown a handful of ways that code can be optimized using unsafe Rust. Our `matrix_multiply` example is performing well, but there's definitely more we can squeeze out of it. And to get better performance, we need to look into using SIMD instructions.

Optimizing with SIMD instructions

One of the most efficient ways to write math-heavy CPU code is to use the SIMD instruction sets available on many processors. **SIMD** stands for **single instruction, multiple data**, and refers to the set of instructions that operate on several values at a time. For instance, if we need to perform some math on a linear array of floating-point numbers, we can use SIMD instructions to do this in blocks of values, potentially up to 512 bits per instruction on modern processors.

In this section, we'll examine how we can make use of SIMD optimizations in Rust through its high-level, cross-platform `std::simd` module, which is currently only available on nightly Rust. To do this, we must first set up the nightly Rust toolchain, then write and benchmark a SIMD implementation of our matrix multiply.

Setting up nightly Rust

Rust exposes intrinsics that map to architecture-specific SIMD instructions in the `std::arch` module. Using these intrinsics effectively requires a significant investment in understanding the low-level instruction sets for each platform you intend to support. And if you are not blessed with a user base that only uses one type of computer, it means writing completely separate implementations for each supported architecture. The challenge of maintaining multiple implementations, as well as the compile time and runtime overhead to select between them, can be overwhelming.

In the wider ecosystem, there are tools to help with this. A notable one is Intel's *ISPC* compiler, which exposes a C-like language for writing kernels of performance-intensive code. This is then compiled down to very efficient architecture-specific SIMD implementations that can be linked into a larger program, significantly reducing the need to maintain multiple architecture-specific solutions.

Rust has a similar high-level SIMD library called `std::simd` built in, but unfortunately, it's not yet stabilized. This means that it's only available in the nightly version of the Rust compiler, but it is planned to move into the stable Rust release at some point in the future. We'll be using the nightly compiler to add some SIMD improvements to our matrix multiplication example.

> **Note**
>
> The Rust crate ecosystem also supplies the `packed_simd` crate, which presents a very similar API to `std::simd`. However, `packed_simd` also requires the nightly compiler, so we'll stick with the standard version for our examples.

First, we must use `rustup` to ensure that we have the latest version of the Rust `nightly` compiler installed. For help with `rustup` or installing Rust in general, please refer to the *Appendix*:

```
$ rustup toolchain install nightly
```

When we have multiple toolchains installed, we can select between them by passing a special flag to Cargo, `rustc`, or any other supported Rust tool:

```
$ cargo +nightly build
$ cargo +stable build
```

Just running `cargo build` will invoke the default toolchain. Throughout the remainder of this section, we'll assume that `stable` is your default toolchain. You can verify this with `rustup toolchain list` or by looking at the version string of either Cargo or `rustc`.

If you need to set the default toolchain back to `stable`, you can run this command:

```
$ rustup default stable
```

We'd ideally like our test project to work under both the `stable` and the `nightly` compiler. After all, we only need `nightly` for a single function. The way that many people faced with this problem in the Rust community handle this problem is by using *features*.

Features are Boolean flags specified in `Cargo.toml`. Each feature can pull in its own set of dependencies, if needed, and we can check whether features are enabled at compile time inside our crate. To support both the `nightly` and `stable` toolchains in our test project, we'll make a `nightly` feature in `Cargo.toml` and use it to gate our `nightly`-only code:

```
[features]
nightly = []
```

This feature definition ends up being very simple, only an empty array. This array can be used to specify that other features must be enabled if this one is enabled. Our crate only has one feature, so this is all we need for now.

Next, we must begin using the feature in our test crate. We can condition code to only be used by a specific feature at compile time with the `#[cfg]` attribute in our code. The most common usage of this is to condition tests to only compile when running `cargo test`:

```
#[cfg(test)]
mod tests {
    #[test]
    fn test_nothing() {}
}
```

In this example, the entire `tests` module will be skipped by the compiler when we're not building tests. However, we need a way to conditionally compile code based on whether a feature is enabled or not. Let's assume our `nightly` code will go into a `src/simd.rs` module. We can then include this module only when our `nightly` feature is enabled by putting these lines into our `src/lib.rs` file:

```
#[cfg(feature = "nightly")]
mod simd;
```

Configuration attributes can also be inverted with the `not` modifier. We can use this to define our function to be benchmarked as `simd::matrix_multiply_simd` when our `nightly` feature is enabled, but define it to be `matrix_multiply_unsafe_indexing` (our current fastest iteration) when `nightly` is not enabled:

```
#[cfg(feature = "nightly")]
pub use simd::matrix_multiply_simd as matrix_multiply;

#[cfg(not(feature = "nightly"))]
pub use matrix_multiply_unsafe_indexing as matrix_multiply;
```

There's one final step we must take before writing any code that uses `std::simd`. When dealing with `unstable` features in the `nightly` compiler, the crate must explicitly declare which `unstable` features will be used at the top of the crate's root file. In our case, `std::simd` is gated by the `portable_simd` feature flag, so we'll need to insert this declaration as the first line of `src/lib.rs` to enable it:

```
#![feature(portable_simd)]
```

But wait! We wanted our crate to compile under both the `stable` and `nightly` compilers. Certainly, the `stable` compiler won't let us get away with declaring our intent to use an `unstable` feature. For these types of situations, Rust provides the `#[cfg_attr]` attribute. This lets us conditionally set an attribute based on a `#[cfg]` string. Our declaration ends up looking like this:

```
#![cfg_attr(feature = "nightly", feature(portable_simd))]
```

Now, we'll only tell the compiler that we're using the `portable_simd` feature if we're using our `nightly` feature.

To benchmark with `nightly` features, our command line will look like this:

```
$ cargo +nightly bench --features nightly
```

This selects the `nightly` compiler and enables the `nightly` feature. Finally, we have our project set up, and we are ready to write a SIMD version of our `matrix_multiply` function.

Writing a SIMD function

Rust's portable SIMD library works by providing a structure that abstracts over a type of data and a width. The library defines this as `std::simd::Simd<T, N>` and provides several aliases for us to work with. For example, `f32x4` is `Simd<f32, 4>`, representing a 128-bit type with four floating-point numbers packed together, usually into a single SIMD register. This can be thought of as either a four-element array, `[f32; 4]`, or as a four-element vector.

The `std::simd` library provides aliases for packed types as small as `f32x1` and as large as `f32x64`. For any type that's not directly supported by hardware, the compiler will generate normal non-SIMD, scalar operations that match the functionality of the SIMD code, but at a performance cost. Thus, even though we're abstracting over different hardware implementations, it's still very important to know the capabilities of your target hardware.

In order to apply this to our code, we'll need a strategy, and a strategy often starts with understanding where we can compress the operations we are performing into a `Simd<T, N>` type. Looking at our `matrix_multiply` function, we can see that in our innermost loop, we step through the `a[i]` array linearly, one element at a time:

```
for k in 0..a_cols {
    sum += a[i][k] * b[k][j];
}
```

What if we could do this same operation on four elements at the same time, instead? The `b` matrix is pesky here, though, because we are stepping through the columns rather than the rows of the matrix. Matrices define a *transpose* operation that flips the matrix along its primary diagonal axis, allowing us to index what would have previously been columns as if they were rows. If we transposed the `b` matrix, we could perhaps speed up this algorithm by stepping through both matrices linearly in memory. This isn't an optimization we'll attempt in this chapter, but it is an interesting exercise to pursue.

Our initial strategy will be to attempt to load and process the `a` matrix's rows efficiently in 128-bit registers. For the `b` matrix, we will also use 128-bit registers, but we will just accept some inefficiency in loading the columns into them and hope that the SIMD operations are still effective enough to get us a performance boost.

We'll also need to handle `sum`. If we're processing four elements of `a` and `b` at a time, that leaves us with four separate values in the `sum` variable. Each component of this `f32x4` vector is the sum of every fourth value we computed in each iteration of the loop. To get the actual sum, we must add all the components of our vector together.

Let's start reconstructing the inner loop with this strategy in mind. We'll begin by modifying our loop to advance the index of `k` forward by four values each time through the loop:

```
for k in (0..a_cols).step_by(4) {
}
```

This is, of course, because we're processing four values with each iteration now instead of one.

Next, we must load our two vectors from memory:

```
let a_vec = f32x4::from_slice(&a[i][p..p+4]);
let b_vec = f32x4::from_array(unsafe {
    [
        *b.get_unchecked(p + 0).get_unchecked(j),
```

```
            *b.get_unchecked(p + 1).get_unchecked(j),
            *b.get_unchecked(p + 2).get_unchecked(j),
            *b.get_unchecked(p + 3).get_unchecked(j),
        ]
});
```

For a_vec, we know that we're loading sequential values in memory, so simply loading it from a slice is easiest and fastest. This incurs a bounds check for each side of the slice, which should be small relative to the amount of data loaded. Still, we could try to avoid this with an unsafe block if we wanted.

Loading b_vec is trickier, as explained previously. We first construct a four-element array containing the values we wish to load, and we then load this into our SIMD data structure. I chose to use unsafe operations to omit bounds checks here because it's relatively straightforward to do so and because our earlier testing showed that the gains we get from doing so are significant.

After we have our data in the SIMD structure, the actual math is straightforward, and the underlying complexity is hidden by the library:

```
sum += a_vec * b_vec;
```

This completes our inner loop, but we still have to store the sum in its appropriate spot in the target matrix:

```
sum += simd_swizzle!(sum, [1, 0, 3, 2]);
sum += simd_swizzle!(sum, [2, 2, 0, 0]);
unsafe {
    *out.get_unchecked_mut(i).get_unchecked_mut(j) = sum[0];
}
```

The first two lines may look like magic, but they are actually relatively straightforward. The simd_swizzle! macro changes the order of the elements of a SIMD vector. This operation, called swizzle, is extremely common in SIMD code. The array passed as the second argument is an array of indices describing how we want to construct the resulting vector.

If we think of the sum vector as having four elements, x, y, z, w, corresponding to indices 0–3 respectively, then we can see that the vector we're constructing with simd_swizzle! is y, x, w, z. When we add this vector to our original, we get x + y, y + x, z + w, w + z.

Another round of this adds `w, w, x, x` to our sum, giving us the result of `x + y + z + w` in each element of our resulting vector. We can then choose to write out any of the elements to the correct spot in our `out` matrix. We choose `sum[0]` here for simplicity.

This gives us a first pass at a SIMD implementation of our multiply. Now, we'll run some benchmarks to see how it compares to our other attempts. We've already set up our project to call the SIMD multiply if using the `nightly` feature, so benchmarking our improvements just looks like this:

```
$ cargo +nightly bench --features nightly
```

The results on my machine show an even further improvement despite the inefficiencies we incur from loading `b_vec`:

```
multiply 100x100          time:   [207.73 µs 208.60 µs 210.07 µs]
                          change: [-41.677% -41.465% -41.251%] (p = 0.00 < 0.05)
                          Performance has improved.
```

We're left with a great speed up from SIMD, and several potential improvements. We could transpose our `b` matrix, we could further investigate removing bounds checks, or we could try dropping to `std::arch` to hand-tune things even more. Also, our implementation has some limitations in that it assumes that all our matrix sizes are multiples of four.

Despite all the room for improvement, we've seen that SIMD is the gold standard for computational tasks on CPU and that `std::simd` presents an approachable API for unlocking its capabilities. When this API is stabilized, it will position Rust as an even stronger competitor when it comes to writing high-performance programs.

Summary

Throughout this chapter, we've examined the unique performance issues affecting Rust code. We then constructed an example program and learned how to measure its performance. Using that info, we worked to produce several speed-ups to the code, resulting in a significant improvement over the original implementation.

In the next chapter, we'll take a look at another way to improve the performance of our programs: **multithreading**.

Get this book's PDF version and more

Scan the QR code (or go to `packtpub.com/unlock`). Search for this book by name, confirm the edition, and then follow the steps on the page.

UNLOCK NOW

Note: Keep your invoice handy. Purchases made directly from Packt don't require an invoice.

11

Multithreading in Rust

While the static safety guarantees of Rust work extremely well in programs using only one thread, the act of running code concurrently across multiple threads complicates nearly every aspect of programming. As we'll see, Rust is still able to provide some compile-time safety guarantees in multithreaded environments. This is a claim that very few other languages can make, and it led Rust's creators to describe it as a language of "fearless concurrency."

In this chapter, we'll examine several aspects of writing multithreaded code with Rust, including Rust's safety guarantees in concurrent environments and common techniques for working with threads.

In this chapter, we're going to cover the following main topics:

- Creating and managing threads
- Multithreading safely in Rust
- Synchronizing data across threads
- Useful multithreading techniques

Technical requirements

Examples in this chapter use Rust 1.82.0, but they will also work with any newer version.

If you need help installing Rust, please see the *Appendix*.

You can find the code files for this chapter in this book's GitHub repository: `https://github.com/PacktPublishing/Rust-for-CPP-Developers`.

Creating and managing threads

Before we can explore the ins and outs of multithreaded programming, we must learn how to create and run code on threads. In this section, we'll explore the Rust standard library's support for threads with some additional help from the crate ecosystem.

Spawning new threads

Every program starts with a single thread, which we often call the *main thread*. Each thread used by the program holds its own stack and instruction pointer and, unless directed otherwise, performs its work independently of any other thread. In order to spawn new threads, we must interact with the OS and runtime facilities to create a thread and allocate resources for it. Then, we must give it some work to do. In C++, these tasks can be accomplished by the `std::thread` API or any number of platform-specific APIs.

Rust similarly places its thread creation functionality in the `std::thread` module. The easiest way to create a thread in Rust is with the `std::thread::spawn` function. This function interacts with the OS to create a thread and begins executing the closure passed in as an argument. We can construct a very simple example using some prints:

```
println!("1. Hello world from main!");
std::thread::spawn(|| {
    println!("2. Hello world from thread!");
});
println!("3. Hello world from main!");
```

When our program uses more than one thread, we have limited control over the relative order in which operations on different threads execute. In the preceding program, the `"2"` and `"3"` prints may happen in either order. In some language environments, a similar program might even interleave the output of concurrent prints, but Rust does work behind the scenes to ensure that prints from different threads don't interfere with one another.

A thread like the one we've created in this example is called *detached* in Rust terminology. This means that we have no control over when the thread completes its execution relative to the rest of the program. The program may even exit before code begins executing on the thread. However, it's often necessary to have control over thread execution. For this, the `spawn` function returns a `JoinHandle` object that we can use to ensure that the thread's operations have completed. To *join* a thread means to wait until it has run to completion:

```
println!("1. Hello world from main!");
let handle = std::thread::spawn(|| {
```

```
    println!("2. Hello world from thread!");
});
handle.join().unwrap();
println!("3. Hello world from main!");
```

When we call the `join()` function, our program's main thread will wait until the thread represented by `handle` has completely finished its work before proceeding further. In this case, we should now see the three prints occurring in the same order every time.

A closure in Rust implicitly *captures* variables that are used inside of it, meaning that it automatically borrows any variable from the enclosing scope referenced inside the closure. If we need to pass data into the thread, we must do so by using the captures on our closure. This functionality is similar to the analogous C++ features of lambdas, although without specific capture modes for each variable. Rather, the Rust compiler decides how to capture each variable, whether as `&T` or `&mut T`, based on its usage inside the closure. Let's try passing data into the thread to see what happens:

```
println!("1. Hello world from main!");
let message = String::from("2. Hello world from thread!");
let handle = std::thread::spawn(|| {
    println!("{}", message);
});
handle.join().unwrap();
println!("3. Hello world from main!");
```

If we attempt to run this, we'll quickly see that it does not compile. The closure attempts to borrow the `message` variable, but the compiler cannot guarantee that the closure will be finished executing by the time the `message` variable that we're borrowing is dropped. The compiler must be able to prove that the borrowed value will remain valid for the entire lifetime of the spawned thread, or Rust's safety rules would be violated.

This is actually an extremely easy mistake to make in C++ when using lambdas that move across threads. Occasionally, programmers will mistakenly capture a variable by reference, but the data being referenced will be deconstructed while the thread is still executing. Rust helpfully catches this situation for us.

To fix this problem, we must use a different capture mode. Rust provides *move closures*, which take ownership of all captured variables instead of borrowing them. Let's try the same example from before using a move closure instead:

```
println!("1. Hello world from main!");
let message = String::from("2. Hello world from thread!");
let handle = std::thread::spawn(move || {
    println!("{}", message);
});
handle.join().unwrap();
println!("3. Hello world from main!");
```

Now, things work as expected. The thread's closure takes ownership of the `message` data and is now responsible for dropping the data on its own schedule. If we try to use the `message` variable after it is captured by the closure, the Rust compiler will produce an error just as it does with any attempt to use data that has changed ownership in a single-threaded program.

But let's investigate this a little more deeply. Why did the Rust compiler error originally occur? We can see that the thread was joined long before the `message` data went out of scope, causing it to be dropped. It shouldn't have caused any lifetime or safety problems for the thread to borrow that data. Why can't the compiler see this?

The answer is that the `std::thread::spawn` function requires that its closure has a `'static` lifetime. Remember that the `'static` lifetime requires a reference to point to valid data for the entire lifetime of the program. The closure's lifetime is propagated to any references it captures. In this way, Rust allows threads to run beyond the scope in which they were declared, but cannot statically reason about behavior such as early joins. For data that does not need to be shared with the main thread, using a move closure is typically the safest and simplest solution to this problem. The `'static` lifetime requirement can be quite limiting, since it is uncommon for Rust objects to live for the duration of the program. For some situations, we can sidestep this problem by using *scoped threads*.

Scoped threads

Scoped threads are a concept that doesn't exist in standard C++. In Rust, they provide the borrow checker with extra information about how long our threads live so that it can make better decisions about what constructs to allow and disallow. In particular, scoped threads make it possible for us to have immutable data without a `'static` lifetime borrowed by multiple threads at the same time.

The `std::thread::scope()` function creates a scope and provides an object, traditionally named s, that we can use to spawn new threads that are attached to this scope. Threads that we create within the scope are automatically joined when execution reaches the end of the scope. Let's visualize this with an example, again using prints:

```
std::thread::scope(|s| {
    s.spawn(|| {
        println!("Hello from thread one!");
    });
    s.spawn(|| {
        println!("Hello from thread two!");
    });
});
```

As before, we have no guarantees about the order in which the two messages are printed. What we *do* have is a compiler-enforced guarantee that both the threads that we've spawned and anything captured into them are released before s is dropped. Previously, when using `std::thread::spawn`, the compiler could not enforce any guarantees about when the thread would finish executing. With scoped threads, the compiler now knows exactly when each thread will complete, and it can make full use of the borrow checker within a much more specific lifetime.

We can immediately make use of this to share immutable, non-static data between the two threads as mentioned:

```
let message = String::from("Shared message");
std::thread::scope(|s| {
    s.spawn(|| {
        println!("Hello from thread one: {}", message);
    });
    s.spawn(|| {
        println!("Hello from thread two: {}", message);
    });
});
```

Everything we capture into the scope must outlive the s object, so the `message` object still must be declared outside of the call to `std::thread::scope`. But this is much better than the restrictions under which we had to operate when using `std::thread::spawn()`.

Spawning threads, whether scoped or not, can be an expensive operation. If our work can be split into many small tasks, it's often inefficient to spawn a new thread for each task. Rather, we can make use of *thread pooling*.

Thread pooling

Thread pooling is a technique where several threads are spawned (either at program start or on demand) and placed into a waiting state. When new work arrives, rather than spawning a new thread on the spot and executing it, a waiting thread from the pool is chosen if one is available. The workload executes on the chosen thread, and the thread is returned to a waiting state after it completes. In this way, we can run large amounts of work across threads without incurring the OS overhead and allocation costs of spawning a new thread each time we have to perform some work.

Rust has no thread pooling functionality in the standard library, but the crate ecosystem offers several high-quality options. The popular `rayon` crate exposes very similar versions of `std::thread::spawn()` and `std::thread::scope()` that execute workloads on a shared thread pool behind the scenes. By default, `rayon` will create its thread pool based on the OS-reported number of logical CPUs on the system. While this can be adjusted, it's often a sensible default.

Adjusting our previous scoped example to work with `rayon` is straightforward:

```
let message = String::from("Shared message");
rayon::scope(|s| {
    s.spawn(|_| {
        println!("Hello from thread one: {}", message);
    });
    s.spawn(|_| {
        println!("Hello from thread two: {}", message);
    });
});
```

A small difference here is that the `spawn` function in `rayon`'s scoped threading implementation passes a parameter to the closure. This is another spawner object, much like `s`, and it exists to allow spawned threads to add more work to the thread pool from within themselves. When this functionality is not needed, the parameter can be ignored by using the special `_` variable name.

When using a thread pool for large amounts of work, it may become important to understand how the work is scheduled across the available threads in the pool. A popular scheduling methodology used by `rayon` is called *work stealing*. In a work-stealing scheduler, each thread in the thread pool has a queue associated with it. When work arrives, the scheduler can freely add the work to any thread's queue. The threads will then execute each of the workloads in their queue until the queue is empty.

The work-stealing part comes into play when a thread exhausts the work in its queue. Before going into a waiting state, it will check whether there is unprocessed work in any other thread's queue. If so, it will "steal" the work and process it on its own queue. This methodology ensures that work is always being processed efficiently and distributed well across the threads in the pool, even when the thread pool is saturated.

When working with thread pooling libraries, keep in mind that each different library typically manages its own thread pool. Libraries have no general way of knowing whether other thread pools already exist in the program. It can be disappointing to look at the threads of your program in a debugger or profiler and observe that you have two or three times as many as expected. Threads in modern programs are not necessarily a scarce resource, so this can be fine. But it's important to be aware of this situation because it can affect the overall performance and memory usage of your program. It's best to keep to one thread pool whenever possible so that work can be scheduled optimally and resource usage can be kept under control.

Having taken a look at different ways to create and manage threads in Rust, let's move on to discuss what makes multithreaded programs challenging to write and how Rust helps.

Multithreading safely in Rust

Multithreaded code can run into several different problems that single-threaded code doesn't have to worry about. As a result, it has gained a reputation for being difficult and error-prone. Still, many of these problems are reduced and even eliminated in safe Rust. In this section, we'll examine a few of these problems and learn how Rust deals with them.

Understanding race conditions

One of the most common problems with multithreaded code is known as a *race condition*. The term evokes the imagery of vehicles racing against one another. The track in this analogy is a section of our code, while the cars are the different threads competing against one another to finish executing it. However, in programming, we're less concerned with the winner of the race than with the order in which each car passes each point on the track.

When we talk about race conditions in code, we're talking about a situation where the code has malfunctioned due to different threads executing the same code in an unexpected order. Consider a simple increment of a mutable integer, which looks identical in C++ and Rust:

```
i += 1;
```

Depending on the CPU and compiler in use, this simple line of code can represent a race condition when multiple threads are used! Or, more specifically, it represents a *data race*, which is a race condition related to the order in which writes to data occur relative to reads across each thread. The increment is a simple example of a *read-modify-write* operation. To perform the increment, we must first read the value from memory or a register to understand its initial state. We then modify it by adding 1 and write the result back to the same register or memory location from which we read it.

As a read-modify-write operation, our increment happens in three steps. Between each step, another thread could come in and run any combination of the same three steps. This can work totally fine, in a situation like this:

```
Thread 1                 |   Thread 2
-------------------------|----------------------------
read, value = 1          |
increment, value = 2     |
write, value = 2         |
                         |   read, value = 2
                         |   increment, value = 3
                         |   write, value = 3
```

But when the cars in our metaphorical race are moving at just slightly different speeds, you can get something like this:

```
Thread 1                 |   Thread 2
-------------------------|----------------------------
read, value = 1          |
                         |   read, value = 1
increment, value = 2     |
write, value = 2         |
                         |   increment, value = 2
                         |   write, value = 2
```

We have two threads doing two increments, but one of them is lost, and our code results in an incorrect value of 2 rather than the expected value of 3. Despite working perfectly in a single-threaded context, this code is broken when multiple threads are involved.

This type of problem is subtle and may not be obvious at first because it depends on a specific ordering of execution across multiple threads. This means that these types of problems can appear to come and go based on conditions outside the programmer's control, which highly complicates multithreaded programming and debugging.

In multithreading parlance, we call an operation *atomic* if it happens in a single step that cannot be interrupted while it's in progress. For code to be correct when run by more than one thread, or *thread-safe*, we must ensure that every operation that can modify data shared by one or more threads is atomic. This is an exceptionally difficult problem for many programming languages, because, like C++, they offer very little in the way of language-level resources for identifying and correcting data races.

Safe Rust, however, can statically validate the absence of data races. While this does not cover every possible multithreading issue, it takes one of the largest problems in the space and makes it a non-issue. This allows us to write multithreaded code with much higher confidence in Rust. Let's take a look at how Rust achieves this.

Data races and the borrow checker

For a data race to occur, we must have at least one thread writing to a memory location or register while another thread also attempts to read from or write to the same location. Many programming languages are not at all concerned about when or how one writes to memory, but this is actually a central concern in Rust due to the borrow checker. As it turns out, the set of restrictions enforced by the borrow checker is a very close match to the conditions needed to ensure that no data race can occur in a multithreaded program.

To ensure thread safety, we must ensure that no other thread is reading memory while one thread is writing it. Rust's approach to this is to use the borrow checker to enforce the same sharing and mutability restrictions across multiple threads as it does with only one thread. A great way to begin to understand this behavior is to try to break it, so let's look at some examples:

```
let mut v = vec![1, 2, 3, 4, 5, 6];
std::thread::spawn(move || v.push(7));
std::thread::spawn(move || println!("{:?}", v));
```

If Rust allowed this, we could print the vector while it was in the process of being modified. But we instead get a compile error thanks to the borrow checker. The v vector has been moved into the first thread and cannot be accessed outside of it. The restrictions of the borrow checker here are identical to those of a single-threaded program. Data can have only one owner, so once it has been moved into a scope, nothing in the outer scope can access it.

What if we try it without `move`? We saw a similar example earlier:

```
let mut v = vec![1, 2, 3, 4, 5, 6];
std::thread::spawn(|| v.push(7));
std::thread::spawn(|| println!("{:?}", v));
```

In this case, the example does not compile because the closure may outlive the value of `v` that it is borrowing. This is thanks to the `'static` lifetime on the closure, as we talked about in the previous section.

What if we try a scoped thread?

```
let mut v = vec![1, 2, 3, 4, 5, 6];
std::thread::scope(|s| {
    s.spawn(|| v.push(7));
    s.spawn(|| println!("{:?}", v));
});
```

Again, we hit a standard borrow checker error here: "`cannot borrow v as immutable because it is also borrowed as mutable`". The `v` object is borrowed into the first thread as mutable, and thus no other thread can borrow it until the scope ends. Between normal borrow checker behavior and correct lifetime annotations, Rust's standard library has all of the bases covered. As long as we're not using the `unsafe` keyword, we cannot accidentally get into a situation where one thread can read or write data while another thread is writing it.

The standard library does have to jump through hoops in some cases, though. Consider the `Rc<T>` type. This type acts like `std::shared_ptr<T>` in C++. Whenever the type is cloned, a reference is added, and a new owned type is created, pointing to the same underlying data. When the reference count reaches zero because all outstanding references to the data have been dropped, the underlying data is also dropped. This is a special implementation of `clone`, which creates multiple owned versions of the same `Rc<T>` type, all pointing to the same internal object and reference count. This threatens to derail Rust's data race safety if there's any way for the internal data to become mutable.

As it turns out, the `Rc<T>` type is often used to hold a `RefCell` type. `RefCell` exposes what is called *interior mutability*. This is a way of skirting around the borrow checker's restrictions, with the trade-off that making mistakes will cause a panic. While it's not always a good practice to use it, `RefCell` is allowed in safe Rust with the caveat that it turns a compile-time safety check into a runtime one. When `RefCell` is held by an `Rc<T>` type, we could theoretically pass a mutable object around to multiple threads. If the compiler allowed this, it would mean that we could create a data race in safe Rust code.

To deal with situations like this one, Rust defines two traits: `Send` and `Sync`. Both `Send` and `Sync` are marker traits, meaning they define no associated types or functions and only exist to provide metadata to the compiler. The `Send` trait states that a type is safe to send from one thread to another through a move. On the other hand, when a type is marked with the `Sync` trait, it specifies to the compiler that it's safe for multiple threads to share a `&T` reference to an object of that type. Thus, `Send` is concerned with whether we can pass owned data to a thread, and `Sync` is concerned with whether we can pass borrowed data to a thread.

The `Send` and `Sync` traits are automatically propagated by the compiler. This is unique among Rust traits at the time of writing. It means that any type will automatically be `Send` or `Sync` if the respective trait applies to all component parts of the type. The vast majority of standard library types implement both `Send` and `Sync`, so most types we can create in our programs will also implement `Send` and `Sync` without any work on our part.

A handful of types in the Rust standard library don't implement various combinations of `Send` and `Sync`, because their usage can never be guaranteed to be safe when multiple threads are involved. Raw pointers fall into this category, restricting both `Send` and `Sync`. `RefCell<T>`, for instance, implements `Send` if `T` also implements `Send`, but does not implement `Sync`. In the case of `Rc<T>`, the increment and decrement of the reference count are not atomic and could be subject to a data race if they were allowed to be passed across threads, so it does not implement `Send` or `Sync`.

Between the borrow checker and the `Send` and `Sync` traits, Rust can effectively guarantee the absence of data races in safe code. This does not mean that the Rust language protects us from all potential multithreading issues, but by giving us a pathway to eliminate data races, it takes care of one of the most common and hard-to-verify problems in multithreaded programming.

Still, we might think that the borrow checker's restrictions here are too limiting and heavy-handed. After all, we do occasionally want to share data across threads. Often, that's actually a requirement to get any useful speed up from multithreading. In the next section, we'll look at how Rust enables us to share data across threads safely.

Synchronizing data across threads

Shared data must be *synchronized* across threads to be shared properly. This means that *reads* and *writes* must both be atomic operations. Many languages offer a suite of *synchronization primitives* to allow users to deal with these issues, and Rust is no exception. In this section, we'll examine how Rust deploys these special types of objects while still disallowing data races in safe code.

Mutual exclusion

Synchronization primitives are a special set of objects that can be used to make data operations in a section of code occur atomically relative to every other invocation of that section of code. The most common synchronization primitive is a *mutex*, which stands for "mutual exclusion." Mutexes are called other names in some platform APIs, such as *critical sections*, but in the end, the goal of a mutex is to ensure that only one thread can execute a specific section of code at a time.

Typical usage of a mutex in most APIs involves calling a `lock()` function at the start of the protected section of code and calling a corresponding `unlock()` function when the protected section ends. While the mutex is locked, only the locking thread can proceed. Any other thread that attempts to lock the mutex will be placed into a waiting state until the mutex is unlocked, and it can proceed. Many languages provide "scoped" APIs that lock and unlock a mutex automatically when the scope object is constructed and destructed. This helps to avoid the critical programmer error of forgetting to unlock the mutex, which could cause any other thread attempting to lock the mutex to wait infinitely.

Rust exposes a mutex with the `std::sync::Mutex<T>` struct. In Rust, the mutex object does not protect a section of code, but rather it protects a specific piece of shared data. The `Mutex` type serves as a wrapper around the shared data and only allows the data to be modified when the mutex is locked.

Let's take a look at an example. Instead of our previous, unsafe increment, we can wrap a simple increment in a mutex to ensure that it works safely across threads:

```
use std::sync::Mutex;
fn increment_safe(i: Mutex<u32>) {
    let mut i = i.lock().unwrap();
    *i += 1;
}
```

The `lock()` function of our `Mutex` type returns a `MutexGuard` object. The guard object exists both to allow access to the underlying data and to ensure that the mutex is unlocked when we are done with the present scope. We unwrap the `Result` of the lock. While `unwrap()` can sometimes be a bad practice, an error when locking implies that a panic was triggered while the mutex was held on another thread, so propagating the panic with `unwrap()` is appropriate in this specific situation.

This example, unfortunately, is not generally useful because our `Mutex` is moved into this function. Since ownership rules generally prevent us from having multiple owners, we cannot use this function to share data across multiple threads in the current implementation. To solve this, we may wish to revisit the `Rc<T>` type, but we saw earlier that this type is not `Send` or `Sync`. So, if it can neither be sent to another thread as owned data nor shared with one as borrowed data, how can it solve our problem?

Atomic reference counting

The Rust standard library provides yet another smart pointer: the `std::sync::Arc<T>` type. This type has the same basic functionality as `Rc<T>`, meaning that it works like `std::shared_ptr<T>` in C++. However, `Arc<T>` is specifically designed to allow sharing across threads. This means that it implements both `Send` and `Sync` so long as the generic `T` type it holds also implements `Send` and `Sync`. The "A" at the start of `Arc` stands for "atomic," indicating that this type does not run into thread safety problems when incrementing or decrementing its reference counts.

Data inside an `Arc` type is generally not mutable. There are a few exceptions to this rule, but by and large, for multithreading purposes, it will be holding something purpose-built to deal with mutability, such as a `Mutex`. Thus, `Arc<Mutex<T>>` is a common way to share and synchronize specific pieces of data across threads in Rust. The `Mutex` ensures that we only have one thread reading or writing the data at once, and the `Arc` type ensures that we can pass the same `Mutex` object to multiple threads as owned data without creating lifetime issues. And underneath it all, the `Send` and `Sync` traits ensure that everything behaves properly together.

Revisiting one of our previous examples, let's make it thread-safe:

```
let mut v = vec![1, 2, 3, 4, 5, 6];
std::thread::spawn(|| v.push(7));
std::thread::spawn(|| println!("{:?}", v));
```

We start with a `Vec` of integers, with one thread adding to the list and another printing the resulting list. Previously, Rust would not let us compile this example because of the data race on `v`. Armed with `Arc<Mutex<T>>`, we can make this work, but with some additional code required to handle lifetimes and synchronization:

```
let v = vec![1, 2, 3, 4, 5, 6];
let owned_data = Arc::new(Mutex::new(v));

let data = Arc::clone(&owned_data);

let thread_a = std::thread::spawn(move || {
    let mut locked = data.lock().unwrap();
```

```
        locked.push(7);
    });

    let data = Arc::clone(&owned_data);

    let thread_b = std::thread::spawn(move || {
        let locked = data.lock().unwrap();
        println!("{:?}", *locked);
    });

    thread_a.join().unwrap();
    thread_b.join().unwrap();
```

As before, we start with a vector, `v`, but we immediately wrap it in `Arc<Mutex<T>>`. The `Mutex` takes ownership of `v`, and the `Arc` manages the lifetime of our mutex. By calling `Arc::clone` before passing the data into each thread, we create a new, owned `Arc` object that can be passed cleanly into the `spawn` closure. We call `Arc::clone` here rather than `.clone()`. Although either works, `Arc::clone` is usually preferred for clarity because this specific implementation of `Clone` is incrementing the reference count of an existing object rather than creating a completely new object like a normal `clone()` call.

We should notice here that we're calling the `Mutex`'s `lock()` function directly from `Arc<Mutex<T>>`. We can do this because `Arc<T>` is set up to be able to incorporate `Deref` into its containing `T` type. If we recall the concept of deref coercion in Rust, this means that we can call functions from `T` using the `Arc<T>` object without any extra syntax. `Mutex`'s guard object uses the same trick, allowing us to call `Vec::push` from the guard object, as in `locked.push(7)`. When not calling a function, we have to use * to dereference the guard object manually, such as when we pass it to the `println!` macro.

The end result of this work is a program that safely manipulates and reads the same data from multiple threads without corrupting the data or exposing either thread to a partial operation. The ordering of the threads is still arbitrary. If we run this example in the Rust playground or locally, we'll observe that sometimes it prints six values, and sometimes it prints seven, based on the order in which the two threads hit the `Mutex`.

While this program's output may not be very useful, the program is still sound from Rust's perspective because it is free of data races. Rust has no ability to protect against race conditions created by the order in which threads are scheduled. Various hazards, such as *deadlocks*, where two threads each wait for a resource held by the other, are perfectly possible traps to fall into in safe Rust. Care must still be taken when writing multithreaded code, but we shouldn't let this overshadow just how important it is that Rust enforces data race freedom at compile time.

Now that we understand the basics of multithreading and synchronization in Rust, we'll explore some useful multithreading patterns that show up frequently in Rust.

Useful multithreading techniques

While the number of multithreading techniques in software development can probably fill multiple books, Rust specifically supports some especially powerful ones. In this section, we will look at a handful of specific techniques that work in Rust and are well-supported across the standard library and crate ecosystem.

Parallel iterators with Rayon

In the C++ ecosystem, libraries such as OpenMP, Microsoft's concurrency runtime ConCRT, and Intel's Thread Building Blocks allow us to implement parallel versions of the normal C++ `for` loop. In a parallel loop, the processing of each iteration of the loop is pushed to a thread pool for execution. When the loop ends, all threads are joined. When it's safe to use this construct, it can produce significant program speedups and introduce multithreading optimizations in a way that's very accessible to most programmers.

In Rust, we can make use of something similar built on top of the standard iterator interface. We encountered the `rayon` crate earlier in our discussion of thread pooling, but one of the most popular features of this crate is its support for parallel iterators. When Rust's iterator library and its freedom from data races are combined, the result is an easy-to-use, high-confidence method of converting existing code to be parallel in a safe and robust way.

Many crates offer a `prelude` submodule that can be used to auto-import several definitions at once. After adding the `rayon` crate to our project with `cargo add rayon`, importing the prelude at the top of our program is the only setup we need to make use of parallel iterators:

```
use rayon::prelude::*;
```

Then, we just need an iterator expression to execute in parallel across a thread pool. We'll start with something simple:

```
let v = vec![0, 1, 2, 3, 4, 5];
let doubled = v.iter().map(|x| x * 2).collect::<Vec<_>>();
println!("{:?}", doubled);
```

This iterator expression simply doubles every number in our list and collects them into a new vector, which we then print. The program's output, predictably, is `[0, 2, 4, 6, 8, 10]`.

The work of multiplying by 2 is not especially CPU-intensive, but to move this work into a parallel iterator, all we have to do is change `iter()` to `par_iter()`:

```
let v = vec![0, 1, 2, 3, 4, 5];
let doubled = v.par_iter().map(|x| x * 2).collect::<Vec<_>>();
println!("{:?}", doubled);
```

Perhaps surprisingly, the output is still `[0, 2, 4, 6, 8, 10]`, even though the work is now happening on the `rayon` thread pool. We might expect the output to be interleaved since the work is parallelized across multiple threads. However, `rayon` does work internally to ensure that collected outputs maintain the same relative order as the inputs, even though any work happening to them is threaded.

The parallel iterator concept is extremely powerful. It gives us similar ease of use to C++ parallel `for` constructs while maintaining the safety of Rust's multithreading guarantees. Because of its high quality and practicality, `rayon` is one of the most popular crates in the Rust ecosystem.

Using channels

Channels represent a queue that is used to pass data between different threads. A channel is defined in terms of its *producers*, or the set of threads adding to the queue, and its *consumers*, which is the set of threads taking values out of the queue.

Channels come in different flavors depending on the number of producers and consumers allowed. These fall into the "single" or the "multiple" category, where "single" usually implies an optimization for performance or complexity purposes. We term these queues with abbreviations such as **MPSC** for **multiple-producer, single-consumer** and **MPMC** for **multiple-producer, multiple-consumer**. An MPMC queue is a superset of the other two types of queues.

The MPSC queue is generally the most useful, and this is the only channel implemented by the Rust standard library in its stable release. However, an MPMC queue is in development in the nightly versions of Rust. An MPSC queue allows us to perform some processing on values as they are added to the queue by multiple threads.

The `std::sync::mpsc` module contains two types of channels. The first, `channel()`, never blocks on the producer side and uses a conceptually infinite queue size. The second is called `sync_channel` and requires a maximum queue size to be passed. If this queue size is exceeded, any producer adding to the queue will block until space becomes available in the queue.

Each type of channel returns a tuple when created. The objects in the tuple are respectively called the *transmitter* and the *receiver* and are often denoted as `tx` and `rx`, respectively:

```
let (tx, rx) = std::sync::mpsc::channel();
for i in 0..10 {
	let tx = tx.clone();
	std::thread::spawn(move || {
		tx.send(i).unwrap();
	});
}

drop(tx);
for i in rx.iter() {
	println!("{}", i);
}
```

In this example, we send 10 events from separate threads on a channel and print them all from the main thread. We'll see, if we run this example in the playground, that the integers print in a jumbled order, as they're added to the channel in an unpredictable order. The iterator produced by `rx.iter()` will block each time the iterator's internal `next()` function is called if it is still waiting for the next value to be transmitted into the queue.

The transmitter behaves a bit like an `Arc` in that we must clone it before passing it a thread. This increases the internal tracking of how many producers exist, which is required for the receiver to know whether it should be waiting for more values or not. Each thread adds a value to the queue and then dutifully drops its copy of `tx`, decreasing the reference count. When the reference count is zero, the receiver knows that there can be no further values added to the queue and stops waiting for one to show up.

Because we have one clone of `tx` for each thread and one remaining for the main thread, we must explicitly drop the main thread's copy of `tx` before we call `rx.iter()` or our `for` loop will block forever waiting for a value from the main thread that will never come. If we know exactly how many events we expect to be in the queue, such as in this case, where we know there will be exactly 10, we can wait for them individually and forego dropping the main thread's `tx`:

```
let (tx, rx) = std::sync::mpsc::channel();
for i in 0..10 {
	let tx = tx.clone();
```

```
        std::thread::spawn(move || {
            tx.send(i).unwrap();
        });
    }

    for _ in 0..10 {
        println!("{}", rx.recv().unwrap());
    }
```

In this case, each `rx.recv()` call blocks waiting for the next value to be added to the queue by a transmitter.

Channels prove to be an excellent and efficient abstraction for passing values between threads. They're often more efficient and ergonomic than using, for example, `Arc<Mutex<Vec<T>>>` or `Arc<Mutex<Deque<T>>>`.

Atomics and lock-free programming

We recall that an operation is atomic if it cannot be seen by any thread in a partially completed state. Most modern CPUs have special features for constructing atomic operations. In C++, the `std::atomic` class exposes this functionality in a platform-independent way. Similarly, in Rust, the `std::sync::atomic` module contains several types implementing atomic versions of each of the Rust primitive integer and boolean types.

Earlier, we talked about increments as a read-modify-write operation. One of the most basic uses of CPU-level atomics is to make the increment operation on integral types into an atomic computation. This, in turn, makes it safe to call from multiple threads, which can be useful for things such as allocating the next free slot in a fixed-size pool of objects or implementing a thread-safe bump allocator.

In Rust, we can demonstrate an atomic increment like this:

```
use std::sync::atomic::{AtomicUsize, Ordering};
let atomic = AtomicUsize::new(0);
std::thread::scope(|s| {
    s.spawn(|| atomic.fetch_add(1, Ordering::SeqCst));
    s.spawn(|| atomic.fetch_add(1, Ordering::SeqCst));
    s.spawn(|| atomic.fetch_add(1, Ordering::SeqCst));
});
println!("{:?}", atomic);
```

There are several things to talk about here. First, why are we able to mutate the `AtomicUsize` object from multiple threads? Doesn't this break the borrow checker's restrictions?

The atomic objects in Rust, much like `RefCell` and `Mutex`, use interior mutability. This means that the object looks to the borrow checker as if it's immutable, but internally uses or exposes tricks to manipulate the data safely. The `fetch_add` method specifically is defined so as not to require a mutable `AtomicUsize`. Because the underlying implementation is atomic at the processor level, manipulating the value of this object is thread safe despite the API intentionally misrepresenting its behavior to the borrow checker.

A second thing to note is the `Ordering` enum we must pass to `fetch_add`. The different values of the `Ordering` enum match the constants in C11 and C++11. These constants control the compiler and hardware's ability to reorder operations. Compiler and memory reordering is a complex topic explained in the C++ and Rust documentation, but it's important to know that `Ordering::SeqCst`, standing for "sequentially consistent," is always the most conservative option and disallows any reordering at all. Other options may provide some speedup, depending on the algorithm and architecture, but must be used with great care.

In C++ `std::atomic`, the memory ordering parameters exist, but default to sequentially consistent. C++ code is free to ignore them as a result. However, Rust, not having default arguments in the first place, requires that the memory ordering be explicitly specified for each atomic operation.

After all that, what's the value printed by our example? Of course, it's always `3`. No matter which order the threads execute in, they can never malfunction due to one thread catching another at just the wrong time because all the operations are atomic and cannot be observed in a partial state.

While it's nice to have access to convenient methods such as `fetch_add`, the `std::sync::atomic` types also enable a very powerful multithreading technique called *lock-free programming*. Lock-free programming is extremely complex and error-prone, even with Rust's guarantees, but it can result in significantly lower contention between threads than other synchronization methods such as mutexes.

Briefly, an algorithm is considered lock-free if at least one thread is always making progress. This progress might not necessarily be useful. In fact, depending on the hardware, lock-free programs can repeat the same operation multiple times before it is successful. But in a lock-free program, it's impossible to get into a situation where no thread is making progress. This is welcome news because it eliminates several notorious multithreading issues around *priority inversion*, where a high priority thread is waiting on some work that may never be executed because it is scheduled to occur on a very low priority thread.

Different processors expose different building blocks for lock-free algorithms, but the C++ and Rust atomic APIs generalize them into one basic operation, the **compare and swap (CAS)**. The CAS can be thought of as a special kind of assignment, except that we must specify both an expected value and a new value instead of just the new value. The processor first atomically compares the current value to the expected value. If the value matches the expected value, the new value is assigned; otherwise, the operation failed and must be retried.

In the Rust atomic API, the CAS concept goes by the similar name `compare_exchange`. Here's an example of what an atomic increment might look like using Rust atomics:

```
let atomic = AtomicUsize::new(0);
loop {
    let expected = atomic.load(Ordering::SeqCst);
    let new = expected + 1;
    if atomic
        .compare_exchange_weak(
            expected,
            new,
            Ordering::SeqCst,
            Ordering::SeqCst,
        )
        .is_ok()
    {
        break;
    }
}
println!("{:?}", atomic);
```

We've implemented the increment as a loop because it must retry until we're able to successfully perform the CAS operation. First, we load the current value so that it can be compared against. Next, we specify the new value to be an incremented version of the current value. After we have these two values, we call `compare_exchange_weak` to attempt to perform the CAS.

If the current value has not changed, the CAS will succeed, and we'll exit the loop; our increment will be successfully completed. If the current value has changed, it means that another thread has altered the data, and we must restart our operation from scratch. Remember that in lock-free programming, one thread is always making progress, so while a retry may seem complicated and inefficient, it's actually a technique that often leads to very low contention over resources.

There are two other things to note about this example. First, we used `compare_exchange_weak` in the example. The `weak` suffix implies that the function is allowed to fail even if the current value has not changed. This can be required as part of the implementation of the CAS technique on some processors. The second oddity of this function is that it takes two separate `Ordering` parameters. In this case, the first ordering is applied on a successful swap, and the second ordering is applied on failure. Again, you can always use `Ordering::SeqCst` as the most conservative option.

The topic of lock-free programming is massive, and this is only a very brief introduction. Lock-free algorithms are the product of research papers and extensive validation. But it's a great tool for when maximum throughput is needed, and well-supported by Rust.

Summary

In this chapter, we went over the basics of creating and using multiple threads in Rust. We examined the safety guarantees of Rust in multithread environments and learned how to make use of Rust's unique take on the problem space to share data across threads. Then, we looked at several powerful techniques supported by Rust to help create safe, reliable, and efficient multithreaded programs.

In the next chapter, we'll take a look at Rust's powerful macro system.

12

Metaprogramming with Macros

Metaprogramming is the practice of writing code that generates or manipulates other code. In many programming languages, metaprogramming capabilities rely on a type of macro expansion system. Macros are a powerful tool in many programming languages, including C++, where they function as a system to generate code through expansion and replacement of text.

The Rust macro system is fundamentally different from C++, and it gives programmers a great deal of additional power. In fact, the Rust macro system encompasses several different types of macros, divided into the categories of **declarative macros** and **procedural macros**. This chapter examines the differences between C++ and Rust's macro systems and shows several examples of how to use the Rust macro system to improve our programs.

In this chapter, we're going to cover the following main topics:

- Pitfalls of the preprocessor
- Declarative macros
- Procedural macros
- Macro best practices

Technical requirements

Examples in this chapter use Rust 1.82.0, but they will also work with any newer version.

If you need help installing Rust, please see the *Appendix*.

You can find the code files for this chapter in this book's GitHub repository: `https://github.com/PacktPublishing/Rust-for-CPP-Developers`.

Pitfalls of the preprocessor

While this book is about Rust more than it is about C++, it's instructive to look at common problems with the C++ preprocessor to better understand Rust's approach to its macro system. In this section, we'll note some common problems with the C++ approach and observe how Rust handles them.

Syntactic fragility

The C++ macro system, inherited from C, does all of its work in a completely separate phase called the **preprocessor**. The preprocessor performs macro substitution as a purely textual process. It assumes that the compiler, which runs on its output, will catch any errors created by the transformation. An effect of this system is that by the time the compiler sees the expanded text, it has lost any contextual information about the macros and cannot distinguish between generated and written code.

To be sure, the C++ macro system exposes some powerful metaprogramming capabilities and has been used to great effect throughout the history of C and C++. But it also has subtle problems that programmers must be aware of to use it effectively. A classic example is the following macro, which can create unintended behavior when expanded as part of an `if` statement:

```
#define PRINT_TWICE \
    printf("Hello World\n"); \
    printf("Hello World\n");

if( condition )
    PRINT_TWICE;
```

When `condition` is `false`, this will print one copy of `"Hello World\n"` because only the first statement in the macro is considered to be part of the `if` statement by the compiler, and the second is executed unconditionally. In this case, the macro author likely did not intend the macro to be used in this way. But since the macro system is a simple text replacement, the compiler has no way to understand and warn about the programmer's error here.

Simple text replacements exhibit fragility in other ways, as well. Notably, we can never specify or limit in any way the arguments passed into a macro. Because there is no contract enforced by the compiler or preprocessor about what kinds of expressions are valid inputs to each macro, it's easy to cause unintended behavior when the author and users of the macro are not on the same page.

For instance, imagine this simple macro to double a value:

```
#define DOUBLE(x) x * 2
```

When used with a single identifier, this works well, but if passed an expression, we can get unexpected behavior:

```
int main() {
    int x = 0;
    int y = 1;
    std::cout << DOUBLE(x) << std::endl;
    std::cout << DOUBLE(y + x) << std::endl;
}
```

A user of the macro might reasonably expect this program to print out `0` for the first line and `2` for the second, but instead, the second expression prints `1`.

The reason for this is that the macro expanded to `y + x * 2`, or `1 + 0 * 2` when the variable values are subbed in. Due to operator precedence, the multiplication is evaluated before the addition.

These problems are well-known in C and C++, and several workarounds have been created over the years. In the case of our `DOUBLE` macro, the correct workaround would be to use parentheses to ensure that expressions are evaluated in the order we expect:

```
#define DOUBLE(x) ((x) * 2)
```

Another common technique is to enclose the contents of a macro in a `do`/`while` statement. This effectively prevents any syntactical surprises from the semantics of single-line `if`, `while`, and `for` statements. Applying it to our preceding `PRINT_TWICE` macro, we see something like this:

```
#define PRINT_TWICE \
    do { \
        printf("Hello World\n"); \
        printf("Hello World\n"); \
    } while (0)
```

Workarounds like these can often solve the most obvious and problematic issues, but ultimately, C++ macros must be crafted with large amounts of care to ensure that they can't be used in syntactically fragile ways that result in unintended behavior.

There are two primary ways that Rust's macro system deals with syntactic fragility problems. The first is that macro expansion occurs directly in the compiler rather than in a separate preprocessor phase, allowing the compiler to reason about the scope and context of the macro while expanding it. Second, it specifies exactly which types of language constructs are allowed for each input to a macro. For instance, a macro can distinguish between an identifier, an expression, and a type, and can define different behavior for each.

Macro systems predate C and C++, and many of them exhibit another problem that's vexed enough people throughout the years to gain its own terminology.

Variable capture

The term *hygiene* has been applied to macro systems in programming language theory since the 1980s to describe how systems prevent the problem of **variable capture**. To understand variable capture, we'll think of macros in terms of two different sites: the **definition site**, where the macro is defined, and the **invocation site**, where it's used or expanded. Variable capture occurs when a variable that exists in the scope of the invocation site is unintentionally read, written, or shadowed by the macro expansion.

A macro system is considered *unhygienic* if it has no restrictions or safeguards against variable capture. A purely textual macro evaluation and expansion strategy, such as the one used by C++, is inherently unhygienic. A simple example might be a macro that increments a global counter:

```
int x = 0;
#define INC_GLOBAL_X() x += 1
```

This macro might work fine until someone happens to use it in a scope where their own x is defined:

```
int x = 0;
#define INC_GLOBAL_X() x += 1
int main() {
    int x = 1;
    INC_GLOBAL_X();
}
```

In this case, the local x is incremented instead of the global one. Although this example is contrived, this problem shows up in surprising places when working with C++ macros. A common way to deal with this is by attempting to create symbol names that are unlikely to clash with anything else. Accordingly, a custom `ANON()` or `UNIQUE_ID()` macro can be a problem-solver in heavy C++ macro deployments. This type of macro attempts to create a unique symbol name for use inside the macro, often by using token pasting to combine an identifier name with the value of the `__LINE__` or the non-standard `__COUNTER__` macro. While there is no guarantee, it is much less likely for the new symbol name to conflict with anything in the code base.

While it's good to have workarounds for the limitations of the preprocessor, it's even better to have safer defaults. *Hygienic* macro systems achieve this by creating rules and safeguards around how variables from the definition site and invocation site can be used, preventing unintentional variable capture. Hygienic systems vary in both their strategy and restrictiveness. For the purposes of our discussion, we're only concerned about the strategy chosen by Rust, which is called **mixed-site hygiene**.

Mixed-site hygiene specifies exactly which types of identifiers are resolved at the definition site and which are resolved at the invocation site. In Rust's strategy, local variables, along with loop and block labels, are looked up at the definition site, while all other identifiers are looked up at the invocation site. This creates a predictable set of rules that always apply, no matter how the macro is defined or used.

Rust's strategy fits well with the language's focus on predictability and safety, but learning to use it requires mastering these rules. In the next section, we'll examine how to create and use declarative macros as we construct a small macro of our own.

Declarative macros

Rust offers two types of macros, with the first and simplest being **declarative macros**. Declarative macros are also sometimes called "*Macros by example*" in Rust documentation. While many of the capabilities of C++ macros can be achieved with Rust's declarative macros, in keeping with Rust design goals, they are safer, more hygienic, and more expressive.

In this section, we'll learn how to define and use declarative macros by working through a practical example. We'll then explore some oddities and best practices around these kinds of macros.

Creating declarative macros in Rust

Rust uses the `!` symbol after an identifier to denote a macro invocation. We've already encountered this syntax many times in previous chapters, and indeed it is one of the first things a Rust programmer encounters in the language due to common operations such as `println!` and `vec!` being implemented as macros by the standard library. To dive deeply into how the declarative macro system in Rust works, we'll create our own version of the `vec!` macro in this section. We'll call our version of the macro `v!` and use it to illustrate the syntax, matching rules, and expansion behavior of declarative macros.

Creating our first macro

We'll recall that the `vec!` macro we wish to duplicate creates an initialized `Vec`. Let's start with a very simple version of our `v!` macro. We'll simply define a macro that takes no arguments and produces a new, empty `Vec`:

```
macro_rules! v {
  () => { Vec::new() };
}

fn main() {
  let v: Vec<u32> = v![];
  println!("{:?}", v);
}
```

We can see that a macro declaration begins with the `macro_rules!` keyword. The three parts of a Rust macro are all contained in this block. The first is an identifier matching the macro's name. After this follows a list of **rules**, each containing a **matcher** on the left side and a **transcriber** on the right. When the compiler encounters a macro invocation such as `v![]`, it looks through the macro's rules from top to bottom and chooses the first rule that matches the arguments passed. The transcriber is then invoked to expand the macro to its final form.

In this example, our matcher simply matches an empty argument list, and the transcriber expands to `Vec::new()`, which produces an empty vector. What would happen if we tried to pass an argument, such as `v![0]`? The Rust compiler cannot match anything in our set of rules, and reports `error: no rules expected '0'`. To turn this macro into something useful, we'll need to add more rules. Let's expand our macro to allow an initial value to be passed, creating a vector with one element:

```
macro_rules! v {
  () => { Vec::new() };
  ($x:expr) => { Vec::from([$x]) };
}

fn main() {
  let v: Vec<u32> = v![0];
  println!{"{:?}", v};
}
```

The matcher section of each rule has a small syntax of its own. Here, the syntax `$x:expr` is used to capture a **syntax fragment** that can be used in the transcriber. This syntax fragment has two parts separated by a colon: the `$x` *metavariable* holding the captured syntax fragment, and the *fragment specifier* denoting which kinds of syntax fragments match this rule. There are several allowed fragment specifiers, but a few common ones are `expr` to capture an expression, `block` to capture a series of statements, and `ty` to denote a type name. A full list of fragment specifiers is available in the Rust documentation.

In this rule, we've used `Vec::from` in the transcriber, creating an array on the stack to pass to our `Vec`. When this happens, `Vec::from` will create a copy of the array on the heap. This is obviously inefficient and is not the way that the standard `vec!` macro behaves, but it will allow us to demonstrate the macro behaviors that we need while producing working code.

Expanding our capabilities with repetition

At this point, we must note that a macro that only allows us to initialize a `Vec` with either zero or one elements is still very limited. Let's modify our rules so that they can accept any number of arguments. To do this, we must use **repetition**. A repetition is a special syntax for both the matcher and transcriber that lets us capture and expand multiple arguments, respectively.

Repetitions make use of a **repetition operator** to specify the exact number of arguments that are accepted by the matcher and transcriber. Repetitions use operators similar to those found in many different regular expression libraries, with * meaning zero or more arguments, + meaning one or more arguments, and ? meaning zero or one argument. The tokens and metavariable matches to be repeated are placed inside `$(...)`, followed by an optional token specifying our argument separator (such as a comma) and then one of the repetition operators.

Putting it together, we wish for our macro to accept any number of arguments, such as `v![0, 1, 2]` or `v![0, 1, 2, 3, 4]`. We end up with `$($x:expr),+` on the matcher side, giving us a rule that matches one or more expressions separated by a comma. Let's put this into our macro before discussing the transcriber side of things:

```
macro_rules! v {
  () => { Vec::new() };
  ($($x:expr),+) => { Vec::from([$($x),+]) };
}

fn main() {
  let v: Vec<u32> = v![0];
  println! {"{:?}", v};
  let v: Vec<u32> = v![0, 1, 2, 3];
```

```
    println!("{:?}", v);
}
```

When running this, we'll see the expected output:

```
[0]
[0, 1, 2, 3]
```

Our macro now accepts any number of arguments, and we see that the transcriber syntax is nearly identical to the matcher syntax. That is, we place the tokens and metavariables we wish to expand inside a `$(...)` expression, followed by a separator and a repetition operator.

When using repetitions, the number of expanded arguments in the transcriber must exactly match the number captured by the matcher. This is normally the case unless we're attempting to mix together different repetitions from the matcher side of the rule. For example, an operation called `zip` in some languages can combine two tuples together, for example, going from `((0, 1, 2), (3, 4, 5))` to `((0,3), (1, 4), (2, 5))`. In macro form, it might look like this:

```
macro_rules! zip {
    (($($l:expr),*), ($($r:expr),*)) => {
        ($( ($l,$r) ),*)
    };
}

fn main() {
    let out = zip!((0, 1, 2), (3, 4, 5));
    println!("{:?}", out);
}
```

The macro looks imposing, but if we break it down, we see that it's matching two sets of tuples, `$l` and `$r`, of arbitrary length separated by a comma. In the transcriber, we then combine these two tuples into one, zipping their elements.

Our example works as compiled, printing `((0,3), (1,4), (2,5))` as expected. However, if the two input sequences have different lengths, as in `zip!((0, 1, 2), (3, 4))`, the compiler will not allow us to expand the macro, giving this message:

```
error: meta-variable `l` repeats 3 times, but `r` repeats 2 times
```

The repetition syntax can be hard to read, but this is a powerful feature once we get a handle on it. But we're still not quite done with our example v![] macro yet.

Matching explicit tokens

Our v![] macro is now functioning well, but we've forgotten one other syntax accepted by the corresponding vec![] macro. Arrays can be initialized with a default value and the number of elements separated by a semicolon. Using what we already know, it shouldn't be too difficult to add this behavior, so let's complete our v![] macro now:

```
macro_rules! v {
  () => { Vec::new() };
  ($val:expr; $count:expr) =>
    { Vec::from_iter(std::iter::repeat_n($val, $count)) };
  ($($x:expr),+) => { Vec::from([$($x),+]) };
}

fn main() {
  let v = v![0u32; 5];
  println!("{:?}", v);
}
```

The only new thing to us in this example is the semicolon as a literal token in the matcher. In macros, we can mix metavariables such as `$val:expr` and literal tokens such as `;` freely, but the `$` token is explicitly reserved by the macro language and cannot be escaped.

As a small optimization, we use the `Vec::from_iter` function to construct our vector. This ensures that we don't waste huge amounts of stack space constructing the array that we'll convert into a vector. We didn't worry about this when using `Vec::from`, but the workaround here is straightforward. As we can guess, the output of this program is `[0, 0, 0, 0, 0]`, meaning that our example v![] macro is now feature complete!

With that, we've covered the basics of declarative macros, and we have created our own version of vec! in the process. Next, we'll dive more deeply into some of the practical considerations around creating declarative macros that do their job well.

Practical considerations for declarative macros

While Rust's declarative macros are often significantly safer than a strict textual replacement system, they have nuances and best practices that will be helpful to understand both when writing macros and when using them.

Choosing delimiters

The topic of **delimiters**, or the pair of tokens used to denote the macro arguments, can be a confusing aspect of declarative macros. The Rust macro language allows three separate pairs of delimiters. Parentheses are most often used for macros that represent function calls, such as `println!()`. We've also seen that brackets can be used when dealing with macros that behave somewhat like arrays, as in `vec![]` or our previous `v![]` macro. The third type of delimiter is braces, and they are often used when the macro arguments represent a code block or a series of statements.

These delimiters are interchangeable in most cases. For instance, this small variation of `"Hello World"` compiles and runs without issue:

```
fn main() {
    println!("Hello World, parentheses");
    println!["Hello World, brackets"];
    println! {"Hello World, braces"};
}
```

For clarity and consistency, most Rust programmers use the delimiter that best matches the macro's usage, be it parentheses for function-like, braces for block-like, or brackets for array-like macros.

We can also use any combination of delimiters when defining the macro rules. For instance, the following examples are all valid and equivalent:

```
macro_rules! nil {
  () => ( () );
}

macro_rules! nil (
  [] => [ () ];
);

macro_rules! nil [
  {} => { () };
];
```

Note that when defining macro rules with `()` or `[]`, we are required to follow them with a semicolon. While using any of the three sets of delimiters in these situations is allowed by the language, in practice, almost all macros we will see in the wild will use braces, {}, for defining the macro rules and parentheses, (), for defining the matchers and transcribers.

Implications of mixed-site hygiene

As discussed earlier, Rust's macro hygiene strategy prevents capture of local variables and loop or block labels by looking up and resolving their symbols at the definition site. This is intended to catch the most egregious variable capture issues, but still allows the possibility that we could reference some things unexpectedly. Let's look at an example in practice:

```
macro_rules! double_x {
    () => {
        x *= 2
    };
}

fn main() {
    let mut x = 1;
    double_x!();
    println!("{:?}", x);
}
```

A quick glance at this code might give us the impression that it would print 2, as it might in a purely-textual C++ preprocessor expansion. However, the compiler reports an error instead:

```
error[E0425]: cannot find value `x` in this scope
```

The mixed-site hygiene rules under which Rust macros operate dictate that x must be in scope at the definition site, not the invocation site. What if we try with a function instead?

```
macro_rules! double_x {
    ($x:ident) => {
        $x = double($x)
    };
}

fn double(x: i32) -> i32 {
    return x * 2;
}

fn main() {
```

```
    let mut x = 1;
    double_x!(x);
    println!("{:?}", x);
}
```

The results here are much different. We indeed get the 2 print that we were expecting, because function names are looked up at the invocation site rather than the definition site. This allows the macro to access them safely.

This behavior can cause similar issues to the C++ preprocessor when it comes to functions, structures, traits, or global constants. The solution in Rust is to fully qualify the names of the identifiers we must use inside our macro. This ensures maximum robustness, especially if our macro will be distributed as part of the public interface of a crate.

We can adjust our v! macro from earlier to comply with this recommendation as follows:

```
macro_rules! v {
    () => { ::std::vec::Vec::new() };
    ($val:expr; $count:expr) =>
        { Vec::from_iter(::std::iter::repeat_n($val, $count)) };
    ($($x:expr),+) => { ::std::vec::Vec::from([$($x),+]) };
}
```

Declarative macros also provide the special $crate metavariable. This resolves to the current crate in a transcriber, so that identifiers local to the crate can also be fully qualified. A key point to remember is that because lookup only occurs at invocation time, we will not be able to test the correctness of a rule unless the compiler actually expands it. In other words, if we had made a typo in the fully qualified name of any type, the compiler would not catch it unless we happen to encounter a use of the macro that matches the errant rule. Some time spent writing unit tests that match each rule is highly recommended to avoid this problem.

Now that we have a good handle on how to create declarative macros and some idea of best practices around their authoring and maintenance, it's time to explore the second category of macro offered by Rust, the procedural macro.

Procedural macros

Procedural macros in Rust allow for extremely powerful code-generation abilities, at the cost of significantly greater development complexity than declarative macros. These macros are at the heart of some of the most powerful and compelling features in the crate ecosystem. This includes ergonomic serialization using crates such as `serde_derive` and intuitive command-line parsing using crates such as `clap` and `argp`.

In this section, we'll explore the different types of procedural macros Rust offers and construct a short example for each.

Common properties of procedural macros

Rust currently supports three separate types of procedural macros: custom derives, custom attributes, and function-like procedural macros. We'll investigate these three types of procedural macros in the order in which a programmer is most likely to encounter them. But first, we'll begin by looking at the properties shared by all three types.

One of the most notable characteristics of procedural macros is that each must live in its own crate. Procedural macro crates are compiled into dynamic libraries that are loaded by the compiler. This allows the compiler to invoke them in line with other compile stages. A procedural macro crate is designated by setting `proc-macro` to `true` in the `[lib]` section of the crate's `Cargo.toml` file.

Each procedural macro crate must export at least one public function, which is tagged with an attribute specifying which of the three kinds of procedural macro it is implementing. A single procedural macro crate can export more than one function, but all exported functions must be tagged with one of the procedural macro attributes.

All procedural macro functions both operate on and produce a *token stream* of the `proc_macro::TokenStream` type. The `proc_macro` crate is provided by the compiler and does not need to be listed in `Cargo.toml`, but can only be used or referenced in procedural macro crates. Since they use token streams directly, procedural macros operate at a very low level. Normally, only the compiler would operate at this level of abstraction. Fortunately, we aren't required to manually parse the token stream into an abstract syntax tree as a compiler would. The frequently-used `syn` and `quote` crates exist to help us in parsing and generating the token stream.

We'll now dive in by creating our first procedural macro crate. We'll be using one of the most powerful types of macros in all of Rust: the custom derive.

Custom derive

We've seen and used #[derive] attributes throughout this book. While several of these are implemented by the compiler for standard traits such as Debug, Copy, or Clone, the procedural macro system exposes derive functionality to the crate ecosystem. At its heart, #[derive] is intended to automatically generate implementations that extend the behavior of a type. This capability is showcased most prominently by the flagship Rust serialization serde crate and its accompanying custom derive macro crate, serde_derive.

To explore custom derives on our own, we'll write a simple pretty-printer for structures. While we'd normally use Debug for this, implementing our own derive makes for an excellent "Hello World" example for procedural macros. Let's start by setting up a new crate to hold our macro:

```
$ cargo new --lib prettyprint_derive
$ cd prettyprint_derive
$ cargo add syn quote
```

It's a common convention for custom derive crates to use the _derive suffix, but it is not enforced by the compiler.

At this point, we must edit Cargo.toml to tell the compiler that this is a procedural macro crate. We must open the file and add this section:

```
[lib]
proc-macro = true
```

Let's now open src/lib.rs and add the skeleton of our procedural macro:

```
use proc_macro::TokenStream;

#[proc_macro_derive(PrettyPrint)]
pub fn pretty_print_derive(input: TokenStream) -> TokenStream {
  todo!()
}
```

The #[proc_macro_derive(PrettyPrint)] attribute tells the compiler that we're defining a procedural macro function that can be used with #[derive(PrettyPrint)] once it's imported. The identifier passed to this attribute often corresponds to a trait name, but this is not required. To keep our example a little simpler, we won't define a PrettyPrint trait for it.

At this point, the macro craft builds, but our macro does not provide any useful functionality. To start adding some, we'll need to add the syn crate to our imports and parse the input tokens:

```
use proc_macro::TokenStream;
use syn::{DeriveInput, parse_macro_input};

#[proc_macro_derive(PrettyPrint)]
pub fn pretty_print_derive(input: TokenStream) -> TokenStream {
  let input = parse_macro_input!(input as DeriveInput);
  todo!()
}
```

The syn crate provides the `parse_macro_input!` macro to parse the input token stream into a useful structure. In this case, we're asking it to parse into a `syn::DeriveInput` structure. It's important to understand the use of the `as` keyword when passed to this macro. While this keyword is normally used for casts between simple types, here, it is expected by the macro match rules of `parse_macro_input!` to denote the type of structure for the macro to return.

Recall that when we're using `#[derive]`, we're using it as an attribute attached to a structure or enum. The `DeriveInput` structure, in most cases, will tell us all the info about the attached type needed to implement our macro. For the purposes of our `PrettyPrint` macro, this includes the name of the structure and the name and type of each member.

To start generating our output token stream, we'll use the `quote` crate. Generally, we only need to import one thing from this crate, the `quote!` macro. This macro allows us to write the Rust code that we're generating in a natural, readable form, while still giving us a way to create the `syn::TokenStream` required as the return value of our procedural macro.

Let's finally remove our `todo!()` and replace it with a `quote!` block that generates some initial code:

```
use proc_macro::TokenStream;
use quote::quote;
use syn::{DeriveInput, parse_macro_input};

#[proc_macro_derive(PrettyPrint)]
pub fn pretty_print_derive(input: TokenStream)-> TokenStream {
    let input = parse_macro_input!(input as DeriveInput);
    let name=&input.ident
    let output = quote! {
```

```
        impl #name {
            pub fn pretty_print(&self) {
            }
        }
    };
    TokenStream::from(output)
}
```

As we can see, the quote! macro allows us to use the values of variables that are in the local scope in the generated code. Here, we used #name to create an impl block for the structure we've been passed. If we were filling out an actual trait definition instead, we'd do something closer to impl PrettyPrint for #name. We've also generated an empty function, pretty_print, which will show up on every structure using our custom derive, although we have yet to fill out the implementation.

Now is a good time to set up a second crate to test our procedural macro. We can do all of our testing in this crate from here on out:

```
$ cd ..
$ cargo new prettyprint_test
$ cd prettyprint_test
$ cargo add --path ../prettyprint_derive prettyprint_derive
```

Let's set up a structure in src/main.rs for this crate and call its pretty_print() function:

```
use prettyprint_derive::PrettyPrint;

#[derive(PrettyPrint)]
struct TestStructure(u32, u32, u32);

fn main() {
    let x = TestStructure(0, 1, 2);
    x.pretty_print();
}
```

Now, we're exercising our PrettyPrint derive with a simple test structure, but as expected, it does not yet print anything when we run cargo run for this crate. Let's go back to our quote! block in the prettyprint_derive crate and add some functionality. The main thing we'll want is a way to iterate over the members of our structure and generate some code for each.

First, we'll need to begin digging into `DeriveInput` to pull out the information about our structure:

```
let fields = match input.data {
    syn::Data::Struct(data) => data.fields,
    _ => unimplemented!(),
};
```

Here, we only support deriving on `struct` types in our procedural macro. The `unimplemented()!` macro will raise a panic if a user tries to use our macro on an `enum` or `union` type. While this is far from production quality, it's good enough for our current example. We'll look into proper error handling later in the chapter.

The field data is wrapped in another structure, so we'll need to pull it out with another pattern match:

```
let fields = match fields {
    syn::Fields::Named(ref fields) => &fields.named,
    syn::Fields::Unnamed(ref fields) => &fields.unnamed,
    syn::Fields::Unit => &Default::default(),
};
```

Here, `syn::Fields::Named` holds the fields of a normal structure with named members. Similarly, `syn::Fields::Unnamed` holds info about the members of tuple-like structures, such as the one we're using in our test crate. These members are accessed with names such as `.0`, `.1`, and so on. Lastly, `syn::Fields::Unit` represents an empty structure, such as `struct MyStruct()`. For this case, we'll just return an empty default value.

The `fields` variable holds a reference to a possibly-empty list of comma-separated fields. We can now iterate over these fields to begin generating code to pretty-print them:

```
let field_prints = fields
    .iter()
    .enumerate()
    .map(|(i, f)| {
        if let Some(field_name) = f.ident.as_ref() {
            quote! {
                println!("  {}: {:?}", stringify!(#field_name), self.#field_name);
            }
        } else {
            let index = syn::Index::from(i);
```

```
            quote! {
                println!(" .{}: {:?}", #index, self.#index);
            }
        }
    })
    .collect::<Vec<_>>();
```

Here, we simply check each field's identifier. If it exists, we create a `TokenStream` that prints out the name and value of the field, using the built-in `stringify!` macro to convert the identifier to a string literal. If the identifier is `None`, then we're dealing with an unnamed tuple field and will just generate a print of the index and its value. We then collect all of these generated token streams into `Vec<TokenStream>` in preparation for our final step:

```
let output = quote! {
    impl #name {
        pub fn pretty_print(&self) {
        #(#field_prints)*
        }
    }
};
TokenStream::from(output)
```

We amend our final output using the `#(...)*` syntax provided by `quote!` to output each element of our vector in order.

Moving back to the `prettyprint_test` crate, we can use `cargo run` with it to see the results of our code generation in action:

```
 .0: 0
 .1: 1
 .2: 2
```

We now have a working procedural macro of the custom derive flavor, and we successfully used both `syn` and `quote` crates to parse and generate a `TokenStream`. We'll get more practice working with these crates as we move on to the second kind of procedural macro that we'll explore.

Attribute-like macros

We've encountered attributes before. They take the form `#[identifier]` and are placed directly before the *item* they're intended to modify. An item in practice is most often a function, structure, or enum, but attributes can also modify other parts of the language. Many of the attributes in Rust are built into the compiler, such as `#[test]`, `#[inline]`, or `#[doc]`. But Rust's procedural macro infrastructure gives us the opportunity to provide our own attributes as part of the crate ecosystem.

Attribute-like procedural macros are similar in structure to custom derive macros, but with two important differences. First, the procedural macro function receives two input `TokenStream` arguments. Second, the output `TokenStream` *replaces* the input tokens when the macro is executed, rather than adding new tokens as with custom derive macros.

To use an attribute-like procedural macro, we must create a new crate just as we did with our custom derive macro. This crate must be set to `proc-macro = true` in the `Cargo.toml` file, and it must export at least one public function tagged with the `#[proc_macro_attribute]` attribute.

Let's set that up now. As an example, we'll be building a small attribute-like macro called `log_call` that can be applied to a function to automatically print a log message at the start and end of each call:

```
$ cargo new --lib log_call
$ cd log_call
$ cargo add quote
$ cargo add syn --features full
```

We add the `full` feature to our `syn` crate, because it's needed by `syn::ItemFn`, which we will use later.

As before, we must next specify that this is a procedural macro crate in `Cargo.toml`:

```
[lib]
proc-macro = true
```

Now, let's sketch out the start of our macro crate:

```
use proc_macro::TokenStream;

#[proc_macro_attribute]
pub fn log_call(_attr: TokenStream, item: TokenStream) -> TokenStream {
```

```
    item
}
```

As we can see, there isn't much difference here versus our earlier custom derive macro crate. As mentioned, there are two input token streams for an attribute-like macro. The first argument, which we've called `_attr`, contains the tokens of the attribute itself, which, in our case, starts with `#[log_call]`. This allows macro authors to pass additional arguments to the macro. For instance, if we wanted to allow an argument such as `#[log_call(verbose = True)]`, we would use the first `TokenStream` to parse the arguments. Since we aren't using it in this example, we prefix it with an underscore to avoid compiler warnings about unused variables.

The second `TokenStream` argument, which we've called `item`, contains the tokens of the item to which the attribute is attached. In our simple test, we're just returning the item directly, making this attribute macro a no-op.

To properly implement our `#[log_call]` attribute, we'll make a wrapper function around the actual implementation of our tagged function. This will not only ensure that we print an ending message regardless of the function's control flow, but it also allows us to print more info about the function, such as the return value, as part of our logging.

To set this up, we'll first need to parse the item's `TokenStream` with `syn::parse_macro_input!` as in our custom derive macro. In this case, we will parse into `syn::ItemFn`, which represents an item that is specifically a function. This way, `parse_macro_input!` will give users a useful compile error if they try to use our attribute on any other kind of item:

```
use proc_macro::TokenStream;
use syn::{parse_macro_input, ItemFn};

#[proc_macro_attribute]
pub fn log_call(_attr: TokenStream, item: TokenStream) -> TokenStream {
    let item = parse_macro_input!(item as ItemFn);
    todo!()
}
```

Next, we'll make aliases for some useful pieces of data inside `ItemFn`:

```
use proc_macro::TokenStream;

#[proc_macro_attribute]
pub fn log_call(_attr: TokenStream, item: TokenStream)-> TokenStream {
    let item = parse_macro_input!(item as ItemFn);
```

```
    let sig=&item.sig
    let name=&item.sig.ident
    let body=&item.block
    let vis=&item.vis
    todo!()
}
```

Here, `sig` is the full function signature, including its name, arguments, and the return type. We'll pull the function's identifier out into `name`, its body (including starting and ending braces) into `body`, and `vis` will either contain the `pub` token or nothing at all. These end up being the only pieces of information we need to implement our logging.

We might wonder about function arguments; shouldn't we be pulling them out of `sig` somehow to use them in our new function's body? It turns out that function arguments in Rust are quite complicated, even after `syn` has parsed them into something structured, so we'll use a small trick to make our implementation easier. Rather than trying to parse the arguments, we'll wrap the body of the function in an immediately invoked closure. This closure will capture the arguments by reference, making them available for use inside our closure without any changes to the original function's body. Finally, we'll begin our `quote!` block:

```
let output = quote! {
    #vis #sig {
        println!("start {}", stringify!(#name));
        let result = (|| #body)();
        println!("end {}, result {}", stringify!(#name), result);
        return result;
    }
};
TokenStream::from(output)
```

The `quote!` block makes a new outer function with both the exact same visibility and signature as our tagged function. The body of our original function is then inserted into an internal closure, which captures our arguments as we discussed and then is called immediately. We store the result, print it, and then return it from our new outer function. In the end, we have transparently wrapped the tagged function and augmented it with new behavior.

While this wrapped function approach is quite powerful, it's only one possible use of attribute-like macros. The `syn` crate lets us parse other types of items in a similar way, but in the crate ecosystem, we find this function-wrapping style somewhat frequently around profiling instrumentation crates.

Hopefully, we're becoming more comfortable working with `TokenStream` types at this point, but we still have one more type of procedural macro to investigate.

Function-like macros

Function-like procedural macros look almost exactly like declarative macros when they are used in code. But instead of going through the `macro_rules!` matchers as declarative macros do, they operate directly on a `TokenStream` like the other kinds of procedural macros.

Similar to attribute-like macros, function-like macros replace the input `TokenStream` with the returned stream. It's tempting to think that there is a lot of overlap with declarative macros in terms of functionality, but many function-like macros in the crate ecosystem focus on token manipulation tasks that can't be done in any other way.

As an example, let's build our own version of the compiler built-in `stringify!` macro, which we've already seen several times so far in this chapter. As we know, this takes an identifier and turns it into a string literal. We'll start the same way as our other procedural macro crates, but we won't need to add `syn` for this particular example:

```
cargo new --lib stringulate
cd stringulate
cargo add quote
```

As always, when making a procedural macro, we must edit `Cargo.toml` appropriately:

```
[lib]
proc-macro = true
```

And we can then begin setting up our `src/lib.rs` file:

```
use proc_macro::TokenStream;

#[proc_macro]
pub fn stringulate(input: TokenStream) -> TokenStream {
    todo!()
}
```

Again, we see a lot of similarities with past procedural macros that we've created. Function-like macros are designated with the `#[proc_macro]` attribute, and we take in and return a

TokenStream. The next step seems like it should be quite easy. Can we simply use quote! to place our input TokenStream inside a pair of quotation marks?

```
use proc_macro::TokenStream;
use quote::quote;

#[proc_macro]
pub fn stringulate(input: TokenStream) -> TokenStream {
    TokenStream::from(quote! {
        "#input"
    })
}
```

Unfortunately, this doesn't work. The quote! macro treats this as a literal string and won't properly substitute in our input. However, we're not quite out of ideas yet. We may be surprised and pleased to find that TokenStream contains a .to_string() method! This makes our finished, working macro quite simple as well:

```
use proc_macro::TokenStream;
use quote::quote;

#[proc_macro]
pub fn stringulate(input: TokenStream) -> TokenStream {
    let input = input.to_string();
    TokenStream::from(quote! {
        #input
    })
}
```

Now, we've seen and used each of the three types of procedural macros. Put together with our understanding of declarative macros, we should be well equipped to read the implementations of any macros we encounter and have a great foundation for writing our own. Let's continue looking into Rust macros in the next section by examining some best practices for using them.

Macro best practices

As with any powerful tool, care must be taken when using Rust macros to achieve the best results. In this section, we'll go over best practices and tips to make your macro development safer and easier.

Error handling

Because macros are expanded by the compiler behind the scenes, proper error handling is essential to help understand what's going wrong, both when authoring a macro and when using it in code. In this section, we'll focus specifically on best practices around error handling in procedural macros.

There are two general ways to handle errors in procedural macros. The first is to panic. The panic is picked up by the compiler when it runs your macro and returned as a compile error. The second approach is to return a `TokenStream` containing a call to the `compile_error!` macro.

Both of these methods will correctly stop macro evaluation and report a compile error, but an error message that helps the user resolve the problem can be tough to craft. To help solve this, the `syn` crate provides the `syn::Error` structure. This can be used to generate a nicely-formatted `compile_error!` containing contextual info from the parsed syntax tree produced by `syn`.

The best practices vary by macro type. For function-like macros, our previous `stringulate` macro can make a good test case:

```
#[proc_macro]
pub fn stringulate(input: TokenStream) -> TokenStream {
    panic!("Bad input: {}", input);
    let input = input.to_string();
    TokenStream::from(quote! {
        #input
    })
}
```

The compile error produced by this is actually quite good for a function-like macro:

```
error: proc macro panicked
  --> src/main.rs:21:22
   |
21 |     println!("{:?}", stringulate!(1 + 1 + 1));
   |                      ^^^^^^^^^^^^^^^^^^^^^^^
   |
   = help: message: Bad input: 1 + 1 + 1
```

To use `compile_error!` in our macro, we must return a quoted expression that invokes it:

```
return TokenStream::from(quote! {
    compile_error!("Could not parse input")
});
```

This doesn't give us much different behavior from the panic when used with the function-like macro:

```
error: Could not parse input
  --> src/main.rs:21:22
   |
21 |     println!("{:?}", stringulate!(1 + 1 + 1));
   |                      ^^^^^^^^^^^^^^^^^^^^^^^^
   |
   = note: this error originates in the macro `stringulate` (in Nightly builds,
run with -Z macro-backtrace for more info)
```

The compiler helpfully tells us that the error originated in our macro, which was made explicit by the `panic` method. For function-like macros, the output is similar enough to recommend the simpler `panic!` in all cases.

Things become less simple when using custom derive or attribute macros. In our `PrettyPrint` custom derive macro, we already have a panic from the `unimplemented!()` macro that fires if we use the macro on something that isn't a structure:

```
let fields = match input.data {
    syn::Data::Struct(data) => data.fields,
    _ => unimplemented!(),
};
```

We noted earlier that this isn't production quality. Let's see what the compiler says when we raise this error. We can trigger it easily by attempting to use our macro with an `enum` type:

```
#[derive(PrettyPrint)]
enum TestEnum {}
```

The compiler message we get is nowhere near as helpful as with the function-like macro:

```
error: proc-macro derive panicked
 --> src/main.rs:5:10
```

```
  |
5 | #[derive(PrettyPrint)]
  |          ^^^^^^^^^^^
  |
  = help: message: not implemented
```

While this correctly indicates a failure, it does not clearly explain what is wrong or highlight the correct source location. It would be nice to be able to tell the user the actual part of the code causing the error. In this case, that's the `enum` declaration.

Let's examine how we can do this with `syn::Error`:

```
let fields = match input.data {
    syn::Data::Struct(data) => data.fields,
    _ => {
        return syn::Error::new(
            input.ident.span(),
            "PrettyPrint custom derive only supported on structures",
        )
        .to_compile_error()
        .into();
    }
};
```

While this is verbose, it gives us much more control over the formatting of our error. In this case, we've chosen to highlight the identifier, since the `enum` keyword is not readily available after converting to `DeriveInput`. The resulting message is much more helpful:

```
error: PrettyPrint custom derive only supported on structures
 --> src/main.rs:6:6
  |
6 | enum TestEnum {}
  |      ^^^^^^^^
```

Panics can be useful, especially if they have informative messages associated with them, but `syn::Error` gives you the most control over your error messages. A little time spent here can have big returns both for the development of the macro and for end users. But error messages aren't the only important part of macro development. When we get into unexpected situations, we need a way to debug and test our macros.

Debugging and testing

Debugging macros can be challenging because they are expanded at compile-time. While many errors will be caught by the compiler, the experience can still be frustrating if things don't go to plan.

The easiest way to debug any macro, whether declarative or procedural, is to look at the expansion performed by the compiler. In an editor with **Language Server Protocol** (**LSP**) tooling, macro expansions may be displayed as a feature of the `rust-analyzer` language server. While LSP is useful, the most common tool for debugging macros is found in the crate ecosystem. The `cargo-expand` crate provides a plugin for Cargo that will expand all macros in a crate and print the resulting code. While this tool is a small wrapper around lesser-known `rustc` compiler flags, it provides a convenient and easy way to examine macro expansions.

To use `cargo-expand`, we must have a `nightly` toolchain installed. We do not have to invoke it with the `nightly` toolchain; it simply needs to have a `nightly` version of `rustc` available. We installed a `nightly` toolchain for SIMD usage in *Chapter 10*, so there may be one already on your system. If not, you can install it with `rustup`.

As a demonstration, we can create a test crate that uses the `#[log_call]` attribute macro defined earlier:

```
#[log_call]
fn square(x: u32) -> u32 {
    x * x
}
```

This function is now wrapped by the procedural macro, which inserts logging statements at the beginning and end of the function body.

At this point, `cargo-expand` is simple to use. Assuming a crate that compiles correctly and a `nightly` install available on our machine, the following commands can give us the expansion of our function:

```
$ cargo install --locked cargo-expand
$ cargo expand
```

By default, cargo-expand runs a formatting pass over the expansion to make it easier to read. The resulting expansion looks something like this:

```
fn square(x: u32) -> u32 {
    {
        ::std::io::_print(format_args!("start {0}\n", "square"));
    };
    let result = (|| { x * x })();
    {
        ::std::io::_print(format_args!("end {0}, result {1}\n", "square",
result));
    };
    return result;
}
```

Note that the tool expanded not only our procedural macro, but also the `println!` macros inside of it. It stops expanding when it encounters built-in macros such as `format_args!`. These are tagged as `#[rustc_builtin_macro]` in the library source and implemented directly inside the compiler itself, so they have no source-level expansion available.

The ability to expand macros is a great debugging aid, but what if we want to ensure their continued correctness? Then, we need to look into unit testing, but if we try writing tests for a procedural macro, we'll very quickly figure out that using the `proc_macro::TokenStream` type outside of a procedural macro is not allowed, and our test will panic and thus fail.

To solve this, the crate ecosystem provides the `proc_macro2` crate. To write a unit test for our macro, we must rewrite it in terms of `proc_macro2::TokenStream`. After we use `cargo add proc_macro2`, we can refactor our procedural macro crate into something that looks like this:

```
use proc_macro2::TokenStream as TokenStream2;

fn log_call_internal(_attr: TokenStream2, item: TokenStream2) -> TokenStream2 {
}

#[proc_macro_attribute]
pub fn log_call(attr: TokenStream, item: TokenStream) -> TokenStream {
    return log_call_internal(attr.into(), item.into()).into();
}
```

Now, we've moved all of our functionality over to the `proc_macro2` version of `TokenStream`, converting to and from `proc_macro::TokenStream` in our actual procedural macro entry point. Let's fill out the definition of `log_call_internal` for completeness:

```
fn log_call_internal(_attr: TokenStream2, item: TokenStream2)-> TokenStream2 {
    let item: ItemFn = syn::parse2(item).expect("Failed to parse fn");
    let sig=&item.sig
    let name=&item.sig.ident
    let body=&item.block
    let vis=&item.vis
    let output = quote! {
        #vis #sig {
            println!("start {}", stringify!(#name));
            let result = (|| #body)();
            println!("end {}, result {}", stringify!(#name), result);
            return result;
        }
    };
    output
}
```

This is identical to our previous implementation, except using `proc_macro2::TokenStream` as the API. We notice one significant change. We're no longer using `syn::parse_macro_input!`, but rather a `syn::parse2` function. The reason for this is that the `parse_macro_input!` macro only works with `proc_macro::TokenStream`. We must use the (mostly) equivalent `syn::parse2` instead when working with `proc_macro2`.

Now, we should be able to set up some tests. There could be several properties to test about this function, but in this example test, we'll just write out the expected expansion directly and compare. Directly in our `lib.rs`, we can drop the following code:

```
#[cfg(test)]
mod test {
    use super::*;
    #[test]
    fn test_expansion() {
        use quote::quote;

        let input = quote! {
            fn square(x: u32, y: u32) -> u32 { x * x }
```

```
        };

        let expected = quote! {
            fn square(x: u32, y: u32) -> u32 {
                println!("start {}", stringify!( square ) );
                let result = (|| { x * x }) ();
                println!("end {}, result {}", stringify!( square ), result);
                return result;
            }
        };

        let attr = TokenStream2::new();
        let item = input;

        let output = log_call_internal(attr, item);

        assert_eq!(output.to_string(), expected.to_string());
    }
}
```

This is a lot of code, but mostly straightforward. We first set up our boilerplate test module and test function, ensuring that it only compiles in a test config. We then set up an input and expected `proc_macro2::TokenStream` types using `quote`, and call our internal procedural macro. The assert compares the output and expected as strings. Tokens are normalized in the resulting string, so there's no need to worry about formatting, but we do have to ensure that the tokens in our expansion match exactly.

Running `cargo test` on the procedural macro crate, we should now see that our test passes. The ability to test procedural macros in this way can be a large help to both the development and maintenance of the macros.

Summary

In this chapter, we explored the general topic of Rust macros, starting with traditional sources of unsafety and misuse in macro systems and showing how Rust chooses to avoid these problems. We then constructed an example macro of each type allowed by Rust, learning how to work not only with `macro_rules!` but also with the `syn` and `quote` crates. Finally, we explored some best practices around macro usage.

In the final chapter, we'll conclude our exploration of Rust and talk about some potential next steps to take on our learning journey.

Get this book's PDF version and more

Scan the QR code (or go to `packtpub.com/unlock`). Search for this book by name, confirm the edition, and then follow the steps on the page.

UNLOCK NOW

Note: Keep your invoice handy. Purchases made directly from Packt don't require an invoice.

13

Continuing with Rust

After reading through this book and following along with the examples, you should have a strong base upon which to build some serious Rust expertise. We'll now explore ways to continue our journey with Rust, with a focus on deliberate practice.

In talking with other professionals, I've found that for many, the biggest frustration with learning a new technology is taking time away from their work or family. With that in mind, this chapter will focus on ways to practice Rust that don't monopolize your free time.

Of course, some readers may be ready to dive in and start using Rust in a professional context. If that's you, we'll explore some ways to make the transition as easy as possible without alienating your coworkers.

In this chapter, we're going to cover the following main topics:

- Practicing Rust at home
- Navigating Rust in the workplace
- Keeping up with Rust

Practicing Rust at home

Many of us may be interested in Rust as a language for hobbies or personal projects. These projects can be used to keep our technical skills sharp, or maybe they're even just for fun. As with all hobbies, the amount of time spent can be overwhelming if we don't manage it properly.

This section contains several suggestions for ways to keep yourself in practice with Rust without sacrificing every last scrap of your free time.

Online challenges

Online challenges are a fun and productive way to become more familiar with new programming languages. The "challenge" parts of these sites are often algorithmic in nature, but solving them in Rust can give you lots of practice with file I/O, string manipulation, and iterators.

One of the best sites for practicing new languages is *Advent of Code* (`https://adventofcode.com`). This site provides themed challenges on the first few days of December each year. The site is competitive in nature, with users aiming for the correct solutions in the smallest amount of time each day. However, the themed puzzles from previous years are all archived to allow you to practice at your own pace.

The *Advent of Code* puzzles increase in difficulty each day of the year, but every day requires at least some light parsing of text-based input. This can give you excellent opportunities to practice writing ad hoc parsers and string-to-binary conversions using the standard library. If you're not yet comfortable using strings in Rust, this is one of the quickest ways to improve.

The algorithmic parts of the puzzles often require the use of standard containers such as `Vec`, `HashMap`, and `HashSet`. Often, they can also give practice using iterators such as `filter` or `map`. The puzzles ramp up in difficulty quickly, but the early days of each year can often be solved with only a modest time investment.

Another great way to practice Rust is *LeetCode*, found at `https://leetcode.com`. While it is popular for job interview preparation, LeetCode is also excellent for practicing programming languages. It offers a very large number of algorithmic puzzles of all difficulties to challenge both your brain and your programming language skills.

Lastly is *Exercism*, found at `http://exercism.org`. This site is similar to LeetCode, but is specifically designed to teach programming languages. Each language supported by the site has an individual learning track and graded exercises. The exercises can either be solved on the site or downloaded and completed with offline tooling.

While these sites are great for practice, a number of you will quickly want to jump into something more substantial. This is where we can begin to graduate into hobby projects.

Hobby projects

Hobby projects are an excellent and often productive way to practice new languages, but they can quickly become complicated. Rust itself, after all, started as a hobby project. In this section, I'll suggest a few hobby projects that are engaging and will help you practice Rust, but don't require more than a weekend or so of your time.

First is the excellent *Ray Tracing in One Weekend* series. These books, found at `https://raytracing.github.io`, gently guide the user through creating a hobby ray tracer from scratch. As the title claims, these projects do not take much time to execute but are an accessible journey through a small slice of graphics programming. At the time of writing, this series encompasses three books.

The books use C++ with minimal dependencies. Following the books in Rust involves some transliteration from language to language and a bit of detective work to figure out idiomatic strategies in Rust. But with the foundation we've built throughout this book, especially with respect to optimization and multithreading, a motivated reader could find a lot of interesting directions to take one of these hobby ray tracing projects.

Another project I recommend for Rust practice is to write a Z-machine. What is a Z-machine? The game *Zork* was released in 1977 and became one of the first and most well-known examples of the interactive fiction genre. Cleverly, the authors built the entire game on top of a virtual machine that they called the "Z-machine," allowing improved portability to many architectures and creating a development platform ultimately used by hundreds of other games.

The Z-machine today is well-documented, and implementing it gives us a small bit of insight into a bygone era of game development. Completing this project also allows us to play a number of interactive fiction games on a virtual machine we ourselves wrote.

> **Note**
>
> The original *Zork* games were open sourced under the MIT license in November 2025. Many public domain or otherwise freely available Z-machine games are hosted at the *Interactive Fiction Archive* at `https://www.ifarchive.org`. Be sure to carefully check license terms before downloading any games.

The best place to start when implementing a Z-machine is the standards document available at `https://inform-fiction.org/zmachine/standards/index.html`. This document describes the instruction set and data formats used by the version 3 virtual machine used by *Zork*, as well as subsequent versions. Another handy resource is the **CZECH** project, which stands for **Comprehensive Z-Machine Emulation Checker**. This project houses unit tests for most instructions, which can be an essential debugging aid when implementing the project.

In addition to a ray tracer and Z-machine, there are plenty of other fun hobby projects. Historical console emulators, operating systems, databases, and toy programming languages are all excellent choices. But these two projects should provide great practice in Rust while not filling all of your free time. In the next section, we'll move away from writing Rust in our free time and begin discussing writing Rust professionally.

Navigating Rust in the workplace

While Rust is packed with technical value, it's still often a controversial choice for C++ developers to introduce it in the workplace. This is often for good reasons, such as team familiarity and the costs of rewriting legacy code in time, money, and stability. But while Rust can be a challenge to integrate into your professional life, this section offers some tips to make it easier to do so when appropriate.

Introducing Rust to professionals

While I hope this book has given you ample reasons to be excited about Rust, it's often best to take it slow when advocating the language in any professional context. We've seen reports from companies such as Microsoft and Google that their developers are happier with Rust, produce fewer bugs, spend less time on code review, and pick up the language quickly. But there's no reason to believe that this success is repeatable in every organization.

Often, the most important aspect of introducing Rust to an organization is empathy. Professionals are often focused on their tasks and don't feel as if they have time to learn a new language on the job. Introducing any new technology without buy-in can lead to resentment and frustration among your peers.

Many companies allow engineers to present talks or tutorials on various topics. This can be a great chance to talk about the pros and cons of Rust and how they relate to your field. Often, the resulting conversations that come out of a talk like this can help you judge how your colleagues might feel about using Rust professionally. Giving a talk can be especially helpful if you have no decision-making authority at your workplace.

A next small step can be to identify parts of the code base that might make sense to become Rust. Anything that is legacy, maintained by a handful of people, and relatively isolated from the rest of the code base is a good candidate, especially if it keeps causing problems. Other candidates might be areas of code that represent a potentially large attack surface and need to be secured.

Once a system where Rust can be of help is identified, the proper approvals can be sought. Keep in mind that while Rust conversions have been quite successful in many companies, there are several trade-offs in terms of performance and developer familiarity that must be considered before choosing Rust. Additionally, every code rewrite creates some risk of introducing new bugs. Therefore, it's essential to have very good testing to ensure that behavior remains stable.

Searching for a Rust career

As the language has become increasingly popular, there has been a marked uptick both in programmers searching for a Rust career and in companies offering Rust jobs. But a strong job market for Rust is still developing.

A number of larger companies appear to have trained their existing engineers to use Rust rather than hiring teams of Rust specialists. While information about how these companies use Rust internally can be sparse, they are making gradual bets on Rust. This implies that their engineers need to work and be proficient in multiple languages.

The result of this is that careers that allow work exclusively in Rust may be limited to smaller companies and start-ups. There are a handful of great ways to find these companies. For one, Rust-specific job boards such as `https://rustjobs.dev` have been created specifically to help match Rust job seekers to companies.

Still, a straightforward way to learn about companies that are using Rust is to browse crates on `crates.io`. Many companies using Rust like to keep at least some presence in the open source ecosystem, and this includes releasing their work publicly as crates to the community.

Another great way to learn about companies using Rust is the *Rust in Production* podcast, available on most podcast platforms. This podcast, hosted by the Rust consulting firm `https://corrode.dev`, features interviews with representatives from companies using Rust. The talks are often candid and feature insights into their positive and negative experiences using the language. While the podcast is interesting for many reasons, it can be a great way to familiarize yourself with companies that may have open roles.

Whether you hope to introduce Rust in your existing role or to find an excellent job writing Rust full-time, the Rust job market is a dynamic and interesting space that seems poised to grow heavily in the coming years. At the same time, it's unlikely for our C++ skills to soon become obsolete professionally. Maintaining expertise in both languages can only make us better engineers and better candidates.

Keeping up with Rust

Rust is a fast-moving language with a vibrant community and ecosystem. New versions of the language are released every six weeks, and marvelous new crates are being released nearly every day. It can be daunting to try to keep up with all of this, especially as a busy developer. In this section, we''ll talk about the organization of the Rust community and how we can keep up with the language from week to week.

Understanding the Rust community

Like most language communities, the Rust community is a loose collection of individuals who are collectively excited about the language and its technical value. Perhaps unlike many communities, the Rust community prides itself on being welcoming to outsiders. The project runs a yearly community survey and regularly finds that users feel welcomed and comfortable in community spaces.

Many of the most popular community spaces are actually unofficial. Hacker News, Reddit, and X (formerly Twitter) often host great discussions about Rust, but they are all unofficial community spaces. Official discussions happen on the Rust users forum at `https://users.rust-lang.org/` and on the official Rust Zulip server at `https://rust-lang.zulipchat.com/`.

While technical discussion often happens in those spaces, the `rust-lang` GitHub organization is also considered an official project space. This is where users can download source code, submit issues, or contribute to the Rust compiler, Cargo, and several official crates.

An important repository under the `rust-lang` organization is the RFC repository found at `https://github.com/rust-lang/rfcs`. The **Request for Comment** (**RFC**) process is how the project navigates proposals to substantially change the language. If you have a great idea for how to improve Rust, this is the place to formally propose those changes to the development team. Accepted RFCs often start as "unstable" features available only in nightly Rust. As the implementation solidifies and becomes stable, they eventually move into the stable distribution of the language.

Community spaces, both official and unofficial, are great ways for learning about popular crates or new features and participating in technical discussions with other Rust users. But how do we keep up with such a fast-moving language?

Staying up to date with Rust

The Rust project understands that 'it's difficult to keep up with a language that releases every six weeks. To help users deal with this, they produce a weekly newsletter to highlight recent events around the Rust world. The newsletter, titled *This Week in Rust*, is located at `https://this-week-in-rust.org/`. Each week features blog posts, tutorials, and project updates about Rust.

The Rust project also makes new releases of the language as easy to digest as possible. Each Rust release is accompanied by extensive release notes and a small blog post highlighting new features of interest. This often highlights APIs that were stabilized in the release, as well as any major new features.

If you rely on a deployment of Rust in production, you should also be aware of beta releases. Each release spends six weeks in the beta channel, available in `rustup`. The beta period gives both the Rust developers and users of the language a chance to evaluate the new features before they are released as stable. This can be an excellent way to ensure that an upgrade 'isn't going to hurt your deployment should you wish to move to the newest Rust version.

Keeping up with Rust can be a challenge, especially if 'you're not using it daily in a professional setting. But between the community spaces, release notes, and the weekly newsletter, 'it's easy to pick the best way to stay updated that works for you.

Summary

Throughout this book, we've explored many aspects of Rust as a programming language, its associated tooling and libraries, and the exciting ecosystem of software around it. I hope you've come away with not only a healthy respect for the design choices and technical trade-offs chosen by Rust, but also with a strong foundation upon which to build a mastery of Rust that will complement your C++ skills.

More than anything, I hope you now consider Rust to be a part of your engineering toolbox when approaching problems. The world desperately needs better software, and every tool that can help us create it is a valuable one. While Rust is not the only tool that can help us, it has a strong and rapidly growing foothold in the security and systems programming spaces.

Perhaps Rust will become an integral part of your professional work. Perhaps you will simply use it as a toy language for hobby projects going forward. Maybe you'll choose to contribute Rust code to the open source ecosystem. Whatever your choice, I thank you for the time you've allowed us to spend together with Rust, and I hope you can draw on what you've learned in this book to create excellent software.

Get this book's PDF version and more

Scan the QR code (or go to `packtpub.com/unlock`). Search for this book by name, confirm the edition, and then follow the steps on the page.

UNLOCK NOW

Note: Keep your invoice handy. Purchases made directly from Packt don't require an invoice.

Appendix

Setting Up The Development Environment

The first thing any Rust programmer needs is a computer that is properly set up for development. In this appendix, we'll walk through all the steps required to set up a Rust development environment on a clean Linux, macOS, or Windows machine.

This appendix aims to provide you with a useful set of default tools that can take you through the entire development cycle: editing, compiling, and debugging. The recommendations in this appendix are not intended to imply that these tools are the best or only tools available, only that they provide a reasonable set of defaults for a new Rust programmer.

In this appendix, we're going to cover the following main topics:

- Installing Rust development tools
- Setting up Visual Studio Code for Rust development
- Using Clippy, the Rust linter

Installing Rust development tools

Rust development tools can be installed in several different ways for different operating systems. Package managers on several different operating systems all have their own individual distributions. In this section, we'll focus on the official set of installation tools created and maintained by the Rust project. This has the advantage of providing a nearly uniform set of installation instructions across all major operating systems.

Obtaining Rust development tools

The minimal Rust development setup consists of three major tools. `rustup` is the tool that manages and modifies the Rust installation, including updating to newer versions and installing ancillary development tooling. `rustc` is the Rust compiler, which is, of course, needed to compile Rust programs. Finally, Cargo is the Rust build and packaging tool, which is used for project and dependency management. Rust also needs a linker, which is often provided by the system. If you can develop C++ code on your machine, chances are good that you already have an appropriate linker installed.

Our three major development tools are installed by the `rustup-init` program. This program can be found at the `https://rustup.rs/` website. This website will detect the operating system of the client and provide users with the option to download and install `rustup-init` by themselves, which can then be run at the user's leisure. Another option provided is a single-line shell command that can be copied and pasted into the user's terminal to perform the download and run it in one step.

After it is run, the Rust installer will prompt the user as to what they want to install. Accepting the defaults is usually best for a new Rust programmer. If external requirements exist, the program will warn about that as well. For instance, on Windows, the installer will ask the user whether they wish to install Visual Studio. The requirements on external software may change in the future, for instance, if the Rust project begins to ship its own linker.

> Note
>
> **Visual Studio licensing**
>
> If Visual Studio is needed when installing Rust on Windows, the installer will download and install a copy of Visual Studio Community Edition. This edition is free for many uses, but Rust users on Windows should double-check to ensure that the Community Edition license is appropriate for them. Rust can also use a paid version of Visual Studio or the MinGW-w64 open source toolchain based on `gcc`.

After the user acknowledges all the prompts, the Rust development tools will be downloaded and installed. The installer will print a success message when it completes and instruct the user on how to import required environment variable modifications into their current shell. The user can also choose to close and reopen their shell or terminal program to have the new settings applied.

If all goes well, we now have the Rust development tools installed, and we can begin our Rust journey. The first step will be verifying that everything works.

Verifying installation

Next, we will verify that our tools are correctly installed and usable. One of the best ways to do this is to compile and run a program. Let's start by opening a new terminal window and ensuring that our compiler is installed correctly:

```
$ rustc --version
```

Running this command will ensure that `rustc` exists in our system path and that it did not have any installation problems. The expected output is the installed version of Rust, which is most likely the current version of Rust at the time of installation.

To test compiling and running a program, we can use Cargo to generate a new project. Cargo can generate either a binary or a library crate. Let's first try a binary crate:

```
$ cargo new hello
$ cd hello
$ cargo run
```

We should see some messaging from Cargo indicating that the program is compiling, followed by the usual `"Hello, world!"` message in our terminal. If there are any errors at this point, it may mean that our system is missing development tools such as the system linker.

We can do the same exercise with a library crate. In the case of a library crate, Cargo does not generate a binary, so we cannot use `cargo run`, but we can use `cargo test` to run the automatically generated tests instead:

```
$ cargo new --lib hello_lib
$ cd hello_lib
$ cargo test
```

We should see the `tests::it_works` test created by Cargo pass. Again, any errors here might indicate a problem with the system linker.

If you've gotten this far, you should now have all your development tools installed and have verified that you can compile and run Rust programs and tests. Next, let's look at some of the things we can do with `rustup`.

Managing a Rust installation with rustup

As its name might imply, `rustup` is primarily used to update the Rust installation. Rust is frequently updated, with new releases landing at a six-week cadence. These are often small updates, but there are usually interesting new features in each release. Since Rust is backward-compatible, there should never be any specific need to update the Rust installation. But it can be helpful to stay up to date simply because most of the ecosystem tends to stay close to the latest stable release. To update our installation to the latest version, we simply run the following:

```
$ rustup update stable
```

This will download and install the latest Rust version. Usually, upgrading is a painless process, but occasionally, small bugs slip into a stable release. When this happens, the Rust team is quick to release a minor version update addressing the issue, which can then be installed with the same command.

While we will primarily work with stable Rust, `rustup` also allows us to access additional **channels** as well. A channel is an independent set of development tooling updated at different cadences than the stable version. The beta channel is the next-to-be-released version of Rust, while the nightly channel contains releases from the ongoing development branch. Nightly releases offer access to unstable features, which need further development before they can make their way into the stable version. In the past, some useful crates have depended on unstable nightly-only features, but these types of crates are a rare exception now.

We will not use nightly much in this book, but we'll briefly look at how to install and work with additional toolchains using nightly as an example. The nightly toolchain can be installed with the following command:

```
$ rustup toolchain install nightly
```

We can alter the default toolchain with the `rustup default` command:

```
$ rustup default nightly
```

When more than one toolchain is installed, we can specify which one we want to use when invoking the `cargo` command:

```
$ cargo +nightly run
```

Moving forward, let's ensure that `stable` is our default toolchain. If you have not run any of the preceding commands, this will already be the case. Otherwise, you'll need to run the following command to get our installation back to its initial state:

```
$ rustup default stable
```

Another interesting feature of `rustup` is its ability to install different **targets**. A target refers to an architecture that can be installed for the purposes of cross-compilation. For instance, this could be useful if you wanted to build a WebAssembly or Android version of your program on your Windows or Linux development machine. Cross-compilation can be a large topic, but you can see the available targets with the following command:

```
$ rustup target list
```

The final part of `rustup` that we'll examine is **components**. Components are additional software installed along with a toolchain beyond the standard development tools. Several components are installed along with the Rust development tools, including offline documentation accessible through the `rustup doc` command, and the Rust linter Clippy, which we'll explore in depth later in this appendix.

To view the available components, you can use this command:

```
$ rustup component list
```

You should now have a good feel for how to manage your Rust installation. Now we'll move on to setting up a great editing experience.

Setting up Visual Studio Code for Rust development

Coming from C++, it's likely that you're already comfortable with a specific editor or IDE. If it's a popular editor, there's a great chance that Rust will work well with it. Rust provides tooling that implements the popular **Language Server Protocol** (**LSP**), an editor-independent way of providing language refactoring and analysis features. Because of this, it can be used with all editors that implement LSP.

For those without a strong editor preference already, we'll walk through setting up Visual Studio Code for Rust development here. Visual Studio Code is a free, high-quality editor that works well with both Rust and other languages, but it's far from the only choice available.

Installing Visual Studio Code

Visual Studio Code can be installed by visiting the editor's main website at `https://code.visualstudio.com/`. As with the Rust website, the server will detect your operating system and offer you an appropriate package to download. Depending on your operating system, there could end up being more than one choice, so pick the package that you feel most comfortable installing. After downloading it, you can install the package using the traditional software installation method for your operating system.

Clicking on the download link will send you to a page offering several resources for first-time users of the editor, including intro videos and configuration recommendations. If you're unfamiliar with the editor, I recommend that you spend some time with these videos to familiarize yourself with the user interface, extension system, and what Visual Studio Code calls the **Command Palette**. For those who like to jump right in, opening the editor with no project loaded will offer some in-editor tutorials.

The Rust project distributes a program called `rust-analyzer` that implements LSP as well as an extension for Visual Studio Code that enables several useful features for Rust development. To add this extension to a fresh install of Visual Studio Code, press *Ctrl* + *Shift* + *X* to get to the extensions browser and search for `rust-lang.rust-analyzer`. Click the **Install** button next to the extension's name. If the editor tells you that a reload is required, do that now.

When we get back to the main editor user interface, we'll have full Rust support ready for us to use. Feel free to load one of the skeleton projects we made earlier to try things out. To build a Rust project from within the editor, press *Ctrl* + *Shift* + *B* and choose **rust: cargo build**. The first time we build from the editor, we may need to save a `tasks.json` file generated by the editor to disk. This contains any settings we might want to modify to change how the build works. For instance, we might want to change the default from a debug build to a release build with optimizations or add other options to the list of choices in the build menu.

Using the Rust analysis extension

With Rust support installed, we're now ready to explore the analysis features offered in Visual Studio Code. The Visual Studio Code team maintains documentation for working with `rust-analyzer` in their editor that can be found at `https://code.visualstudio.com/docs/languages/rust`. In the following paragraphs, we'll examine some of the most useful features of the `rust-analyzer` extension for new Rust programmers.

First is access to documentation. When hovering the mouse over an identifier, the extension will bring up the documentation for that function or type in a pop-up window. If the small preview isn't enough help, you can right-click on the identifier and choose **Open Docs** from the context window. This can be especially helpful when looking through the functions in a structure to find the one you need.

Another way to find the functionality you need is through the auto-completion feature provided by the `rust-analyzer` extension. As you type code in the editor, the extension will search for functions and identifiers that make sense in context and suggest them to you. While this can save a little typing, it's also a good way to discover new functionality. For instance, typing an integer literal followed by `.` will bring up a large selection of math functions that can be used on the integer type.

One of the other functions of the `rust-analyzer` extension is to provide you with inline type hints. Since Rust is a type-inferred language, types are often elided from code. The editor uses the analyzer to deduce the type of identifiers that are inferred and displays these together with the code. The font and color scheme differ slightly from the normal syntax highlighting of the code, so the hints can be distinguished from the actual code. While some new Rust programmers will find these hints extremely useful, others may be confused by them while still learning the syntax of the language. If desired, they can be turned off in the `rust-analyzer` preferences.

The `rust-analyzer` extension also compiles code in the background and highlights errors. This can save a lot of time that might have otherwise been spent compiling to discover errors. The extension can sometimes provide suggested fixes for the errors. One of the most interesting uses for these suggested fixes is to avoid typing boilerplate. This deserves a quick demonstration.

Let's say I want to implement the `std::fmt::Display` trait for my structure. We can look at this as providing a way for us to customize how our structure looks when printed to `stdout`. With `rust-analyzer` in Visual Studio Code, I can just define the trait for my `Foo` structure like this:

```
impl std::fmt::Display for Foo {}
```

This isn't valid Rust because the contents of the trait are not defined. The `rust-analyzer` extension highlights the error and gives me a light bulb icon indicating that there are fixes available. When clicking on the icon and choosing **Implement missing members**, the code is replaced with a full definition that compiles correctly and is ready for me to implement:

```
impl std::fmt::Display for Foo {
    fn fmt(&self, f: &mut std::fmt::Formatter<'_>) -> std::fmt::Result {
        todo!()
```

```
    }
}
```

Because the extension filled in the definition for me correctly, I didn't have to look up the specifics of the trait's boilerplate and could focus entirely on the implementation.

There are several other features of the `rust-analyzer` extension that make our lives easier as we read, write, and refactor Rust code. These include automatic code formatting, symbol renaming, and advanced code navigation. For both new and experienced Rust programmers, using the `rust-analyzer` extension is a great time-saver, but it's just one of the features offered in Visual Studio Code. Next, we'll look at another important topic: debugging.

Debugging Rust in Visual Studio Code

Debugging is a core discipline of programming. While many programmers find it quick to insert `print` statements to trace the execution of their programs, nothing comes close to the ability to single-step through a running program and watch as data changes.

Rust is an interesting language for debugging because so much of its behavior is already predictable in stable mode. There's no need to worry about memory overwrites, reading out of bounds, or any of the other hazards of more traditional systems programming languages. When that is put together with built-in testing support, do we still need to debug at all?

Of course! Debugging is still phenomenally important in Rust, although in my own coding, it happens less frequently than in other languages. When I first introduced colleagues and friends to Rust, their first question was often whether it has a debugger.

Because the Rust toolchain produces binaries in the same format as C++ compilers and uses the same debug information formats, any debugger that can debug a C++ program can technically also debug a Rust one as well. Feel free to try out your favorite tools for debugging and profiling, but again, we'll look at how Visual Studio Code tackles the problem at hand.

To start, we must install a debug extension. A popular one that is recommended for all platforms is called `CodeLLDB` and can be found by searching in the extension management user interface, accessible by *Ctrl* + *Shift* + *X*, in the same way we installed the `rust-analyzer` extension. Once this is installed, there are two ways we can begin a debug session.

If you loaded one of the skeleton projects we created, you may have noticed that every `main()` function and every test is annotated with both the **Run** and **Debug** options by the `rust-analyzer` extension. Clicking on the **Debug** option will compile the program in debug mode and begin a debug session at that entry point. This is one of the most convenient ways to start a debug session, although at present, there is no way to pass arguments to the program using this method.

Of course, unless we set a breakpoint, the debugger will most often just run the program and exit cleanly. In order to set a breakpoint, we'll need to move the cursor to the line of code we're interested in and press the *F9* key. On clicking on the **Debug** option again, we'll see that the program stops at our breakpoint, assuming we put it in code that's executed.

The debug user interface in Visual Studio Code is accessible with the *Ctrl* + *Shift* + *D* shortcut. From this window, you can view much of the normal info available in debuggers, such as the contents of local variables, any variables specifically watched for changes, the call stack, and the current list of breakpoints.

Stepping through the stopped program can be accomplished with the *F10* and *F11* keys, much like the highly regarded visual debugger in Visual Studio Code's big brother, Visual Studio. There's also a small widget in the editor at the top of the source code that allows us to control the program's execution and exit the debugging session.

Earlier, I mentioned a second way to start a debug session. In the debug user interface, when there is no current session, a **Run and Debug** button will be visible. Clicking on this for the first time will detect that we are in a Rust workspace and prompt us to allow the automatic creation of a `launch.json` config file. With this file created, we can then launch a new session directly from the debug user interface. We can also edit the JSON config to add any arguments we wish to pass to our program.

At this point, Visual Studio Code is completely configured for us, and we know how to compile, edit, and debug our Rust project in the editor. But there's one further topic to explore before we can consider our development environment complete: linting.

Using Clippy, the Rust linter

Linters have a long history in computer science and exist in many programming languages. As the name may imply, they can take the "lint" out of your code by running a light form of static analysis on your program and highlighting potential problems. Using a good linter is like having a very smart code reviewer sitting at your desk with you.

Working with Clippy

Linters for C and C++ focus heavily, but not exclusively, on the misuse of pointers and other memory safety issues. Rust already protects you from those types of mistakes by default, so the best reason to use Clippy is that it can teach you ways to improve Rust code that wouldn't be obvious to beginners otherwise. These can range from reducing the amount of typing required to perform common tasks to teaching you how to avoid common performance pitfalls.

Linters live and die on their signal-to-noise ratio. Minor issues may be easy to flag with static analysis, but users tend not to want to dig through output containing 100 warnings about minor issues just to find 2 or 3 about major issues. A good linter provides more value than noise. By this standard, Clippy, named after a famously helpful anthropomorphic paperclip, is a great linter. The out-of-the-box experience tends to provide a lot more value than noise, especially for new Rust users.

Clippy is installed by default with the rest of the Rust development tools and is invoked by running the `cargo clippy` command from a terminal application. You may prefer to invoke it from your editor as well. If you're using Visual Studio Code with the `rust-analyzer` extension that we set up earlier, you can find this as one of the options under the build menu, accessible with the *Ctrl* + *Shift* + *B* shortcut.

Clippy also has a mode that can alter your source code to address many of its warnings. This can be invoked using the following command:

```
$ cargo clippy --fix
```

By default, this will fix as many issues as possible. The Clippy team only includes automatic fixes that are highly probable to work correctly and not break your source code.

Configuring Clippy for your project

As a beginner Rust programmer, it's valuable to use Clippy with the default options for a while before looking into turning on or off behaviors. Even often-dreaded stylistic checks can teach you a lot about what idiomatic or commonly accepted styles are used in the wider Rust community. If nothing else, they can teach you about new styles or API calls that you didn't realize were there. Still, as we continue our Rust journey, we may start wanting to change the default behavior.

As with most linters, the primary reason we'll want to alter the configuration of Clippy is to change the behavior of individual checks, or **lints**. Lints in Clippy, much like normal warnings in Rust, have three possible configurations: allow, warn, and deny. A lint set to allow is disabled, meaning that the behavior warned about by the lint is normally allowed by the project. A lint set to warn will issue a warning and recommend that the programmer fix the issue. Finally, a lint set to deny will issue an error rather than a warning. This can be useful to keep specific undesirable behaviors out of a shared code base.

There are several ways to set the status of each lint. The most flexible is to configure them by annotating the source code itself. The Rust language allows us to set the configuration of warnings coming from the compiler at different scopes throughout the program using its

attribute syntax. As an example, we can ignore a warning generated by the Rust compiler that enforces a specific casing style on structure names:

```
#[allow(non_camel_case_types)]
struct test;
```

Normally, we would get a warning suggesting that we change the name of our structure to `Test`, but since we allowed the behavior for this structure, the compiler will no longer complain. As we might expect, we can also use the `warn` and `deny` attributes for Rust warnings depending on our desired behavior for each.

This same system is extended to Clippy by prefixing the name of a lint with `clippy::`. Depending on where the attribute is placed, it can affect an individual type, a function, or the entire project. For instance, to enable all Clippy lints for our entire crate, we can place this attribute at or near the top of our `main.rs` or `lib.rs` file:

```
#![warn(clippy::all)]
```

Notice that when we wish for the directive to affect the entire crate, we must prefix it with `#!` rather than `#`. Rust specifies the former as **inner attributes** affecting the scope that the attribute is inside (in our case, the entire crate) and the latter as **outer attributes** affecting what is immediately following it in the source code.

Configuring Clippy lints in source code can be convenient when we need fine-grained modifications, but for an entire project, it may be more straightforward to specify them in the Cargo configuration for each crate, stored in the `Cargo.toml` file at the crate's root. To perform the same modification as the crate-level attribute we just saw, we can add a section like this anywhere in our `Cargo.toml` file:

```
[lints.clippy]
all = "warn"
```

If there are conflicts between the settings in the source code and the Cargo configuration, the source code will take precedence.

There's more info about Clippy in the official documentation, including a comprehensive list of lints and even more methods of configuring it. But now we should have a good understanding of how it can help programmers who are starting out with the language to discover better ways to structure and write more idiomatic Rust code. If it gets in the way at some point, we know how to selectively enable or disable parts of it to improve the value it provides for our specific projects.

15

Unlock Your Exclusive Benefits

Your copy of this book includes the following exclusive benefits:

EPUB PDF

DRM-Free PDF Version

Download DRM-free PDF and ePub copies of this book.

7-Day Packt Library Access

Get 7-day unlimited access to 8,000+ books and videos. No credit card required.

Available for first-time Packt+ trial users only.

Next-Gen Reader Access

Read this book on Packt Reader with progress sync, dark mode and note-taking.

Follow the guide below to unlock them. The process takes only a few minutes and needs to be completed once.

Unlock this Book's Free Benefits in 3 Easy Steps

Step 1

Keep your purchase invoice ready for *Step 3*. If you have a physical copy, scan it using your phone and save it as a PDF, JPG, or PNG.

For more help on finding your invoice, visit `https://www.packtpub.com/en-us/unlock?step=1`.

> **Note**
>
> If you bought this book directly from Packt, no invoice is required. After *Step 2*, you can access your exclusive content right away.

Step 2

Scan the QR code or go to `packtpub.com/unlock`.

On the page that opens (similar to *Figure 15.1* on desktop), search for this book by name and select the correct edition.

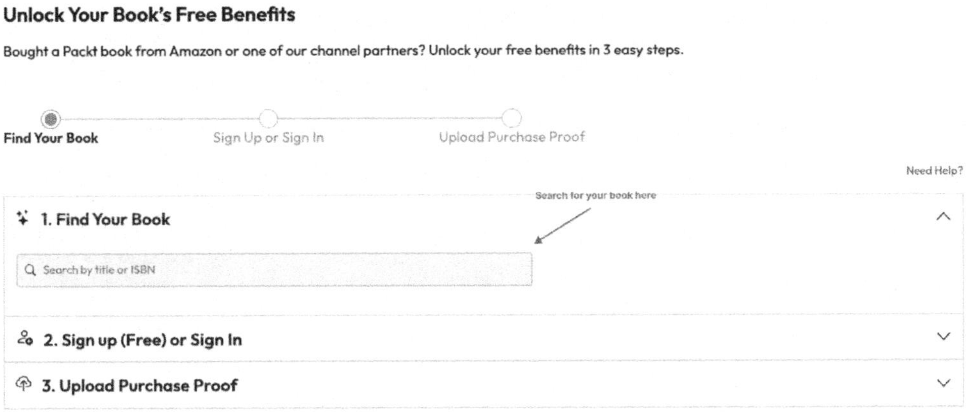

Figure 15.1: Packt unlock landing page on desktop

Step 3

After selecting your book, sign in to your Packt account or create one for free. Then upload your invoice (PDF, PNG, or JPG, up to 10 MB). Follow the on-screen instructions to finish the process.

Need Help

If you get stuck and need help, visit `https://www.packtpub.com/unlock-benefits/help` for a detailed FAQ on how to find your invoices and more. This QR code will take you to the help page.

> **Note**
>
> If you are still facing issues, reach out to `customercare@packt.com`.

packtpub.com

Subscribe to our online digital library for full access to over 7,000 books and videos, as well as industry leading tools to help you plan your personal development and advance your career. For more information, please visit our website.

Why subscribe?

- Spend less time learning and more time coding with practical eBooks and Videos from over 4,000 industry professionals
- Improve your learning with Skill Plans built especially for you
- Get a free eBook or video every month
- Fully searchable for easy access to vital information
- Copy and paste, print, and bookmark content

At `www.packtpub.com`, you can also read a collection of free technical articles, sign up for a range of free newsletters, and receive exclusive discounts and offers on Packt books and eBooks.

Other Books You May Enjoy

If you enjoyed this book, you may be interested in these other books by Packt:

Asynchronous Programming in Rust

Carl Fredrik Samson

ISBN: 9781805128137

- Explore the essence of asynchronous program flow and its significance
- Understand the difference between concurrency and parallelism
- Gain insights into how computers and operating systems handle concurrent tasks
- Uncover the mechanics of async/await
- Understand Rust's futures by implementing them yourself
- Implement green threads from scratch to thoroughly understand them

The Rust Programming Handbook

Francesco Ciulla

ISBN: 9781836208877

- Thoroughly understand Rust's unique programming model and its advantages for software development
- Implement advanced features like smart pointers, concurrency, and error handling to write efficient and secure code
- Seamlessly incorporate Rust into your projects, enhancing both performance and scalability
- Prepare for sophisticated development tasks in systems and web programming using Rust
- Navigate Rust's ecosystem with the latest tools and frameworks to stay ahead in technology

Packt is searching for authors like you

If you're interested in becoming an author for Packt, please visit `authors.packt.com` and apply today. We have worked with thousands of developers and tech professionals, just like you, to help them share their insight with the global tech community. You can make a general application, apply for a specific hot topic that we are recruiting an author for, or submit your own idea.

Share your thoughts

Now you've finished *Rust for C++ Developers*, we'd love to hear your thoughts! Scan the QR code below to go straight to the Amazon review page for this book and share your feedback or leave a review on the site that you purchased it from.

`https://packt.link/r/1836206518`

Your review is important to us and the tech community and will help us make sure we're delivering excellent quality content.

Index

P

R

Made in the USA
Monee, IL
16 September 2026

63035032R00175